S0-CFZ-392

Celtic Contraries

Richard Fallis, Series Editor

Celtic

Contraries

ROBIN SKELTON

SYRACUSE UNIVERSITY PRESS

First Edition 1990
95 94 93 92 91 90   6 5 4 3 2 1

The paper used in this publication meets the minimum requirements of American National Standard for Information Sciences—Permanence of Paper for Printed Library Materials, ANSI Z39.48-1984.∞™

Library of Congress Cataloging-in-Publication Data

Skelton, Robin.
Celtic contraries / Robin Skelton. — 1st ed.
p. cm. — (Irish studies)
ISBN 0-8156-2479-4 (alk. paper)
1. English literature—Irish authors—History and criticism.
2. Ireland—Intellectual life. 3. Ireland in literature.
I. Title. II. Series: Irish studies (Syracuse, N.Y.)
PR8714.S56 1989
821.009′9415—dc20   89-19736
CIP

Manufactured in the United States of America

For

Liam Miller

Ireland's greatest publisher
in tribute to
his life's work and his vision.

Permission to quote from materials listed below is gratefully acknowledged.

Selected short extracts from the poems of W. B. Yeats by permission of A.P. Watt Ltd. on behalf of Michael B. Yeats and Macmillan London Ltd.

"Nineteen Hundred and Nineteen" reprinted with permission of Macmillan Publishing Company from *The Poems of W. B. Yeats: A New Edition*, edited by Richard J. Finneran. Copyright 1928 by Macmillan Publishing Company, renewed 1956 by Georgie Yeats.

"The Apparitions," "What Then?" "Those Images," and "An Acre of Grass" reprinted with permission of Macmillan Publishing Company from *The Poems of W. B. Yeats: A New Edition*, edited by Richard J. Finneran. Copyright 1940 by Georgie Yeats, renewed 1968 by Bertha Georgie Yeats, Michael Butler Yeats, and Anne Yeats.

Selections from the plays of Sean O'Casey reprinted by permission of Macmillan Publishing Company.

"A Bracelet" and "In Disguise" taken from *Collected Poems 1975* by Robert Graves by permission of A.P. Watt Ltd. on behalf of The Executors of the Estate of Robert Graves.

"A Bracelet" and "In Disguise" and fragmentary quotations from *Collected Poems 1975* by Robert Graves. Copyright © 1975 by Robert Graves. Reprinted by permission of Oxford University Press, Inc.

"Aubade" and "The Sunlight on the Garden" reprinted by permission of Faber and Faber Ltd. from *The Collected Poems of Louis MacNeice*.

Selections from the poetry of Thomas Kinsella reprinted with permission of the author.

Selections from the works of Aidan Higgins reprinted with permission of John Calder Publishers Ltd.

Selections from the works of John Montague reprinted with permission of the author and by courtesy of Wake Forest University Press.

"Without Contraries is no Progression"

William Blake

Irish Studies presents a wide range of books interpreting aspects of Irish life and culture to scholarly and general audiences. Irish literature is a special concern in the series, but works from the perspectives of the fine arts, history, and the social sciences are also welcome, as are studies which take multi-disciplinary approaches.

An Anglo-Irish Dialect Glossary for Joyce's Works. Richard Wall
Beckett and Myth: An Archetypal Approach. Mary A. Doll
Celtic Contraries. Robin Skelton
Children's Lore in "Finnegans Wake." Grace Eckley
Cinema and Ireland. Kevin Rockett, Luke Gibbons, and John Hill
Dreamscheme: Narrative and Voice in "Finnegans Wake." Michael Begnal
Fictions of the Irish Literary Revival: A Changeling Art. John Wilson Foster
The Figure in the Cave and Other Essays. John Montague
Finnegans Wake: A Plot Summary. John Gordon
Fionn mac Cumhaill: Celtic Myth in English Literature. James MacKillop
Frank O'Connor at Work. Michael Steinman
Great Hatred, Little Room: The Irish Historical Novel. James M. Cahalan
In Minor Keys: The Uncollected Short Stories of George Moore. David B. Eakin & Helmut E. Gerber, *eds.*
Irish Literature: A Reader. Maureen O'Rourke Murphy and James MacKillop, *eds.*
James Joyce: The Augmented Ninth. Bernard Benstock, *ed.*
Selected Plays of Padraic Colum. Sanford Sternlicht, *ed.*
Selected Short Stories of Padraic Colum. Sanford Sternlicht, *ed.*
Selected Poems of Padraic Colum. Sanford Sternlicht, *ed.*
Shadowy Heroes: Irish Literature of the 1890s. Wayne E. Hall
The Irish Renaissance. Richard Fallis
Ulysses as a Comic Novel. Zack Bowen
Yeats. Douglas Archibald
Yeats and the Beginning of the Irish Renaissance. Phillip L. Marcus

Contents

Robin Skelton is Professor of Creative Writing at the University of Victoria. Author of numerous books, including *The Writing of J. M. Synge* and his own autobiographical *Memoirs of a Literary Blockhead*, he has edited many other works, including *The Collected Plays of Jack B. Yeats* and the Penguin Modern Classic *Poetry of the Thirties*. He is a Fellow of the Royal Society of Literature.

Preface

Although these essays were written at different times and for quite different purposes and audiences over a long period, I discovered, when I began to gather them together, that they all bore directly or obliquely upon two main concerns, and did, indeed, form something approaching a pattern, though it would be an exaggeration to state that they present a thesis. The first concern, which reveals itself most clearly in the essays on W. B. Yeats, the first essay on Synge, and the essays on MacNeice, Graves, Kinsella, and Montague, and partially in that on Wilde, is with verse craftsmanship, with the language and structure of poetry. The second concern, which is apparent in the essays on Jack B. Yeats, Thomas Kinsella, Aidan Higgins, and John Montague, and partially in the second essay on Synge is a concern with the way in which a writer can contrive to bring contraries together fusing all his themes and techniques into unity, so as to present a coherent all-embracing "philosophy" or attitude.

There are, of course, other and less overarching concerns expressed here. The preliminary essay on Wilde attempts to outline certain aspects of Wilde as a lyric poet, and to suggest that he may be regarded as typical of the romantic decadence which W. B. Yeats at first imitated and then transfigured, and which remains a component of much later Irish poetry. The essay on Synge and Petrarch, while it also presents some aspects of Synge's romanticism that are not totally out of keeping with Wilde's, is more concerned to show how the essential unity of Synge's work resides in its dependence upon the inspiration of his private life. The second essay attempts to shed a little light upon his political attitudes—a matter which writers on Synge (including myself) have hitherto neglected. This is, I suppose, an unfashionably "biocritical" essay, but as it includes some information which is not easily available elsewhere I have not allowed its difference of approach to persuade me to leave it out. The theme of the poet and politics also emerges in the essay on Montague.

I cannot pretend that this book is in any way comprehensive. A thorough discussion of my two main interests would have led me, quite inescapably, to tackle James Joyce, Samuel Beckett, and Flann O'Brien among others, and I might well have felt forced into examining F. R. Higgins' and Austin Clarke's use of Gaelic verse forms, and thus to produce a book of quite unmanageable proportions. This is, therefore, not an attempt at providing the kind of book which might be described by a blurb writer as a "standard work" on the "subject"; it is perhaps more a series of sighting shots at very elusive targets.

As I have said, these essays were written at different times and for different purposes over the years. All, however, have been revised, and several have been enlarged. The essay on W. B. Yeats's workshop originated in some parts of two lectures given in the Lantern Theatre Dublin on the occasion of the centenary of Yeats's birth, and at the Yeats International Summer School at Sligo in 1966. It appeared in the magazine *Concerning Poetry* in the fall of 1968. The essay on *W. B. Yeats as Master Poet* appeared first in *Mosaic*, vol. 1, no. 1, in October 1967 under the title *W. B. Yeats: The Poet as Synopsis*. It was republished in a revised form as chapter 8 of my out of print volume, *The Poets Calling* (Heinemann Educational, 1975) under the title *The Problem of Poetic Authority*. It has been further revised for this collection. The analysis of Yeats's poem *Nineteen Hundred and Nineteen* appeared in Oscar Williams's anthology *Master Poems of the English Language* (Trident Press, 1966). The first essay on Synge is an enlarged and rewritten version of my introduction to the limited and bilingual edition of Synge's translations from Petrarch published by the Dolmen Press in 1971. The first part of the essay, *J. M. Synge: The Personal Compulsions and the Political Beliefs* is a paper read to the Royal Society of Literature on 19 March 1970; the second part was delivered as a paper to the Synge Centennial Conference in Dublin in 1971, and published later in *The Massachusetts Review*. The essay on Jack B. Yeats is composed partly of an essay I contributed to the symposium *The World of W. B. Yeats* published by the Dolmen Press and Washington University Press in 1965, and partly of a paper delivered to the annual conference of the Canadian Association for Irish Studies in 1971; this was published later in *Yeats Studies*. The essay on Louis MacNeice was published in *Time Was Away*, a symposium of essays edited by

Terence Brown and Alec Reid on the tenth centenary of the poet's death and published by the Dolmen Press. The essay on Robert Graves was first published in *The Malahat Review* of July 1975 as part of a gathering in celebration of the poet's eightieth birthday. The essay on Aidan Higgins was delivered as a paper to the 1974 conference of the Canadian Association for Irish Studies, and that on Thomas Kinsella to the 1968 conference of the American Committee on Irish Studies; it was later published in the 1969 issue of *Eire/Ireland. Susan L. Mitchell: An Aide to Immortality* and *Division and Unity: AE and W. B. Yeats*, were included in *The World of W. B. Yeats*, and the essay on Sean O'Casey was broadcast by the CBC in 1965. The essays on Oscar Wilde and on John Montague have not previously faced an audience of any kind.

To all the editors and publishers concerned I here express my gratitude, and to no one more than Liam Miller of the Dolmen Press, who encouraged me on my way as he encouraged so many Irish writers and writers on celtic art and literature, and whose death has deprived me of a personal friend and Ireland of a man of genius.

ROBIN SKELTON

Celtic Contraries

I

Oscar Wilde and "The Tomb of Keats"

In the spring of 1877, Oscar Wilde aged twenty-two visited Rome for the first time after touring Greece with J. P. Mahaffy. In a letter to Reginald Harding, written just before his departure, he said "This is an era in my life, a crisis. I wish I could look into the seeds of time and see what is coming." While at Rome, he visited the grave of Keats and was disturbed by what he saw. He wrote an article about the visit and submitted it to the Reverend Matthew Russell, S. J., who was then editor of the *Irish Monthly*, and it was printed, together with a sonnet "Heu Miserande Puer" on the same subject, in the July 1877 number of the magazine. This article has never been reprinted, though the sonnet reappeared in a revised form in Wilde's 1881 *Poems* and in later collections, and it was reprinted in its original state in Stuart Mason's *Bibliography* of Wilde. As this article includes many statements indicative of Wilde's tastes at this time and several phrases which appear to foreshadow his later work, it is, I believe, worth disinterring. It is headed simply:

The Tomb of Keats

by Oscar Wilde

As one enters Rome from the Via Ostiensis by the Porta San Paolo, the first object that meets the eye is a marble pyramid which stands close at hand on the left.

There are many Egyptian obelisks in Rome, tall, snake-like spires of red sandstone, mottled with strange writings, which remind us of the pillars of flame which led the children of Israel through the desert away from the land of the Pharoahs; but more wonderful than these to look upon is this gaunt wedge-shaped pyramid standing here in this Italian city, unshattered amid the ruins and wrecks of time, looking older than the Eternal City itself, like terrible impassiveness turned to stone. And so in the middle ages men supposed this to be the sepulchre of Remus, who was slain by his own brother at the founding of the city, so ancient and mysterious it appears; but we have now, perhaps unfortunately, more accurate information about it, and know that it is the tomb of one Caius Cestius, a Roman gentleman of small note, who died about 30 B.C.

Yet though we cannot care much for the dead man who lies in lonely state beneath it, and who is only known to the world through his sepulchre, still this pyramid will be ever dear to the eyes of all English-speaking people, because at evening its shadow falls on the tomb of one who walks with Spenser, and Shakespeare, and Byron, and Shelley, and Elizabeth Barrett Browning, in the great procession of the sweet singers of England.

For at its foot there is a green, sunny slope, known as the Old Protestant Cemetery, and on this a common-looking grave, which bears the following inscription:

> "This grave contains all that was mortal of a young English poet, who, on his death-bed, in the bitterness of his heart, desired these words to be engraven on his tomb-stone: 'Here lies one whose name was writ in water.' February 24, 1821."

And the name of the young English poet is John Keats.

Lord Houghton calls this cemetery "one of the most beautiful spots on which the eye and heart of man can rest," and Shelley speaks of it as "making one in love with death, to think one should be buried in so sweet a place"; and indeed when I saw the violets, and the daisies, and the poppies that overgrow the tomb, I remembered how the dead poet had once told his friend that he thought the "intensest pleasure he had received in life was in watching the growth of flowers," and how another time, after lying a while quite still, he murmured in some strange prescience of early death, "I feel the flowers growing over me."

But this time-worn stone and these wild flowers are but poor memorials* of one so great as Keats; most of all, too, in this city of Rome, which pays such honour to her dead; where popes, and em-

*Recently some well-meaning persons have placed a marble slab on the wall of the cemetery with a medallion-profile of Keats on it, and some mediocre lines of poetry. The face is ugly, and rather hatchet-shaped, with thick, sen-

perors, and saints, and cardinals, lie hidden in "porphyry wombs," or couched in baths of jasper and chalcedony, and malachite, ablaze with precious stones and metals, and tended with continual service. For very noble is the site, and worthy of a noble monument; behind looms the grey pyramid, symbol of the world's age, and filled with memories of the sphinx, and the lotus leaf, and the glories of old Nile; in front is the Monte Testaccio, built, it is said, with the broken fragments of the vessels in which all the nations of the East and the West brought their tribute to Rome; and a little distance off, along the slope of the hill under the Aurelian wall, some tall gaunt cypresses rise, like burnt-out funeral torches, to mark the spot where Shelley's heart (that "heart of hearts!") lies in the earth; and above all, the soil on which we tread is very Rome!

As I stood beside the mean grave of this divine boy, I thought of him as of a Priest of Beauty slain before his time; and the vision of Guido's St. Sebastian came before my eyes as I saw him at Genoa, a lovely brown boy, with crisp, clustering hair and red lips, bound by his evil enemies to a tree, and, though pierced by arrows, raising his eyes with divine, impassioned gaze towards the Eternal Beauty of the opening heavens. And thus my thoughts shaped themselves to rhyme:

Heu Miserande Puer

Rid of the world's injustice and its pain,
  He rests at last beneath God's veil of blue;
  Taken from life while life and love were new
The youngest of the martyrs here is lain,
Fair as Sebastian and as foully slain.
  No cypress shades his grave, nor funeral yew,
  But red-lipped daisies, violets drenched with dew,
And sleepy poppies, catch the evening rain.
O proudest heart that broke for misery!
  O saddest poet that the world hath seen!
    O sweetest singer of the English land!

sual lips, and is utterly unlike the poet himself, who was very beautiful to look upon. "His countenance," says a lady, who saw him at one of Hazlitt's lectures, "lives in my mind as one of singular beauty and brightness; it had the expression as if he had been looking on some glorious sight." And this is the idea which Severn's picture of him gives. Even Haydon's rough pen and ink sketch of him is better than this "marble libel," which I hope will soon be taken down. I think the best representation of the poet would be a coloured bust, like that of the young Rajah of Koolapoor at Florence, which is a lovely and life-like work of art.

Thy name was writ in water on the sand,
But our tears shall keep thy memory green,
And make it flourish like a Basil-tree.

Rome, 1877.

This article did not reach print without some argument as to the layout. On the 15th or 16th of June 1877, Wilde wrote to Russell:

> Dear Sir, I write in haste to say that my sonnet must be printed in *full large type*: it looks and reads *bad* as it stands. Let the article begin on the *middle* of p. 473, and then 475 will begin, as I wished, with "As I stood beside the mean grave" and the *sonnet will end the page*. Please manage this for me, and send me second proof to look at. You might fill up the space with "winged words" which are always good wherever they come.
>
> I have put "hearts of hearts" in inverted commas; of course you remember *"cor cordium"* is the inscription on Shelley's tombstone.
>
> Please see to the change.
>
> I am sorry you object to the words *"our* English Land." It is a noble privilege to count oneself of the same race as Keats or Shakespeare. However I have changed it. I would not shock the feelings of your readers for anything . . . Yours truly
>
> OSCAR WILDE

Wilde also sent a copy of the sonnet to Lord Houghton, suggesting that he lend his name to an appeal for money to erect "a really beautiful memorial." The word "our" is retained in this copy of the poem. A copy and a similar letter were sent also to W. M. Rossetti, and Harry Buxton Forman was sent a copy of the magazine, together with a request for information as to the whereabouts of some available print of W. B. Scott's etching of Keats's grave. To both Rossetti and Forman he described his "monograph" as "little more than/only a stray sheet from a boy's diary."

As the discussion of the word "our" shows, Wilde was not particularly concerned with his Irish descent. He had recently stopped signing his letters with the fuller, and very Irish version of his name, OSCAR F. O'F. WILDE, and when the sonnet was reprinted in 1881 the word "our" was replaced. The final version of the poem differs in several other ways from the first version, also. It reads:

The Grave of Keats

Rid of the world's injustice and his pain,
He rests at last beneath God's veil of blue.
Taken from life when life and love were new
The youngest of the martyrs here is lain,
Fair as Sebastian, and as early slain.
No cypress shades his grave, no funeral yew,
But gentle violets weeping with the dew
Weave on his bones an ever-blossoming chain.
O proudest heart that broke for misery!
O sweetest lips since those of Mitylene!
O poet-painter of our English Land!
Thy name was writ in water—it shall stand:
And tears like mine will keep thy memory green,
As Isabella did her Basil-tree.

The revisions are partly for metrical reasons. "And tears like mine will keep thy memory green" is a smoother iambic line than "But our tears shall keep thy memory green". The dramatic quality of the poem is intensified by substituting the more powerful "Thy name was writ in water—it shall stand" for the rather confusing "Thy name was writ in water on the sand" which did not, in any case, tie in well with the following reference to the Basil tree. On the other hand, the rather melodramatic reference to the poet's being "foully slain" is removed, and the phrase "early slain" substituted for it. This concentrates more attention upon Keats' youth and adds a useful piece of further information, whereas the emotional force of the word "foully" adds little to the poem, the word "martyrs" having already been used. The three completely altered lines all point in one direction. They increase the sensual vitality of the poem.

But red-lipped daisies, violets drenched with dew,
And sleepy poppies, catch the evening rain.

is pictorially pleasant and may even, in its general tone, remind us usefully of Lycidas. The new version, however, substitutes one complex image for three fairly simple ones and brings the notion of grief much more into the picture. Moreover, the alliteration in "b" adds a necessary toughness to what might otherwise be a rather sickly image.

> But gentle violets weeping with the dew
> Weave on his bones an ever-blossoming chain.

This has also a greater degree of subtlety. "Weeping with the dew" combines the notion of dew as the tears of the violets, and with that the notion of the dew's tears being additional to those of the violets. The same process of intellectual and sensual intensification has occurred with the tenth line of the poem. The rather uneventful: "O saddest poet that the world hath seen!" is replaced by: "O sweetest lips since those of Mitylene."

The greater degree of sensuality is obvious, and the classical reference clearly adds something to the intellectual strength of the poem. Mitylene (or Mytilene) was, of course, the chief city of Lesbos. The lips of Mitylene are, therefore, those of Sappho, and the reference to them brings a sexual ambiguity to the poem which again intensifies its sensuality. Moreover, as this reference is followed by a comparison between the speaker's grief over Keats and that of Isabella for her murdered Lorenzo in Keats's poem "Isabella," the sexual undertone becomes even more apparent. It is at this point, perhaps, that the replacing of the daisies, poppies, and violets of the early version by the violets of the later version might be reconsidered. In his article Wilde referred to Shakespeare, and violets are used by Shakespeare for several elegiac speeches. Perhaps the most celebrated is that by Laertes over the grave of Ophelia.

> Lay her i'th' earth,
> And from her fair and unpolluted flesh
> May Violets spring!

Marina, in *Pericles*, also scatters violets upon a grave. Violets are, in Shakespeare, emblematic of fidelity. It may well be that in discarding the daisies and poppies Wilde was aware of their irrelevant emblematic meanings and deliberately concentrated upon the more valid violets.

If we look back at the poem again, we can see that Keats's death is presented in the context of, firstly, the murder of the "lovely brown boy" St. Sebastian, whose fault was his belief in a socially unacceptable religion; secondly; the weeping violets of fidelity which are laid so often upon the grave of a loved one; thirdly, the comparable beauty of the poetess Sappho whose (wholly justifiable) reputation for poetry was accompanied by a (possibly unjustifiable) reputation for lesbianism; and lastly the grief of Isabella over the murdered Lorenzo whose only fault was his desire for a forbidden love.

I am not trying, as the saying goes, to make a federal case out of it, but it does appear that Wilde's well-known worship of the work of Keats, which led him to discover the "soul of Christ" in Keats's poetry, and to plead for a copy of Keats's *Poems* when in prison, was as much a consequence of his emotional needs as of his critical judgments. His sonnet upon the sale of Keats's letters, which he wrote in 1885, is curiously anticipatory of his own fate.

On the Sale by Auction of Keats' Love Letters

These are the letters which Endymion wrote
  To one he loved in secret, and apart.
  And now the brawlers of the auction mart
Bargain and bid for each poor blotted note.
Ay! for each separate pulse of passion quote
  The merchant's price: I think they love not art
  Who break the crystal of a poet's heart
That small and sickly eyes may glare and gloat!

Is it not said that many years ago,
  In a far Eastern town, some soldiers ran
  With torches through the midnight, and began
To wrangle for mean raiment, and to throw
  Dice for the garments of a wretched man,
Not knowing the God's wonder, or his woe?

Throughout his life Wilde constantly made use of the theme of youthful beauty, its destruction, and its destructiveness. The severed head of Lorenzo may be said to appear again, in a different guise, in *Salomé*. Endymion, in different guises, receives many tributes, and the figure of the person martyred by society occurs in both comic and tragic shapes. Wilde had already written, and published, one or two small pieces before he published his article on "The Tomb of Keats," but it may be that this article and its accompanying sonnet were seminal for his work. A case could certainly be made out for suggesting that his letter to Reginald Harding showed a disturbing amount of insight when he wrote of his visit to Rome. "This is an era in my life, a crisis. I wish I could look into the seeds of time and see what is coming."

The Garden of Eros

Had Wilde looked into the seeds of time, he would have seen that, as a poet, he did not really survive the crisis. His aesthetics, his drama, and his stories have given him an honorable place in Anglo-Irish literature, but his poetry, with the exception of *The Ballad of Reading Gaol* and one or two shorter pieces, has largely been ignored. It is however in Wilde's poetry that we can see the development of a pathologically romantic imagery which, in its excess, defines the literary tradition from which much early poetry of the Irish Renaissance sprang more clearly than does much better and less obsessed work of the period.

Much can be summarized briefly. *Ravenna* (1878) is a dexterous elegiac meditation which, dwelling upon the sad beauty of ruin and the memories of poets long gone, also indulges in a pastoral paganism typical of the period. Wilde's paganism, however, returns us to his Sebastian and to certain aspects of his ideal poetic hero. In the fifth section of *Ravenna* the speaker wanders through the woods.

> Long time I watched and surely hoped to see
> Some goat-foot Pan make merry minstrelsy
> Amid the reeds! some startled Dryadmaid
> In girlish flight or lurking in the glade,
> The soft brown limbs, the wanton treacherous face
> Of woodland god! Queen Dian in the chase,
> White-limbed and terrible, with look of pride,
> And leash of boar hounds leaping at her side!
> Or Hylas mirrored in the perfect stream.

It is, to say the least of it, odd to find Hylas presented as the climax of this list of amorous deities. Hylas, Hercules' minion, was notable only for being beautiful. He went to fetch water one day and the nymph Dryope and her sisters, seeing his beauty, enticed him into the stream to live with them. Wilde's lines link Hylas with Narcissus, who fell in love with his own reflection. It seems that, for Wilde, Hylas the beautiful boy, is an important image, a central symbol.

If we accept the homosexual element here as obvious, and from the description of Diana, also note something of a masochistic flavor, we are part way to understanding the central poetic symbolism of Wilde. After *Ravenna*, which won the Newdigate Prize in 1878, comes the collection, *Poems* (1881), and in this book other developments occur. The "Sonnet to Liberty" is masochistic. Dull-eyed democracies do not please the speaker, but he has a weakness for reigns of terror, and says, with curious candor,

> These Christs that die upon the barricades,
> God knows it I am with them, in some things.

"Ave Imperatrix" sees the British Empire through a bloody mist and mourns the dead who have been sacrificed to create it. There is, however, a lip-smacking relish in the blood and thunder as well as a luxuriating in the sadness of the young dead. Democracy is attacked further in the "Sonnet to Milton," though it is attacked for failing, not for existing. In "Louis Napoleon" the "poor boy" is honored by republican France, which kisses "the mouth of Liberty." Wilde's attitude towards liberty is somewhat inconsistent, however. In "Libertatis Sacra Fames" he refers to the "kiss of anarchy" and says:

> I love them not whose hands profane
> Plant the red flag upon the piled-up street,

and talks of "this modern fret for Liberty" which he sees as leading to the fading of "Art, Culture, Reverence, Honour" and to the triumph of "Treason and Murder." In "Theoretikos" he announces his wish to "stand apart" in dreams of art/ and loftiest culture."

These poems point to Wilde as wishing, perhaps masochistically, to stand apart, and to dream of a culture beyond theological concern. He will be "Neither for God, nor for his enemies."

In "The Garden of Eros," we get one of these dreams. It includes Herakles strewing flowers on the tomb of Hylas, and numerous references to the flowers and goddesses of pastoral classicism. Keats also turns up again as "the boy who loved thee best," "thee" meaning Eros. Swinburne also makes an appearance as the seer of the "grand Greek limbs of young Democracy" and the announcer of "the great Republic," as well as the viewer of Atlanta, the kisser of Proserpine, and the singer of "the Galilean's requiem." Swinburne is followed by Rossetti who, the "Spirit of Beauty" is told,

> "Loves thee so well, that all the World for him
> A gorgeous coloured vestiture must wear,

And sorrow take a purple diadem,
Or else be no more Sorrow, and Despair
Gild its own thorns, and Pain, like Adon, be
Even in Anguish beautiful . . .

The poem closes with a lament for the present time which has chosen to ignore beauty and the old gods.

Mario Praz, in *The Romantic Agony*, has already documented the masochistic element in nineteenth-century poetry, and many critics have shown how the love of rich colors, sensual excess, and spiritual symbolism combined with masochistic passions in the work of the Pre-Raphaelites, Wilde, Swinburne, Francis Thompson, and others. Wilde, however, is not merely a "fleshly" poet. In other of his shorter poems in the 1881 volume, he takes up different themes. In a section called "Rosa Mystica," he praises Rome both for its classicism and its Christianity. Christ is seen, predictably, as suffering, and the speaker, equally predictably, as filled with "sin and shame" and as possessing a "tortured past." The real center of this section, however, is "The New Helen," a femme fatale, linked closely with Venus Erycina, the Roman Aphrodite. Since the fall of Troy, she has been hidden away in a hollow hill with "That discrowned Queen men call the Erycine," so that she need not see

The face of Her, before whose mouldering shrine
To-day at Rome the silent nations kneel;
Who gat from Love no joyous gladdening,
But only Love's intolerable pain,

Thus the Virgin Mary is opposed to Aphrodite, by being the goddess of Love's cruelty. The New Helen, however, appears to be equally unproductive of joy. The speaker asks for kindness from her, though he is in such a condition that he can hardly form the request with his "tremulous lips." He says:

So bowed am I before thy mystery,
So bowed and broken on Love's terrible wheel
That I have lost all hope and heart to sing . . .

He has also a shrewd suspicion that the lady will ignore his request and go back to

> the tower of thine old delight,
> And the red lips of young Euphorion.

Euphorion, according to Goethe (*Faust*, part 2, act 3), was Helen's child by Faust. He was also, we are told, her child by the ghost of Achilles in one classical myth. Wilde, perhaps predictably, emphasizes his attractiveness, and, while the "tower" may remind us of Marlowe's reference to Helen's unfortunate effect upon "the topless towers of Ilium," it also has a rather medieval (or perhaps Gothic-Romantic) quality.

Helen herself was not born as other women are, but apparently rose, like Aphrodite, from the foam. Thus in "The New Helen," Wilde manages to make use of references to three pain-causing women, Helen, Aphrodite, and the Virgin Mary, as well as Euphorion who represented, we are told, Byron and romanticism, and we may choose to remember that Byron's mother was also a giver of much pain to the poet. Wilde apostrophizes Helen finally as

> Lily of love, pure and inviolate!
> Tower of Ivory! Red rose of fire!

The second of these epithets derives surely from the Song of Songs and is more appropriate to masculinity than feminity. Wilde, indeed, in "The New Helen," has presented a sort of symbolic sexual ragout to lay at the feet of his idea of poetry.

That idea never receives an adequate definition in Wilde's actual poems. In "The Burden of Itys," we are once again treated to a description of the fascinations of Greek mythology in a setting of the countryside round Oxford. Clearly affected in structure by Matthew Arnold's "Scholar-Gipsy," it remains undisturbed by logic. There is not much connection between the landscape and the fantastic reverie it arouses. A small daffodil succeeds in reminding the speaker of Jove and Danae, Mercury, and Arachne.

> Men say it bloomed upon the sepulchre
> Of One I sometime worshipped, but to me
> It seems to bring diviner memories
> Of faun-loved Heliconian glades and blue
> nymph-haunted seas,
>
> Of an untrodden vale at Tempe where
> On the clear river's marge Narcissus lies,

The tangle of the forest in his hair,
  The silence of the woodland in his eyes,
Wooing that drifting imagery which is
  No sooner kissed than broken; Memories of Salmacis

Who is not boy nor girl and yet is both,
  Fed by two fires and unsatisfied
Through their excess, each passion being loth
  For love's own sake to leave the other's side
Yet killing love by staying

The poem is populated with cruel beauties (female) and suffering beauties (male) though occasionally such personalities as Philomel provide welcome variety.

Wilde himself said in a letter to Violet Hunt on 22 July 1881, "The poem I like best is 'The Burden of Itys' and next to that 'The Garden of Eros.' They are the most lyrical, and I would sooner have any power or quality of 'song' writing than be the greatest sonnet writer since Petrarch." Wilde's fascination with cruel beauty and amorous youth is also displayed in "Charmides," another of his longer poems. The beautiful youth, Charmides, falls in love with the statue of Pallas Athene in her temple. He strips it of its finery and embraces it. . . . He presses "His hot and beating heart upon her chill and icy breast."

It was as if Numidian javelins
  Pierced through and through his whirling brain,
And his nerves thrilled like throbbing violins
  In exquisite pulsation, and the pain
Was such sweet anguish that he never drew
  His lips from hers till overhead the lark of warning flew.

After this experience he rests in the countryside and is much admired for his beauty by the passing woodsmen, who think he must be an immortal.

and one said
  "It is young Hylas, that false runaway
Who with a Naiad now would make his bed
  Forgetting Herakles," but others, "Nay
It is Narcissus, his own paramour,
Those are the fond and crimson lips no woman can allure."

Charmides is drowned for his blasphemy. His body is adored by a young votaress of Diana, and the Goddess kills her for her unchastity. In Hades, however, Venus contrives that the two young creatures shall meet and love each other. This poem adds to its masochistic and homosexual overtones a touch of necrophilia.

There would be no point in exploring such attitudes were it not that Wilde was at once a product of his age, and a conclusion to it. His brand of romanticism derives clearly from an admiration for the Keats of *Endymion* (he refers to Keats as Endymion not infrequently), the *Adonais* of Shelley, and the "splendid sin" in the more hectic poetry of Swinburne, Rossetti, and the other Pre-Raphaelites. It also, however, derives from a classical aestheticism learnt in his Trinity College days from the great Mahaffy and taken to its extremes at the Oxford of Walter Pater. In writing to Mahaffy in April 1893, Wilde described him as "one to whom I owe so much personally," "my first and my best teacher," "the scholar who showed me how to love Greek things." The long poem "Panthea" takes the view, implicit in all Wilde's poetry and much of his aesthetics, "To feel is better than to know." This explains, or perhaps excuses, the lack of intellectual structure and content in most of his poetry. It also suggests, in combination with the continual worship of ideal immortal figures, a kind of idealistic hedonism which is equally discernible from time to time in Keats and Spenser. Wilde's poetic attempt at a coherent philosophy can be found in "Humanitad." This poem concludes, after much adoration of beauty and art and after a somewhat surprising reference to Wordsworth, with the view that we are

ourselves the sowers and the seeds,
The night that covers and the lights that fade . . .
Lords of the natural world are yet our own dread enemy

Nevertheless, this is a passing condition, and we will survive.

we are crucified, and though
The bloody sweat falls from our brows like rain,
Loosen the nails—we shall come down I know,
Staunch the red wounds—we shall be whole again,
No need have we of hyssop-laden rod,
That which is purely human, that is Godlike, that is God.

"Humanitad," though stating a humanist point of view, by its imagery suggests an idealism that approaches the sensual mysticism of Swinburne. This sensuality reaches its apogee in "The Sphynx," which Mario Praz sees, justly, as a fantasy upon the theme of the fatal woman, La Belle Dame sans Merci, which echoes Keats, Swinburne, Baudelaire, and Poe. Wilde's "Sphynx," however, is even more of a whore than Swinburne's Cleopatra. After coupling with a collection of gods so varied and odd as to remind us of the less restrained pictures of Bosch, she is invited to finally sate herself with a lion or tiger:

if you are grown sick of dead divinities

Follow some roving lion's spoor across the copper-coloured plain,
Reach out and hale him by the mane and bid him be your paramour!

Couch by his side upon the grass and set your white teeth on his throat
And when you hear his dying note lash your long flanks of polished brass

And take a tiger for your mate, whose amber sides are flecked with black,
And ride upon his gilded back in triumph through the Theban gate,

And toy with him in amorous jests, and when he turns, and snarls, and gnaws,
O smite him with your jasper claws! and bruise him with your agate breasts!

This is so preposterous as to compel admiration for its excess. It is also, however, not unimportant to the understanding of the romanticism of the end of the nineteenth century. Wilde's Sphynx is, in its way, the direct descendant of Petrarch's Laura. If the Mistress is cruel, through her chastity or absence, and the lover luxuriates in his suffering; then, sooner or later, the lover is likely to admire the most intense form of cruelty he can discover. Again, the Hylas-Narcissus figure is clearly a descendant of Endymion, and of Adonis; the beautiful boy who causes others to suffer by his chastity or unattainability must sooner or later develop into a figure of death, must, indeed, become the drowned Hylas, the drowned Narcissus, the drowned Charmides. . . . In death the chastity and unattainability are complete; thus the passion which is satisfied upon the dead is the most intense passion of all, and the most triumphant. Again, the "splendid sins" of Wilde's poetry combined with the frequent images of "tortured guilt" can be seen as direct descendants of the "Lord, I am unworthy" cry of Petrarch and of some of the early English sonneteers, not to mention the Provençal lyricists.

Wilde could not combine his images into a coherent pantheon. Nor could he, as a poet, entirely separate himself from his models. He could, however, expose the predicament facing the romantic fantasist in the 1870s and 1880s. The image of the ideal poet, and therefore ideal hero, is of a Keats-Endymion facing a Belle Dame sans Merci. This ideal is beyond the present to accomplish; we may only observe the dead boy, now locked away so firmly in his dream of death as to be a Hylas, a Narcissus. In observing him, we remember also all those other boy-lovers of a terrible Muse, not only Charmides, but also Actaeon, and even the Christian martyrs at the feet of the Holy Virgin-Mother—the combination of virginity with motherly authority has obvious attractions. Our worship of these heroes may appear to be sexually ambiguous; though if we are true Hellenists, the love of man and boy, or of man and man, will not disturb us and may be quite as chaste and ideal as we wish. In 1882 Emma Speed, Keats's niece, gave Wilde the manuscript of Keats's "Sonnet on Blue." Wilde's letter of thanks runs, in part:

> What you have given me is more golden than gold, more precious than any treasure this great country could yield me, though the land be a network of railways, and each city a harbour for the galleys of the world.
>
> It is a sonnet I have loved always, and indeed who but the supreme and perfect artist could have got from a mere colour a motive so full of marvel: and now I am half enamoured of the paper that touched his hand, and the ink that did his bidding, grown fond of the sweet comeliness of his character, for since my boyhood I have loved none better than your marvelous kinsman, that godlike boy, the real Adonis of our age, who knew the silver-footed messages of the moon, and the secret of the morning, who heard in Hyperion's vale the largest utterance of the early gods, and from the beechen plot the light-winged Dryad, who saw Madeline at the painted window, and Lamia in the house at Corinth, and Endymion ankle-deep in lilies of the vale, who drubbed the butcher's boy for being a bully, and drank confusion to Newton for having analysed the rainbow. In

my heaven he walks eternally with Shakespeare and the Greeks, and it may be that some day he will lift

> "his hymenaeal curls from out
> his amber gleaming wine,
> With ambrosial lips will kiss my forehead, clasp the hand of noble love in mine."

"An etching of a lady, by Menpes after W. Graham Robertson, and a Manuscript Poem, by Keats, framed, "was sold at the auction of Wilde's belongings on 24 April 1895; the lot went for 38 [pounds]."

The Seeds of Time

I have not considered all of Wilde's poems; his slight, deft, near-imagistic "Impressions" are better poems than those I have discussed, and his *Ballad of Reading Gaol*, though unduly extended, is moving. I have been concerned only with those poems which most clearly reveal Wilde's central poetic symbolism and his classicism. Wilde—though he regarded himself, according to his letters to Bernard Shaw, as a member of the Celtic movement—was not really a part of the Irish Renaissance. He preferred the glory that was Greece to the glories of ancient Ireland, and is this he was a true product of Mahaffy's Trinity College where classics reigned triumphant over lesser concerns. Nevertheless, in his romantic sadness, his idealism, his mourning of the past, his reveries, he was not totally unlike many writers of the emerging Irish movement. He could easily have turned from classical poetry to Irish myth, as did John Todhunter in his collection *The Banshee* of 1888. He could have found in Oisin, or the story of Liadan and Lumhair, the themes he also found in Greek mythology or, like Austin Clarke, have portrayed pagan innocence in an Irish setting. He could have found an adequate supply of martyrs in Irish history, as did others of his contemporaries and successors. He chose, however, another track, and his poetry remained essentially an extension of the English tradition unenriched by references to other than familiar myths and attitudes.

Nevertheless, Wilde's work is not without its sympathetic connections with the work of the Irish Renaissance. The young Yeats, in *The Island of Statues* (1885), was able to make Alminor announce "All rhapsody hath sorrow for its soul," and the combination of pastoralism and enchantment in this juvenile work is not totally unlike that of Wilde.

Yeats's Byronic "Two Titans" of 1886 makes use of the femme fatale image and, in hectic language, portrays a most melodramatic scene.

When flash on flash once more the lightning came,
The youth had flung his arms around the rocks,
And in the sibyl's eyes a languid flame
Was moving. Bleeding now, his grasp unlocks,
And he is dragged again before her feet.
Why not? He is her own; and crouching nigh
Bending her face o'er his, she watches meet
And part his foaming mouth with eager eye—

To place a kiss of fire on the dim brow
Of Failure, and to crown her crownless head,
That all men evermore may humbly bow
Down to the mother of the foiled and dead.

The Mistress-Mother image is clear here. She is, in her tormented avidity, close to Wilde's "Sphynx" (though that poem appeared later). She is described in terms with which we are now familiar.

A sybil, with fierce face as of a hound
That dreams. She moveth, feeling in her brain
The lightnings pulse—behold her, aye behold—
Ignoble joy, and more ignoble pain.

The Beautiful Boy does not occur significantly in Yeats's early work though there are shadows of him in *The Wanderings of Oisin* (1889). Yeats, in fact, while accepting the Muse figure, with her attendant themes of sorrow and love's despair, and while frequently indulging a descriptive ability akin to that of William Morris, escaped Mahaffian classicism and replaced the Greek pantheon by a native one. He did not, of course, escape Keats. On 5 August 1913 he told his father: "There are always to types of poetry—Keats the type of vision, Burns a very obvious type of the other, too obvious indeed." On 14 March 1916 he corresponded with his father again: "I think Keats perhaps greater than Shelley and beyond words greater than Swinburne because he makes pictures one cannot forget and sees them as full of rhythm as a chinese painting." Earlier, on 28 June 1903 he had written to John Quinn: "Almost the greatest difficulty before good work in the ordinary theatres is that the audience has no binding interest, no great passion or bias that the dramatist can awake. I suppose it was some thought of this kind that made Keats' lines telling how Homer left great verses to a little clan seem to my imagination when I was a boy a description of the happiest fate that could come to a poet." Yeats sees Keats as a message-giver, a man with a task. Wilde sees him as a sacrifice, a suffering, though passionate, boy. Wilde's heroes (in his poetry, and in much other of his work) are the passive prey of forces and circumstances they cannot control. His women may be decisive, as in *Salomé* or in his comedies (consider Lady Bracknell, Mrs. Erlynne), but his men are rarely so.

Yeats's protagonists are not always decisive, being occasionally possessed by forces beyond their control; but such possession is always resented. Wilde exemplifies the masochistic thread in English romanticism; it was Yeats's triumph, as a young man, to work within the tradition but not to fall prey to its disorders. Wilde as a poet never really recovered from the emotional crisis of his youth, or from the crisis of sensibility he adumbrates in his letter to Reginald Harding of 1877. Yeats, with the same initial desire for beauty, the same urge to revive a cultural inheritance, and the same birthplace, carried the romantic tradition whole into the twentieth century and, finally, saw the Circus Animals for what they were.

2

SYNGE AND PETRARCH

WHEN OSCAR WILDE dropped the Irish elements in his name and turned, as a lyric poet, to Greek myth and to the worship of the English romantics, he clearly did so because he found little in the Irish part of his inheritance to stimulate him and a great deal in the Hellenism taught him at Trinity College by the great Mahaffy. He also, it seems, created poetry that, while not truly autobiographical, reflected with almost pathological intensity, the emotional conflicts and complexities of his own life. While he said that he would "sooner have any power or quality of song writing than be the greatest sonnet writer since Petrarch," he emulated Petrarch in many of his emotional attitudes, utilizing the worship of an ideal beauty as a means of expressing his personal philosophy and his sexual tendencies. Wilde was in his twenty-fourth year when he first visited Rome and wrote that sonnet on Keats which I have maintained to be so significant. J. M. Synge first visited Rome in 1896 shortly after his twenty-fourth birthday, and there he, too, found a romantic image and a theme, though in his case the resultant poetry had to wait twenty years for its appearance.

Parallels of this kind may appear to be willful and arbitrary. They are not, however, without interest. In their middle twenties both Wilde and Synge were emotionally overwrought and products of a divided inheritance. Both were products of Trinity College, Dublin, and of its protestant traditions, and both had grown to feel it necessary to oppose the bourgeois morality and narrow religiosity of the period. Both had, moreover, turned to Europe. There are, indeed, enough similarities between the situations of the two young men to make a case for placing their different approaches to the romantic tradition alongside one another.

It was in the last years of his life, as he was beginning work on *Deirdre of the Sorrows*, that Synge turned once more to the enthusiasms he experienced on his first visit to Rome and began to construct his versions of Petrarch. At this period he made his writing an expression of his own fears of approaching death and of his own sense of isolation, just as Wilde expressed the isolation of the aesthete and the martyrdom of the artist in his own romantic poems. In giving a new voice to Petrarch's *Sonnets to Laura in Death*, Synge was anticipating his separation from his own Laura, and also reflecting upon some of the difficulties he found in that relationship.

Synge's interest in Petrarch may have been partly renewed by his love for Molly Allgood, but it had its origin in his studying Italian and reading Petrarch in the original tongue in Rome in 1896. He had gone to Italy with his mind filled with romantic notions of love's suffering and the solitude of the sensitive artist. There he had begun to write (and may, indeed, have completed) the first draft of his *Vita Vecchia*, a sequence of poems linked by passages of prose in which he told the story of a man rejected by his beloved. This work is, in its tone, strongly reminiscent of a then popular and now forgotten collection of verse by Eric Mackay called *Love Songs of a Violinist and Other Poems*. It was first published in 1885 and by 1893 had reached a fifth and expanded edition. It is difficult to believe that a popular and widely available book of poems with this title would not have been read by Synge at a time when he was still thinking of becoming a violinist and was writing poetry. Although there are few close verbal parallels between Mackay and Synge, there are many similarities in approach and attitude. The love in Mackay's book speaks with a hectic insistence that owes something, perhaps, to the work of James ("B.V.") Thomson, and is constantly complaining of his lot. He is beset by dreams and refers frequently to music, to death, and to an ideal beauty. Were it not for the way in which one of Synge's few surviving poems of this period reminds one of Mackay at two points, one might dismiss the notion of "influence" entirely and put the similarities down as due simply to both poets being affected by a popular manner of the time. This poem of Synge is prefaced with the words "My lady left me and I said" and reads:

> I curse my bearing, childhood, youth,
> I curse the sea, sun, mountains, moon,
> I curse my learning, search for truth,
> I curse the dawning, night, and noon.

Cold, joyless I will live, though clean,
Nor, by my marriage, mould to earth
Young lives to see what I have seen,
To curse—as I have cursed—their birth.

The two relevant passages from Mackay are:

Have I not sworn that I will not be wed
But mate my soul with hers on my death-bed
("A Prayer for Light")

I curse thy face; I curse thy hair;
I curse thy lips that smile so well,
Thy life, thy life, and my despair,
My loveless couch, thy wedding bell. . . .
("Sylvia in the West")

If Synge did read Mackay's book, he may well have read in the edition of 1895, or in the original newspaper review, the comments of Joseph Ellis who said, "The writer of the 'Love-Letters' is manifestly imbued with the tone and tune of Italian poetry, and has the merit of proving the English tongue capable of rivalling the Italian "*Canzoni d'Amore*" . . . Unto Britannia, as erst to Italia, has been granted a Petrarch."

Mackay was indeed a student of Italian poetry, had lived in Italy, and had composed poems in Italian. It is tempting to elevate possibility into probability and suggest that when Synge first visited Italy in 1896 and began to read Petrarch, his view of the poet had already been affected by his reading of Mackay.

Certainly, at this time, he must have been very susceptible to Petrarch. He was suffering himself from the pangs of unrequited love, having spent a good deal of the previous summer in trying, without success, to persuade Cherry Matheson to marry him. Cherry Matheson was the daughter of a leader of the Plymouth Brethren and found Synge's atheism an unsurmountable obstacle to their marriage. In Rome, in February 1896, Synge met an American girl, a Miss Capps, and also found that religious differences made close friendship impossible. On 1 May 1896 he left Rome for Florence where he met Marie Antoinette Zdanowska, an art student, who again found his atheism unacceptable and who insisted upon lending him various theological works. On his return to Paris in the spring, he proposed once again to Cherry Matheson and was rejected. It is clear that at the time when Synge first read Petrarch he was in a condition to sympathize deeply with the sonnets to Laura.

It is always difficult to determine exactly how a poet's experiences relate to his works. In the case of Synge's first encounter with Petrarch's Laura, however, we do have a number of clues. *The Life of Petrarch* by Thomas Campbell, which is included in the Bohn Library edition of the poet, contains the following: "Petrarch himself relates that in 1327, exactly at the first hour of the 6th of April, he first beheld Laura in the church of St. Clara of Avignon, where neither the sacredness of the place, nor the solemnity of the day, could prevent him from being smitten for life with human love. In that fatal hour he saw a lady, a little younger than himself, in a green mantle sprinkled with violets, on which her golden hair fell plaited in tresses." From this time onward Petrarch celebrated Laura and his love for her in his *Canzoniere*. These poems are traditionally divided into two collections, those written *in vita di Madonna Laura* and those written after her death in 1348, *in morte di Madonna Laura*; the greater part of the later collection being written at Vaucluse. Petrarch was never Laura's lover. She was a married woman and seems never to have encouraged or much appreciated his passion. She became therefore, for Petrarch, a symbol of spiritual and of unattainable paradise, and the poems to her are as much celebrations of a man's relationship to ideals of beauty and divinity as of sexual obsession.

From 1896 to 1898, after his Italian visit and his rejection by Cherry Matheson, Synge worked on a play which dealt with the love of a young man for a nun. It is clearly related closely to his feelings about Cherry Matheson, whom his German friend, Valeska von Eiken, had nicknamed "the holy one," but I suspect that it may also owe something to his reading of Petrarch. There is a general similarity between the imagery used by the play's hero, Colm, and that used by Petrarch to Laura, and when Sister Eileen decides to abandon her habit and marry the hero, she exchanged her habit for a "green silk dress."

The green dress appeared again in Synge's life in 1898 when he met Margaret Hardon, an American art student, in Paris. He nicknamed her in his diary as "la robe verte," and in 1899 he proposed to her and was rejected. This appears to have been Synge's last serious love affair before 1905 when he fell in love with Molly Allgood, a young actress at the Abbey Theatre. Although his relationship with Molly soon became blessedly un-Petrarchan, Synge's temperament was such as to cause him a good deal of unhappiness and frustration. He was easily roused to jealousy and frequently became upset by Molly's refusal to permit him the indulgence of self-pity. Molly herself was also capable of jealousy, and when on 18 September 1906 he accompanied the American poet, Agnes Tobin, on a visit to Waterford, the home of her ancestors, Molly became extremely annoyed.

Agnes Tobin was already involved in the study of Petrarch when she met Synge. Her book, *Love's Crucifix*, published in 1902 by Heinemann, consisted of translations of ten sonnets and a canzone and was introduced by Alice Meynell. Francis Thompson wrote of it: "The important and cardinal point of all is, that a fine foreign poem should beget a new English poem. . . . For the first time I can understand that Petrarch should have a reputation; before I never could . . . This diction has the beauty and humility of running water." W. B. Yeats wrote to Miss Tobin in 1904: "I have just written many dull and unnecessary letters to all kinds of unnecessary people and now I can give myself the deep pleasure of telling you how I delight in your Petrarch. I have read it over and over. It is full of wise delight—a thing of tears and ecstasy."

Yeats was, indeed, sufficiently impressed by *Love's Crucifix* to recommend it to others, and Katherine Asquith has recorded that, on visiting her home for a weekend, he read several of the poems aloud and showed himself particularly impressed by one which concluded with the line "The rest are words whose sweetness stops the sun."

Agnes Tobin's friendship with W. B. Yeats led her to become an enthusiastic supporter of the Abbey Theatre, and it seems likely that Synge met her at a dinner she gave for the Abbey company in early September 1906. At this time she was busy with the final stages of a new book of Petrarch translations *On the Death of Madonna Laura* which was to include material from both *Love's Crucifix* and her second collection of 1905, *The Flying Lesson*. On 20 September 1906, she wrote to Synge from Claridge's Hotel, London, to tell him that her uncle had died and that she felt she must return instantly to America. She told him: "I cannot do any more about the book— perhaps Mr. Yeats would see to it, or perhaps you would have time (it needs to be punctuated) so I send all the stuff I have—and will you please write to Mr. Yeats. I cannot write more than one letter (not even a telegram). My maid will write to Mr. Heinemann (my publisher)."

On the 24 September she wrote again to say that she had received cablegrams from home advising her not to sail till late October, so that she could deal herself with her book. Synge returned the material to her and she received it on 26 September. During the next few weeks, the correspondence continued. In thanking Synge, on 23 October, for a copy of *The Well of the Saints*, she wrote him: "I feel in it, what I felt in the Shadow of the Glen—that you ought to write verse. It seems to me you are very strong in the peculiar insight and the imaginings of beautiful subtle, and unusual things and feelings, which are the poet's inalienable right." She told him also that "My final proofs of Madonna Laura I expect daily—It ought to be 'out' in two weeks." On 30 November she wrote again to say "I hope Madonna Laura will please you—there was a terrible drain on me went to produce her," and she reported "Arthur Symons was very short with me when I told him you ought to write verse: 'no—no: he is the best dramatist of the lot.' " She expressed the hope of seeing him soon. On 7 December he wrote to Molly from England: "I went up to London today and lunched with Miss Tobin. She was very nice and kind. There is not of course the remotest sign of flirtation about us, but I like her greatly and value her friendship." And, on 27 December he wrote again:

> In the evening now I am reading Petrarch's sonnets, with Miss Tobin's translations. I think I'll teach you Italian too so that you may be able to read the wonderful love poetry of these Italian poets Dante and Petrarch, and one or two others . . . You feel as fully as anyone can feel all the poetry and mystery of the nights we are out in—like the night a week ago when we came down from Rockbrook with the pale light of Dublin shining behind the naked trees till we seemed almost to come out of ourselves with the wonder and beauty of it all.

It was not long after this that Synge began to translate Petrarch himself. While a part of his intention was simply to render that love poetry into English and so share it with Molly, he also used the translations as an exercise in creating prose poetry of the kind he could use in *Deirdre of the Sorrows* on which he had begun work. On 12 April 1908 Agnes Tobin wrote from San Francisco: "My very best wishes for Easter. Has Deirdre completely swallowed you up? And when am I to have The Tinker's Wedding? Above all—when am I to have the Laura Sonnets in Folk Speech?" Later, on 17 December 1908, she wrote from London. "How can we possibly wait till March to see the volume of your poems! It is delightful to think of it."

Synge died on 24 March 1909 and the Cuala Press edition of his *Poems and Translations* was not published until 8 April. This first edition contained eight translations from Petrarch's *Laura in Death*, sonnets 4, 5,

10, 32, 42, 47, 53, and 67. Each translation was given a title in imitation of Petrarch's own manner; though in the *Collected Works* published by Maunsel in 1910, a further series of sonnets were added, the titles being provided by another hand than Synge's. These are sonnets 11, 24, 60, and 75. In 1961 for my edition of Synge's translations I added titles to versions of sonnets 12, 13, 14, 25, and 73. These are all the sonnets that Synge translated in full, though he began work also upon sonnets 75 and 78 and some drafts of the opening lines of these exist in the Synge papers.

It is not possible to say with any certainty what text Synge used for his work on Petrarch. Although he could read Italian, he could not read it without assistance. His versions have little in common with those of Agnes Tobin whose work we know he read and studied. Mr. Liam Miller has pointed out that they do, however, from time to time remind one of some of the versions printed in the Bohn Classical Library edition. It is interesting to compare Synge's version of Sonnet XII with that by Agnes Tobin and with those by MacGregor and Capel Lofft in the Bohn volume.

I do not think that I have ever seen
So many times in one short afternoon
The Lady they call dead.

Tobin

Nowhere before could I so well have seen
Her whom my soul most craves since lost to view

MacGregor

Never till now so clearly have I seen
Her whom my eyes desire, my soul still views

Capel Lofft

I was never anyplace where I saw so clearly
one I do be wishing to see when I do not see

Synge

In her version of this sonnet, Agnes Tobin refers to "the nest that Cypris made for Eros." Capel Lofft translates this passage as "Love not in Cyprus found so sweet a nest." Synge says, "I wouldn't think that Love himself in Cyprus had a nest so nice and curious."

If we turn to Sonnet X, we find Tobin giving the last line as "Had I but died three years ago today!" MacGregor's version in Bohn reads "Death had been sweet today three years ago." Synge's version is "Oh, what a sweet death I might have died this day three years to-day!"

Synge's version of Sonnet XIV is close to the first version in Bohn but not to the second. This second version, by Anne Bannerman, begins:

> When welcome slumber locks my torpid frame,
> I see thy spirit in the midnight dream;
> Thine eyes that still in living lustre beam:
> In all but frail mortality the same.

The first version, by Wrangham, opens:

> O Blessed spirit! who dost oft return,
> Ministering comfort to my night of woe,
> From eyes which Death, relenting in his blow,
> Has lit with all the lustres of the morn:
> How am I gladden'd, that thou doest not scorn
> O'er my dark days thy radiant beam to throw!
> Thus do I seem again to trace below
> Thy beauties, hovering o'er their loved sojourn.

Synge's version of this passage is:

> Sweet spirit you that do be coming down so often to put a sweetness on my sad night-time with a look from those eyes death has not quenched, but made more deep and beautiful:
>
> How much it is a joy to me that you throw a light on my dark days, so that I am beginning to find your beauty in the places where I did see you often.

This is remarkably close to Wrangham, and quite different from Bannerman. In the case of Sonnet XI, however, Synge seems to make use of Bannerman's last line rather than that by Charlotte Smith or Dacre. Bannerman reads:

> Yes, though I seem'd to shut my eyes in night,
> They only closed to wake in everlasting light.

Synge's version of this passage runs:

> when you saw me shutting up my eyes I was
> opening them on the light that is eternal.

In the case of Sonnet XXIV the version by Charlemont seems closest to Synge's.

> Those eyes, sweet subject of my rapturous strain!
> The arms, the hands, the feet, that lovely face,
> By which I for myself divided was,
> And parted from the vulgar and the vain.
>
> Charlemont

> The eyes that I would be talking of so warmly,
> and the arms, and the hands, and the feet, and the
> face, that are after calling me away from myself
> and making me a lonesome man among all people
>
> Synge

The way in which Synge's versions resemble versions by Wrangham, Bannerman, Capel Lofft, Charlemont, and others which have not been gathered together in any place other than the Bohn volume, combined with the certainty that Synge did require assistance of some kind in his translations, makes it very likely that he used the Bohn collection. It seems equally clear that he did not use the Tobin one.

We cannot be sure what Italian text he used. His numbering usually follows that of the Bohn edition, which accepted the arrangement of Marsand. The sonnets numbered 60 and 78 by Bohn and Marsand, however, are numbered 59 and 77 by Synge. This may be totally without significance.

All the sonnets that Synge chose to translate are from *Laura in Death* and express moods which he himself was feeling at this time. His health was not good, and during the spring of 1907 he suffered a serious collapse. The glands in his neck began to swell again, and in April he told Stephen McKenna that he had been ill for two months, "four weeks not even downstairs." In September he had to undergo an operation on his neck, and in December he felt the first pains of the tumor in his side which was to prove the direct cause of his death. It is clear from Agnes Tobin's letter of 12 April 1908 that he had by that time done a good deal of work on Petrarch but had not completed his translations. He entered the Elpis Nursing Home on 30 April; the tumor was discovered to be inoperable. By now he knew that he had not long to live; he had suspected this for some months. His translation of Sonnet IV opens:

> Life is flying from me, not stopping an hour, and
> Death is making great strides following my track.
> The days about me, and the days passed over me
> are bringing me desolation, and the days to come
> will be the same surely.

Over the same period Synge's relationship with Molly Allgood was far from placid. He was jealous of her friendships with other men and on one occasion came back post-haste to Dublin from Kerry because she had not answered one of his letters and he felt that he might have lost her. His translation of Sonnet V ends with the paragraph,

> Let you not be giving new life every day to your own
> destruction, and following a fool's thoughts forever.
> Let you seek Heaven when there is nothing left pleasing
> on the earth, and it a poor thing if a great beauty, the
> like of her, would be destroying your peace and she living
> or dead.

The phrase "the like of her" is an addition to Petrarch. Again in his translation of Sonnet XXXII, he expressed his jealousy,

> What a grudge I am bearing the blessed saints that have
> got her sweet company, that I am always seeking; and

> what a grudge I am bearing against Death, that is standing in her two eyes, and will not call me with a word.

Petrarch's grief at the death of Laura was, I believe, for Synge a poetic analogy for his own grief over his frequent estrangements from Molly, and his awareness that his own death was soon to separate them. Moreover, he could find a parallel in Petrarch for the way in which his illness had come upon him at the exact point at which he and Molly had decided to make their engagement public and plan marriage. Thus the translation of Sonnet XLVII includes the statement:

> The time was coming when Love and Decency can keep company, and Lovers may sit together and say out all things are in their Hearts. But Death had his grudge against me, and he got up in the way, like an armed robber, with a pike in his hand.

Synge, here uses the word *Decency* though *Chastity* would be more accurate and is the usual translation. Petrarch was saying that age had brought Laura and himself to the point where friendship without sexual desire had become possible. The fires that had afflicted him for so long had cooled. The fires that had been "wasting" Synge's heart were perhaps rather different, and by changing Chastity to Decency he may have been attempting to hint rather at a totally accepted marriage than at a platonic relationship.

There is, of course, another and more disturbing side to these translations. Synge chose to present Molly with love poems from *Laura in Death* rather than *Laura in Life*, and he made these translations at a time when he was writing, for her, a play in which she should act the part of a woman whose love brought her man to destruction and who, after grieving over his death, committed suicide. In both *Deirdre* and in the translations, he was utilizing aspects of his own predicament. In his translation of Sonnet LX (which in his manuscript he misnumbered 59), there is a curious substitution of the phrase "living and dead" for the literal translation "living or dead," as if his Laura were poised between life and death.

> It is of her only I do be thinking, and she living and dead, and now I have made her with my songs so that the

> whole world may know her, and give her the love that is her due.
> May it please her to be ready for my own passage that is getting near, may she be there to meet me, herself in the Heavens, that she may call me, and draw me after her.

The similarity of mood in *Laura in Death* and *Deirdre of the Sorrows* is, of course, obvious. In his version of Sonnet LXVI, Synge wrote:

> The air and the earth and seas would have a good right to be crying out, and they pitying the race of men that is left without herself, like a meadow without flowers or a ring robbed of jewelry.

In the third act of *Deirdre of the Sorrows*, Deirdre cries

> I will not leave Naisi who has left the whole world scorched and desolate, I will not go away when there is no light in the heavens, and no flower in the earth under them, but is saying to me, that it is Naisi who is gone forever.

Both works contain similar expressions of nostalgia for departed or threatened happiness, similar expressions of grief and a similar adulation of woman's beauty. They are also, however, similar in more than mood and theme. The language of the translations is highly rhythmical without being metrical. The passage quoted above, for example, falls naturally into three parts, and each of the three parts has almost the same number of syllables and stresses as its companions.

> The *air* and the *earth* and *seas* would have a *good right* to be *cry*ing *out*, (6 stresses, 17 syllables)
>
> and they *pity*ing the *race* of *men* that is *left* with*out* her*self* (6 stresses, 16 syllables)
>
> like a *mead*ow with*out flow*ers or a *ring robb*ed of *jew*ellery (6 stresses, 17 syllables)

The *Deirdre* passage is less regular in construction, but still extremely rhythmical:

> I will *not leave Nai*si (3 stresses)
>
> who has *left* the *whole world scorche*d and *des*olate (5 stresses)
>
> I will *not go* aw*ay* (3 stresses)
>
> where there is *no* l*ight* in the *hea*vens (3 stresses)
>
> and *no flow*er in the *ear*th *un*der them (4 stresses)
>
> but is *say*ing to me that it is *Nai*si who has *gone* for*ev*er (4 stresses)

There is room for disagreement as to the precise number of stresses in each "line" here, but there is no doubt as to the general method; the speeches are constructed of separate musical phrases which present a pattern of stresses that is regular enough to be described as verging upon the metrical.

The rhythmical characteristics of Synge's translations are such as to remind one frequently of the sonnet form itself. If one counts the syllables of his version of Sonnet XXIV, one discovers that the first paragraph contains forty-six syllables, the second forty-eight, and the third seventy-seven: if they had contained forty-eight, forty-eight, and seventy-two, the proportion would have been that of the sonnet form itself, the octet being of eight twelve-syllable lines, and the sestet of six. If we divide the translation up into fourteen lines, we get:

> The eyes that I would be talking of so warmly
> and the arms, and the feet, and the face,
> that are calling me away from myself
> and making me a lonesome man among all people
>
> The hair was of shining gold, and brightness
> of the smile that was the like of an angel's surely,
> and was making a paradise of this earth,
> are turned to a little dust that knows nothing at all
>
> And yet I myself am living; it is for this
> I am making a complaint to be left without the
> light

I had such a great love for, in good fortune and bad,
and this will be the end of my songs of love,
for the vein where I had cleverness is dried up,
and everything I have is turned to complaint only.

In this version all the lines are of between eleven and thirteen syllables with the exception of line ten which has fourteen syllables and of line fourteen which has fifteen. The translation of Sonnet XXV is not so regularly constructed as regards the number of syllables in each speech unit, but if broken up into lines by taking every punctuation mark as indicating a line ending, and the words *that, and*, and *where* as indicating the beginning of a new line, becomes a fourteen-line poem divided into two four-line stanzas followed by two three-line ones. Other translations are less closely related to the sonnet form, but all are highly wrought constructions whose cadences and stress patterns are so arranged as to remind us of the regularities of verse even while the "folk" diction suggests the spontaneity of ordinary speech. In his translations of Petrarch, Synge was not only exploring themes and moods of deep personal significance to himself but also inventing a new kind of prose poem.

The strength and delicacy of these poems are so obvious as to make comment unnecessary. Synge combined in these works a simple vocabulary indicative of the directness and clarity of the speaker's emotions, with an elaborately harmonious prose that indicates the ceremonial element in these tributes to his Muse. To some extent he chose to use images more natural to his own beloved west of Ireland than to Petrarch's France and Italy, but he never strayed so far that the poems fail to bear witness to the romantic pastoralism of his original. Believing as he did that in some ways the West of Ireland was the last surviving home of that combination of pagan strength and Christian idealism which animated European culture in the fourteenth and fifteenth centuries, it was not strange for him to hear Petrarch speak with the accents of Aran and cry "Ohone." Synge was, indeed, deeply concerned to see Ireland as a part of Europe and in his *Sonnets from Laura in Death* he attempted to fuse renaissance Italy with renaissant Ireland in prose poems that could seem as natural to the banks of the Shannon as to those of the Sorga. He completed only eight translations to his own satisfaction during his lifetime, but he had reached the final stages of ten others and begun work on two more before he died.

Synge's translations of Petrarch are not usually regarded as an important part of his canon, but an examination of them does reveal something of the way in which Synge managed to bring into unity his personal and his artistic concerns. He told Padraic Colum once that all his work was subjective, coming out of moods in his own life, and it is not difficult to perceive this in all his work, once that hint has been given. In the case of the Petrarch translations, however, he did more than simply make use of his own "moods." He brought together and unified, two cultures. Devoted, as was Wilde, to the English romantic tradition and deeply interested in the Mediterranean beginnings of that tradition, he chose to bring Petrarch to Ireland rather than leave Ireland for Petrarch. He attempted, in this one work, what Yeats succeeded in doing in those later poems when the whole of European culture is brought to bear upon his themes, and Ireland and Byzantium, Leda and Maud Gonne, and Lear and King Billy coexist in the one poetic universe. Synge, like Yeats, had the dream both of "the noble and the beggarman;" and though, unlike Yeats, he did not live long enough to unify them in the one overmastering persona, he was, I believe, moving in this direction when he died. In his translations of Petrarch, he used those themes of romantic love and love's suffering which pervade the poetry of Wilde and the early poetry of Yeats and gave them new force and direction by means of superlative craftsmanship, inventing in the process a new form of "prose sonnet." Thus Synge opened the way to the "free" and experimental translations, the "versions" and "homages," in which later poets from Pound to Lowell have also clothed their personal emotions and sought to bring together into unity differing and even contrary cultures.

3

J. M. Synge

The Personal Compulsions and the Political Beliefs

Until very recently the plays of J. M. Synge have been generally regarded as attempts to portray Irish peasant life in a vivid and basically naturalistic manner. Of his mature drama only *Deirdre of the Sorrows* cannot be viewed as documentation of rural Ireland. Even *The Well of the Saints* appears to celebrate the glories of the peasant imagination. Moreover, all his plays save the last can be shown to include incidents, characters, and phrases that Synge himself came across in his wanderings in Wicklow, Kerry, Connemara, Mayo, and the Aran Islands. His own defence of *The Playboy* included the statement "in writing *The Playboy of the Western World*, as in my other plays, I have used very few words that I have not heard among the country people, or spoken in my own childhood before I could read the newspapers."[1] Accused of libelling the Irish character his defense was that his statements were true. It was, therefore, natural that many critics should see Synge as a social commentator, as even a somewhat detached observer of the Irish scene. Even his friends took this attitude. Jack B. Yeats wrote:

> All wild sights appealed to Synge, he did not care whether they were typical of anything else or had any synbolical meaning at all. If he had lived in the days of piracy he would have been the fiddler in a pirate schooner, him they called "the music"—"The music" looked on at everything with dancing eyes but drew no sword, and

1. Unless otherwise indicated, all quotations are taken from J. M. Synge, *Collected Works,* 4 vols., ed. Robin Skelton (London: Oxford Univ. Press, 1962–68.

when the schooner was taken and the pirates hung at Cape Corso Castle or the Island of Saint Christopher's, "the music" was spared because he *was* "the music."[2]

The belief that Synge was uninterested in symbolical meaning has no longer many adherents. Such critics as Stanley Sultan have revealed the symbolic complexity of *The Playboy of the Western World*, and others have uncovered archetypal material in *Riders to the Sea* and *The Well of the Saints*. The view that Synge was basically concerned in documenting Irish rural life, with however many symbolic overtones, is still popular, and even *The Aran Islands*, that most subjective of books, is regarded as being a documentary, which it is not, rather than the spiritual autobiography, which it is.

I am concerned here to discuss the way in which all Synge's drama utilizes elements of his own personal emotional experience, not in order to claim it as disguised autobiography but in order to show that Synge the poet, Synge the essayist, and Synge the dramatist are one. Synge's poems relate directly and obviously to his own life, and the same can be said of all his essays. Only the plays appear to be impersonal creations, and yet, I content, they are as profoundly dependent upon the emotional experiences of their author as are all his other works. Synge himself commented several times on the personal element in art. In a notebook of 1896–98 he wrote: "All emotions have neither end nor beginning, they are part of a long sequence of impulse and effort. The only relative unity in art is that of a whole man's lifetime." In the 1901 version of his first play, *When the Moon Has Set*, he wrote: "Every life is a symphony. It is this cosmic element in the person which gives all personal art and all sincere life, and all passionate love a share in the dignity of the world." In 1908, in a draft preface to his volume *Poems and Translations*, he wrote: "Many of the older poets, such as Villon and Herrick and Burns, used the whole of their personal life as their material, and the verse written in this way was read by strong men, and thieves, and deacons, not by little cliques only." On one occasion he told Padraic Colum that all his work was subjective, coming out of moods of his own life.

From the age of one John Synge was fatherless, and the narrow evangelical Protestant faith of his mother and maternal grandmother had enormous effect upon him. In the 1890s in Paris, he surveyed his childhood and youth in a number of autobiographical notes where he tried to identify the seminal experiences of his early days. He attached particular

2. Jack B. Yeats, "With Synge in Connemara," in W. B. Yeats, *J. M. Synge and the Ireland of His Time* (Churchtown, Dundrum: Cuala Press, 1911).

importance to his being introduced at an early age to the notion of hell: "One night I thought I was irretrievably damned and cried myself to sleep in vain yet terrified efforts to form a conception of eternal pain. In the morning I renewed my lamentations and my mother was sent for. She comforted me with the assurance that the Holy Ghost was convicting me of sin and thus preparing me for ultimate salvation . . . Religion remained a difficulty and occasioned terror to me for many years." At the age of fourteen, he came across a book of Darwin's and was deeply disturbed: "I flung the book aside and rushed out into the open air . . . I lay down and writhed in an agony of doubt . . . Till then I had never doubted and never conceived that a sane and wise man or boy could doubt. I had of course heard of atheists but as vague monsters that I was unable to realize. It seemed that I was become in a moment the playfellow of Judas. Incest and parricide were but a consequence of the idea that possessed me."

He satisfied his religious needs by a nationalist ardor, totally at variance with the loyalism of his family, and by a form of nature mysticism. In a notebook of 1896–98 he wrote: "A human being finds a resting place only where he is in harmony with his surroundings, and is reminded that his soul and the soul of nature are of the same organization." This harmony he found first in his childhood friendship with his cousin Florence Ross. Together they bird-watched and kept a large assortment of pets. He later said, "This period was probably the happiest of my life. It was admirable in every way."

His harmonious relationship with the natural world remained, however, a contrast to his inharmonious relationship with orthodox Protestantism. His skepticism led to his being rejected by the first girl with whom he fell in love and was an insurmountable obstacle to intimacy with several other girls. His mother persisted in attempting to change his views, pressing the Bible upon him, and introducing him to religious young ladies. Many of the prose notes and poems that he made in the 1890's dwell upon these matters, and in his two early works, *Vita Vecchia* and *Étude Morbide*, he fictionalized his spiritual struggles and emotional difficulties and even included poems and extracts from his journals relating to his doubts and his arguments with his girl friends. He continued to use journal material in his book on *The Aran Islands*, the first work he completed, and this, while purporting to be a straightforward account of life on the islands, is in reality an account of the inner life of John Synge and his personal search for a place and a culture where he could feel himself in harmony with his surroundings and sense the unity of man and nature. He was seeking to find the "cosmic element in the person," and whether or not he found this, he did find, as in his other wanderings in Kerry and Wicklow, material which he was able to use for his drama.

It was in his early play, *When the Moon Has Set*, however, that he first attempted to give dramatic form to his personal conflicts. The story is simple and tells of a young man persuading a nun, Sister Eileen, to abandon her calling and marry him. He uses as an argument the experience of Mary Costello, a woman who rejected his uncle's love on the advice of priests and thereafter went mad because she had denied the real meaning of her life as a woman. It is obvious that this play is a dramatization of his problems with Cherry Matheson, the daughter of a leader of the Plymouth Brethren, who had rejected him because of his atheism. The play is bad. Sister Eileen is scarcely characterized at all, and the young man is given to philosophizing to an unbearable extent. Nevertheless, Synge did not abandon it after its rejection by Lady Gregory and Yeats but continued to work on it for some years. The play contained too much of his personal life for him to let it go.

The first complete and mature play he wrote was *Riders to the Sea*. Here the dominant figure is the old woman, Maurya, and a central point of the play is her unintentional rejection of her son. Unable to bless his journey, she feels after his death that she has been responsible for it. The parallel is easy to see. Mrs. Synge disapproved wholly of her son's choice of a career, and while heartbroken over his unbelief, she could not bring herself to allow her profound love for him to overcome her opposition to his ways. She was a widow, as is Maurya who also mourns the loss of her menfolk and who says, sprinkling holy water upon the dead body of Bartley: "It isn't that I haven't prayed for you, Bartley, to the Almighty God. It isn't that I haven't said prayers in the dark night till you wouldn't know what I'd be saying." Mrs. Synge continually mourned in her letters to her son Robert and in her diary her son John's loss of faith. Maurya is surely the product of Synge's empathetic understanding of his mother's sense of loss and of her grief at the inefficacy of her prayers. Later, in 1908, when she was dying, he again expressed his deep sympathy for his mother's unswerving faith through his translation, *Prayer of the Old Woman, Villon's Mother*. He was, at this time, as the draft preface to his poems shows, identifying himself to some extent with Villon.

It is in the young women of the later plays rather than in the old ones, however, that Synge's own emotional life is brought into play most clearly. Norah Burke in *In the Shadow of the Glen* is as firmly trapped by convention as was Synge in the bosom of his family. Secretly rebellious, she remains with her unloved and unlovely husband for reasons of social propriety and because of her financial dependence upon him. In 1902, when he wrote the play, Synge was similarly financially dependent. As a young man, he too had been unable to face outright rebellion, and it was not until 1889, when he was eighteen years old, that his mother's insistence upon his talking to her vicar had led to his openly confessing his atheism. Moreover, the materialism of Dan Burke and of Michael Dara is comparable to that of the Synges. Michael Dara only agrees to marry Norah when he is assured of the wealth she will inherit from her supposedly dead husband. Mrs. Synge, when her son John objected to Edward Synge's evicting peasants, inquired in reply, "What would become of us if our tenants in Galway did not pay their rents?" Norah, like Synge, is afraid of committing herself absolutely to independence and the consequent vagrant insecurity. Only the crisis contrived by her husband forces her to make her decision, and she goes off with the Tramp, who comforts her fears, saying:

> Come along with me now, lady of the house, and it's not my blather you'll be hearing only, but you'll be hearing the herons crying out over the black lakes, and you'll be hearing the grouse, and the owls with them, and the larks and the big thrushes when the days are warm, and it's not from the like of them you'll be hearing a talk of getting old like Peggy Cavanagh, and losing the hair off you, and the light of your eyes, but it's fine songs you'll be hearing when the sun goes up, and there'll be no old fellow wheezing the like of a sick sheep close to your ear.

With the Tramp, Norah is promised an escape from a world of joyless concern and an experience of harmony with the natural world. Later in his life Synge signed his love letters to Molly Allgood, "Your Old Tramp," and many of his poems to her celebrate their joyful love in the glens of Wicklow where *In the Shadow of the Glen* is set.

This play is not, of course, about Synge's own predicament, his war with middle-class gentility and propriety and his alienation. Its emotional content, however, relates directly to the emotional currents of his own life. Nowhere does it relate more closely to these than in the creation of the figure of the Tramp. In an essay he wrote: "In the middle classes the gifted son of a family is always the poorest—usually a writer or artist with no sense for speculation—and in a family of peasants, where the average comfort is just over penury, the gifted son sinks also, and is soon a tramp on the roadside."

Synge saw himself as the middle-class equivalent of the Tramp. In another place he wrote: "There is something grandiose in a man who has forced all the kingdoms of the earth to yield the tribute of his bread, and who, at a hundred, begs on the wayside with the pride of an emperor. The slave and beggar are wiser than the man who works for recompense, for all our moments are divine and above all price, though their sacrifice is paid with a measure of fine gold. Every industrious worker has sold his birthright for a mess of pottage."

His dislike of the Protestant middle-class worship of industry as a good in itself combined with his admiration of independence of mind and spirit to make the vagrant a hero in his plays. In an early draft of *The Tinker's Wedding* Mary Byrne, the old Tinker woman, has a dream about the priest: "He was out in a bit of the thrifling field he has, and he with two wild geese yoked to a plough, and there he was blessing and cursing them, and making great persuasion, but not a bit would they stir." Some years later Synge wrote to Molly Allgood: "We're all wild geese at bottom, all we players, artists and writers, and there is no keeping us in a backyard like barndoor fowl." Sarah Casey, one of the wild geese of *The Tinker's Wedding*, is, in some respects, the opposite of Norah Burke in *In the Shadow of the Glen*. Whereas Norah is strugging to escape from stultifying convention, Sarah is eager to become respectable. She is envious of the status of married women, is tempted by the orderliness of conventional religious observances, and wishes to belong to a tradition alien to her inheritance. Mary Byrne points out clearly enough that the world of white dresses and wedding rings cannot be hers. It may seem attractive at a time when her imagination is stimulated by the emotional influences of springtime, the movements of May; but the attraction cannot last.

Synge himself, the vagrant of his family, also experienced nostalgia for an ordered world to which he could never belong. In his essay on *A Landlord's Garden in County Wicklow*, he wrote of:

> the tragedy of the landlord class . . . and of the innumerable old families that are quickly dwindling away. These owners of the land are not much pitied at the present day, or much deserving of pity; and yet one cannot quite forget that they are the descendants of what was at one time, in the eighteenth century, a high spirited and highly cultivated aristocracy. The broken green-houses and mouse-eaten libraries, that were designed and collected by men who voted with Grattan, are perhaps as mournful in the end as the four mud walls that are so often left in Wicklow as the only remnant of a farmhouse.

The house here described as Castle Kevin, a boycotted house that Mrs. Synge rented for the family's summer holidays over a number of years. The reference to the destroyed cottage may be equally personal; Synge's brother Edward was a land agent, and in 1887 he burned to the ground the house of Hugh Lacy on the Synge family estate in Wicklow.

Synge felt, like Sarah Cassey, nostalgia for a tradition that had lost its vitality and that had, in any case, long regarded him as an outsider. The savagery with which the Priest is treated in *The Tinker's Wedding* is a mark of the animosity Synge himself felt towards the Irish middle-class establishment.

He despised the decadence of Irish culture, while admiring its past greatness. It was the decadence of Christianity that he hated and not religious belief itself. In the notes for his first play he wrote:

> There is stagnation in everything that has been once mature . . . The world orchestra has been playing its oratorio for two thousand years and the thing has become effete. Now the players have gone out to gain new powers in lonely exaltation . . . I mean that in the Christian synthesis each separate faculty has been dying of atrophy. The synthesis has fallen. The imagination has wandered away to grow puissant and terrible again, in lonely vigils where she sits and broods among things that have been touched by madmen and things that have the smell of death on them and books written with the blood of horrible crimes.

The failure of Christianity was, for Synge, not the failure of religion itself but the failure of that arid middle-class Protestantism in which he was brought up. "The world," he wrote, "is a mode of the Divine exaltation, and every sane fragment of force ends in a fertile passion that is filled with joy. It is the infertile passions that are filled with death. That is the whole moral and aesthetic of the world." He saw this "infertile passion" in his own "pious relations," and he saw it destroying Norah Burke in *In the Shadow of the Glen*. Mary Byrne and Sarah Casey of *The Tinker's Wedding* however, are, as he wrote elsewhere of other vagrants, two of those who "unite in a rude way the old passions of the earth." Sarah Casey, in harmony with her surroundings and with the disturbance of the earth in springtime after "the changing of the moon" has awoken to new desires as the earth has awoken. She is one of the wild geese that cannot be harnessed to the clerical plough, and though her passion may be absurd, it is clearly a fertile one filled with joy, zest, and determined independence of mind.

There is no similar figure in *The Well of the Saints*, Synge's next play. The two central characters are, however, akin to the Tramp figure of *In the Shadow of the Glen*. Martin and Mary Doul, the two blind beggars, are, like the Tramp, in harmony with the earth—as long as they remain blind. When healed by the saint they lose their sense of intimacy with the movements of the seasons and also are unable to continue believing in their own beauty. On joining the world of laborious actuality, Martin becomes rapidly disillusioned, and even to some extent brutalized. When their sight again fails, the two beggars reject the saint's cure, preferring to remain blind and retain their newly regained belief in each other's attractiveness and their sensitive understanding of the sounds and scents of the natural world. Martin Doul makes a crucial statement when he says, at the very end of the play:

> If it's a right some of you have to be working and sweating the like of Timmy the Smith and a right some of you have to be fasting and praying and talking holy talk the like of yourself, I'm thinking it's a good right ourselves have to be sitting blind, hearing a soft wind turning round the little leaves of the spring and feeling the sun, and we not tormenting our souls with the sight of the grey days, and the holy men, and the dirty feet is trampling the world.

It is as outright a rejection of the world of work, material comfort, and conventional social attitudes as that made in the sixties by some of the so-called "hippies." It is an attack upon the do-gooder (Synge's brother Samuel was a missionary and, when at home, abetted their mother in her efforts to bring him back to God), and it implies that those who attempt to improve the lot of people whose culture they do not understand often cause more distress than they alleviate. It is also, of course, a cry for liberty of speech and action, and reminds one that Synge had good cause to make that cry, for he had been attacked very bitterly for the picture he presented in *In the Shadow of the Glen* and was told that his play was un-Irish.

The attack upon conventional beliefs in *The Well of the Saints* disquieted many, but *The Playboy of the Western World* caused riots. Much of the trouble was caused by the play's language. The name of God is regularly taken in vain by all but the widow Quinn. Moreover, there are other elements to offend the religious-minded. The parable of the Good Samaritan is parodied when Sawn Keogh, the pious suitor of Pegeen Mike, is too frightened to help the groaning man in the ditch, and the binding, burning, and threatened execution of Christie Mahon cannot fail to remind the intelligent spectator of the sufferings of Christ after his betrayal. It has been argued, indeed, that Christie Mahon is intended to remind us of Christ Messiah throughout the whole play, and there can be much discussion of this and other elements in the play's symbolism. Here I am only concerned to suggest that Christie's rejection of his father's authority is another utilization of Synge's rejection of his family faith. There is even a passage in which Old Mahon describes Christie in terms which recall Synge's boyhood bird-watching, and of his being suspected (it seems) of voyeurism, for when he bought a telescope it caused trouble and was confiscated. "If he seen a red petticoat coming swinging over the hill, he'd be off to hide in the sticks, and you'd see him shooting out his sheeps' eyes between the little twigs and leaves, and his two ears rising like a hare looking out through a gap."

Christie Mahon is not, of course, in any way a portrait of John Synge. Pegeen Mike, however, closely resembles Synge's fiancée, Molly Allgood, for whom he wrote the part. Her outbursts of rage are similar to Molly's. Her intolerance of self-pity and whining are derived from Molly's outspoken dislike of Synge's own frequent complaints about his health. Her desire to escape from the drab world of her upbringing parallels Molly's successful bid to transform herself from shopgirl to actress, and her restless delight in the vivid and lively is again a part of Molly's make-up. Even her savagery owes something to Molly. When Synge asked Molly if she would go to his funeral, she replied passionately "No, for I could not bear to see you dead and the others living." Synge used the incident for a poem.

I asked if I got sick and died, would you
With my black funeral go walking too,
If you'd stand close to hear them talk or pray
While I'm let down in that steep bank of clay.

And, No, you said, for it you saw a crew
Of living idiots, pressing round that new
Oak coffin—they alive, I dead beneath
That board,—you'd rave and rend them with your teeth.

The Playboy of the Western World not only makes use of Synge's rejection of faith and family and the character of his fiancée, but the play also comments obliquely upon the consequence of his own feeling of rejection by his kin and his countrymen. Considered both by his family and by zealots of Irish nationalism as a man lost to God, a heathen, a traducer of "holy Ireland," he did, in fact, in *The Playboy of the Western World*, attack decadent Christianity, elevate the breaking of several commandments into heroism, and ridicule the ignorance and superstition of the rural Irish. Like Christie Mahon, who became the hero he was falsely believed to be, Synge became the mocking satirist he had been labelled. This is, of course, gross oversimplification, but it is surely now high time to admit that Synge's picture of county Mayo in *The Playboy of the Western World* was deliberately calculated to offend the pious and the believers in holy Ireland. By a stroke of fortune which Synge could not, however, have calculated too precisely, he created a masterpiece, and though rejected by his country as Christie Mahon had been, like him Synge left the scene in triumph, having said his say and asserted his independence.

It was, indeed, at this time in his life that Synge achieved his own independence. He at last faced the task of telling his family about his proposed marriage and was surprised at the mildness of his mother's and his brother Samuel's reactions. His sister Annie and her husband were less amenable. We must remember that he had chosen for his bride a comparatively uneducated papist, an ex-shop girl turned actress, who was fifteen years younger than himself and moreover (for he was now a director of the Abbey Theatre) one of his own employees. He could not have broken more completely with the family gods.

It was after the *Playboy* riots and after establishing his independence so completely that Synge turned to writing *Deirdre of the Sorrows*. He regarded it as a vehicle for Molly from the very start. It proved a hard play to write. His health had worsened, and it was not long before he realized that he had not many more months to live. That concern with death which many critics have noted in his work and which may well have had its origins in his childhood sickliness and fear of damnation now became a central theme of his poetry and drama. Deirdre faces death as soon as she decides to run away with Naisi; moreover, her decision to elope with him is both a sin against the rules of her class and an instance of fornication. She offends against the laws of society and against morality, choosing a way of life that must lead to destruction in order to preserve her human dignity. Her "sincere life" and "passionate love" may give her a "share in the dignity of the world," but it must also make her an outcast, just as Synge's own writings had made him an outcast.

Nevertheless, Deirdre is one of those in harmony with the natural world. The play is filled with pastoral imagery and with allusions to the harmony between human love and natural surroundings. Deirdre is not, however, simply a victim of natural forces. Unlike Sarah Casey, she knows what is moving her. Unlike Norah Burke, she embraces her destiny with complete awareness of what she is doing; unlike Christie Mahon her heroic role is not thrust upon her but eagerly embraced in the teeth of opposition. Unlike the Douls she does not need to support her belief in all that she is bringing to pass. Deirdre is ruthless in that she involves the initially unwilling Sons of Usna in her downfall. She brings to Naisi love and death in the same breath and is intolerant of all waverings.

Deirdre of the Sorrows is not Synge's best play. It is, indeed, incomplete, and in his last months of life he was desperately attempting to strengthen and improve it by adding more elements of the grotesque and more conflict between the characters. It is, however, as deeply personal as was *When the Moon Has Set*, his first play, for in *Deirdre* is all his feeling for the harmonies of nature, all his delight in love, and all his awareness that that love had only a brief time to be enjoyed. He had fallen in love with Molly at a time when his health had begun to break down, and as their love increased so his health declined. It was as if he himself were in Naisi's position, granted happiness on the condition that it should be brief. He wrote the play, it might be said, for his own Deirdre who would be obliged to stand upon the stage and lament the death of her lover, who had never been her husband, in words which surely embody Synge's own passionate despair at the shortness of his life, and perhaps, too, his dream of the grief his death must cause his mistress:

> who'll pity Deidre has lost the lips of Naisi from her neck, and from her cheek forever: who'll pity Deidre has lost the twilight in the woods with Naisi, when beech-trees were silver and copper, and ash-trees were fine gold?
>
> It was sorrows were foretold, but great joys were my share always, yet it is a cold place I must go to be with you, Naisi, and it's cold your arms will be this night that were warm about my neck so often. . . . It's a pitiful thing to be talking out when your ears are shut to me. It's a pitiful thing, Conchubor, you have done this night in Emain, yet a thing will be a joy and triumph to the ends of life and time.

Deirdre of the Sorrows was in the writing when Synge's mother died. Synge himself, a sick man, was in Germany. From there he wrote to

Molly: "I am trying to be cheerful again and to think happily of my poor old mother as I know she would have wished . . . My going home now will be very sad—I can hardly bear to think of going to Glendalough House. She was always so delighted to see me when I came back from a journey—I can't go on."[3] His mother had, indeed, been a source of strength for him all his days. Though he had rejected her religious and political beliefs, she had always existed for him as a stable point of reference, and his use of old women as counsellors in his plays surely derives from this, although none of them are in any way portraits of Mrs. Synge. After the death of his mother John Synge did not live long.

It has not been my concern to write about the meaning or the importance of Synge's dramas. I have tried to make one point only. From the very first notebooks through the highly personal essays and poems and all the plays to the very end, Synge made use of his personal emotions to a greater extent than is commonly supposed. His dialogue, his plots, and his characters were almost invariably derived from his observations of Irish country life, but more importantly, the themes and emotional currents of his plays derive from his own personal feelings and frustrations. He was not the withdrawn observer some thought him. Nor was he wholly the consciously cunning symbolist that some have supposed. He was a man who, deeply affected by his childhood experiences and by his early environment, was compelled to make drama from his own emotional problems and needs. Scarred more deeply and more intimately by his personal experience of ascendant extremism than many others of his generation, he was more completely, and perhaps instinctively, involved in the labor pains of renascent Ireland than the majority of his contemporaries. The fight against long-detested authority was for him a personal battle; the attempt to discover new roots in a living tradition was for him a personal need. Inextricably involved in class consciousness himself, Synge was forced to attack false conceptions of the Irish peasant and to attempt to see Ireland as an Irishman and not as an Englishman in exile. It was a personal pilgrimage that John Synge undertook. He wrote nothing that did not derive, at the most profound level, from his own emotional life, and it is, I believe, this that gives all his mature work that passionate vitality and sincerity which have gained for him, as man and as dramatist, "a share in the dignity of the world."

3. David H. Greene and Edward M. Stephens, *J. M. Synge, 1871–1909* (New York: Macmillan Co., 1959).

No man can claim a "share in the dignity of the world" however, if he removes himself entirely from the world's concerns, and while Synge's writings arose directly from his personal experience of conflicts and contraries, they did not ignore the society in which he found himself. He was not, as was AE, a political activist. He belonged to no party. This may have deluded Yeats who, with that capacity for vast generalization which invalidates so much of his criticism and dignifies the greatest of his poems, considered J. M. Synge "unfitted to think a political thought." The comment tells us, perhaps, more about Yeats than about Synge, but it also directs our attention towards the nature of Synge's political views, for it seems a bit unlikely that a man whose plays aroused so much ire in so many politicians should have no political attitudes at all. Synge himself clearly felt that he had some kind of a political program, for in resigning from Maud Gonne's Irish League in April 1897, he wrote:

> You know already how widely my theory of regeneration for Ireland differs from yours and most of the other members of *Jeune Irlande*. I do not wish to enter the question which of us may be in the right but I think you will not be surprised to hear that I cannot possibly continue to be a member of a society which works on lines such as those laid down for the *Irlande Libre*. I wish to work in my own way for the cause of Ireland, and I shall never be able to do so if I get mixed up with a revolutionary and semi-military movement.

This letter does not suggest a refusal to be involved in political activities but rather a rejection of what we would now call "activism"; it also states clearly that Synge *did* have a "theory of regeneration for Ireland" and was intent upon working "for the cause of Ireland."

Before attempting to discuss the nature of Synge's theory, it might be as well to summarize briefly those aspects of his background and his studies that most clearly contributed to his political viewpoint.

He was born of a long-established Protestant family which at one time had owned considerable estates in Ireland. The family Protestantism was of the most extreme kind; his maternal grandfather, Robert Traill, the rector of Schull in county Cork, was an Antrim man and an extreme anti-Catholic and his views were shared by his wife and by Synge's mother. This puritanism extended to a total opposition to the theater, and during Synge's lifetime only his cousin Florence Ross, of all his relations, is known ever to have visited a theater. The politics of the family were aggressively conservative and pro-British. Synge's brother Edward was a land agent and frequently involved in evictions of the Catholic tenantry on the estates that he administered. As we have seen Synge himself, as a youth, objected to the brutality of these evictions, but his mother approved of them and asked him what would become of *them* if their tenants refused to pay their rents. Mrs. Synge was a dominant figure in Synge's life, for his father died when he was only a year old, and when Synge admitted that he had lost his faith in Christianity, she and her youngest son, Samuel, spent much time in attempting to get him back into the fold, though without success.

It was shortly after his rejection of his family's faith that Synge also rejected the family politics and turned to what he called in a notebook of 1896–98, "a temperate Nationalism." The word *temperate* is explained by his using it at a time when he had been introduced to the extreme militancy of Maud Gonne's political viewpoint. He added, "Everything Irish became sacred . . . and had a charm that was neither quite human nor divine, rather perhaps as if I had fallen in love with a goddess, although I had still sense enough not to personify Erin in the patriotic verse I now sought to fabricate!" None of this patriotic verse has survived; what has survived from the notebooks of those early years, however, indicates that it was the narrow puritanism of Irish bourgeois morality that most disturbed him in his country. His early play, *When the Moon Has Set*, indicates this both clearly and crudely, and this concern with the spiritually debilitating effect of a negative approach to sexuality remained with him all his days.

Synge's political and social views, however, were not founded only in his detestation of puritanism and landlordism and in his rebellion against his family gods. During his years in Paris, he studied the theory of socialism. He attended two lectures by Sebastian Faure, the anarchist, in 1895 and found them "Tres interessant, mais fou." In 1896, however, he read *The Communist Manifesto*, the works of William Morris, and several other books on socialism and anarchism. At this point he regarded himself as a socialist, which disturbed his mother a great deal. It was with this background of anticlericalism, anti-Protestantism, socialism, and anarchism that he approached Maud Gonne's Irish League and found it unacceptable.

The writings of the years before 1902 and the creation of *Riders to the Sea* do not dwell explicitly upon political matters, but *The Aran Islands*, which was written over the years 1898–1901, sheds a good deal of light on Synge's views of the ideal society. He finds much to praise on the islands, and while a great deal of what attracts him is inextricably bound up with his almost mystical admiration of primitivism, some is not. Thus he says of the islanders' belongings:

> Every article on these islands has an almost personal character, which gives this simple life, where all art is unknown, something of the artistic beauty of medieval life. The curaghs and spinning-wheels, the tiny wooden barrels that are still much used in the place of earthenware, the home-made cradles, churns, and baskets, are all full of individuality, and being made from materials that are common here, yet to some extent peculiar to the island, they seem to exist as a natural link between the people and the world that is about them.

This may well remind us of William Morris who wrote in *The Aims of Art* (1887): "the true secret of happiness lies in the taking a genuine interest in all the details of daily life, in elevating them by art instead of handing the performance of them over to unregarded drudges and ignoring them." Synge was at one with Morris in opposing the artificially created appetites and the materialism of the world of commerce. He wrote of the islanders: "Their way of life has never been acted on by anything much more artificial than the nests and burrows of the creatures that live round them, and they seem in a certain sense to approach more nearly to the finer types of our aristocracies—who are bred artificially to a natural ideal—than to the labourer or citizen, as the wild horse resembles the thoroughbred rather than the hack or cart-horse." In the third book of *The Aran Islands*, the similarity of Synge's thought to that of Morris is even more noticeable. Synge wrote: "It is likely that much of the intelligence and charm of these people is due to the absence of any division of labour, and to the correspondingly wide development of each individual, whose varied knowledge and skill necessitates a considerable activity of mind." Morris, in *The Aims of Art* prophesied: "men will find out that the men of our days were wrong in first multiplying their needs, and then trying, each man of them, to evade all participation in the means and processes whereby those needs are satisfied; that this kind of division of labour is really only a new and wilful form of arrogant and slothful ignorance."

When Yeats suggested that Synge should visit Aran, he did so, at least according to his own testimony, in order that Synge should "express a life that has never found expression." I wonder, however, whether

Synge himself, opposed as he already was to the bourgeois materialism of his background and already fascinated by the language and the way of life of the peasants of Brittany as well as Ireland, was not also affected by William Morris's words in *Art and Socialism* (1884):

> Do not let us deceive ourselves, the class of victims exists here as in Russia. . . . And how can we of the middle classes, we the capitalists and our hangers-on, help them? By renouncing our class, and on all occasions when antagonism rises up between the classes casting in our lot with the victims: with those who are condemned at the best to lack of education, refinement, leisure, pleasure and renown; and at worst to a life lower than that of the most brutal savages—in order that the system of competitive Commerce may endure.

Had Synge read this pamphlet, as seems not improbable, he would surely have mentally substituted "Landlordism" for "Commerce" and remembered his mother's enquiry, "What would become of us if our tenants did not pay the rent?"

Though Synge saw the virtues of Aran life through spectacles provided in part by William Morris and though he considered himself a socialist, he did not follow Morris's example by lecturing or pamphleteering for the cause. He turned, instead, to the theater and to the writing of essays in which the values he wished to present were rather implied than argued. In 1902, after completing the Aran book, he wrote two plays, *Riders to the Sea* and *In the Shadow of the Glen*; in these and in *The Tinker's Wedding* the battle between conventional morality and the needs and intuitions of the individual is presented with real vigor.

It was *In the Shadow of the Glen*, of course, which brought Synge into headlong conflict with the Nationalist Irish newspapers. Their accusations that the play was un-Irish, that it was based upon the story of the widow of Ephesus, and that it was written by a man out of touch with true Irish character are too well known for me to elaborate upon them here. The reason for the savagery of this attack, however, does deserve some comment, for it relates directly to the political situation of the time.

The two newspapers which attacked Synge most severely were the *Irish Independent* and the *United Irishman*. The former had been founded to support Parnell at the time of the disintegration of the Nationalist party and his fall from power; it continued to support parliamentary nationalism and the gaining of Irish freedom by constitutional means. The latter was founded as a weekly paper by Arthur Griffith in order to support a movement for total independence and a dual monarchy on the Hungarian model; Griffith saw himself as leader of this movement and did indeed, in 1906, found the Sinn Fein party of which de Valera was later to become the leader. At the time which Synge wrote his play the shadow of Parnell lay heavily upon Ireland, and it seems not unlikely that Griffith, who was not a stupid man, saw in Synge's play an opportunity to assert that he, though a fervent nationalist, was dissimilar to Parnell in refusing to tolerate adultery and in revering Irish womanhood. He even went so far as to say that Irishwomen were the most virtuous in the world. He saw this production of the Irish National Theatre Society, if regarded as part of the political nationalist movement, as likely to arouse once again clerical opposition. There is no doubt of course that sheer puritanism had a hand in the opposition to the play, but so did politics.

It is hard to determine whether or not Synge himself saw the play as having political significance. He clearly did see it, as the *Irish Times* saw it, as an attack upon "the wrong of mercenary marriages." He wrote to Stephen MacKenna: "I think squeamishness is a disease, and that Ireland will gain if Irish writers deal manfully, directly and decently with the entire reality of life. I think the law-maker and the law-breaker are both needful in society—as the lively and volcanic forces are needed to make earth's crust habitable." He might well have added "without contraries is no progression." He told MacKenna, using the old form of the word obsessed, that he too was opposed to "morbid, sex-obseded drama" but added that "no drama can grow out of anything other than the fundamental realities of life."

His view was not that of the majority of the nationalists. James Connolly stated that "at present we need a National Theatre, not for the purpose of enlarging our national vanity, but of restoring our proper national pride," and Maude Gonne referred bleakly to writers who allow foreign influences to distort their presentation of the people of Ireland.

Synge's reaction was interesting. In *National Drama: A Farce*, he ridiculed the philistinism, muddleheadedness, and prurience of his critics, and he suggested that good art is always national in that, while dealing with "eternal human elements," it takes its "attributes" from its local and national environment. He suggested that "an Irish drama that is written in Ireland about Irish people and not on a foreign model, will and must be national in so far as it exists at all." He did not finish this satirical farce, however, and it was not published until 1968. Nevertheless, it shows that at this time Synge was distrustful of what he called, in another place, "wilful nationalism," and of the narrow-mindedness and bigotry to which it all too frequently led. Though he was passionately concerned with the welfare of Ireland and particularly devoted to the cause of the peasants, his viewpoint was European, and his interpretation of the role of the artist in society combined the idealism of William Morris with the skepticism of Anatole France. Indeed, in an unfinished essay on Anatole France, he stated:

> The half-cynical optimism which he has shown so admirably in the books dealing with Monsieur Bergeret, and elsewhere, is simply the frank philosophy of large classes among the French, who are kept healthy by an ironical attitude towards their own distress. No one, it is possible, will consider this humorous optimism, even when completed, as Anatole France completes it, by socialistic ideals, as a high form of practical philosophy, but some may ask where at the present time we can find a better one that is fearless and perfectly healthy.

Synge's own "ironical attitude" and his own "humorous optimism" did not lead him, as they led Anatole France, into political action. He admired France for speaking out on the Dreyfus affair and praised his "practical effort to bring justice and peace into the world," but he did not emulate him. Indeed only in the series of articles which he wrote on the Congested Districts for the *Manchester Guardian* and in the unfinished *Letter to the Gaelic League* did he touch upon practical politics. It might be as well to consider these here.

The *Letter to the Gaelic League by a Hedge Schoolmaster* is headed "Can we go back into our Mothers' womb" and opposes the view that "Irish is gaining the day in Ireland and that this country will soon speak Gaelic." It suggests that it is absurd to believe that people will "cumber" themselves "with two languages where one is enough" and attacks the fanaticism of the Gaelic League with vitriolic fervor.

> I believe in Ireland. I believe in the nation that has made a place in history by seventeen centuries of manhood, a nation that has begotten Grattan and Emmet and Parnell will not be brought to complete insanity in these last days by what is senile and slobbering in the doctrine of the Gaelic League. There was never till this time a movement in Ireland that was gushing, cowardly and maudlin, yet now we are passing England in the hysteria of old women's talk. A hun-

> dred years ago Irishmen could face a dark existence in Kilmainham Jail, or lurch on the halter before a grinning mob, but now they fear any gleam of truth. How are the mighty fallen! Was there ever a sight so piteous as an old and respectable people setting up the ideals of Fee-Gee because, with their eyes glued on John Bull's navel, they dare not be Europeans for fear the huckster across the street might call them English.

This takes up a point made earlier in an article published in *The Academy and Literature* of 6 September 1902. Here he stated: "With the present generation the linguistic atmosphere of Ireland has become definitely English enough, for the first time, to allow work to be done in English that is perfectly Irish in its essence, yet has sureness and purity of form." He suggested that the "new blossom" was due to "the final decay of Irish among the national classes of Leinster" and expressed a fear that if Gaelic were to become influential,

> the feeling for English which the present generation has attained would be lost again, and in the best circumstances it is probable that Leinster and Ulster would take several centuries to assimilate Irish perfectly enough to make it a fit mode of expression for the finer emotions which now occupy literature. . . . If however the Gaelic League can keep the cruder powers of the Irish mind occupied in a healthy and national way till the influence of Irish literature, written in English, is more definite in Irish life, the half-cultured classes may come over to the side of the others, and give an intellectual unity to the country of the highest value.

This viewpoint is certainly that of a member of the Anglo-Irish ascendancy, and it was a viewpoint echoed by Yeats when he said in a speech to the Irish senate: "I am proud to consider myself a typical man of that minority. We are the people of Burke; we are the people of Grattan; we are the people of Swift; the people of Parnell. We have created the most of the modern literature of this country. We have created the best of its political intelligence." Yeats's fellow senators were not wholly pleased with this speech. It smacked too much of the days of the Big House, and it was patronizing. Synge's view of the Congested Districts was not patronizing. Soberly he recorded what he saw there, and soberly he refrained from any outburst of passion at the suffering he encountered and the abuses he discovered. Only towards the end of the series did he allow himself to suggest possible remedies, and these were sensible enough. He praised the Congested Districts Board for its ideals and many of its projects, but he suggested that "one does not always pardon a sort of contempt for the local views of the people which seems rooted in nearly all the official workers one meets with through the country." Synge praised the Gaelic League for its improving local morale, but he shook his head sadly over the probability that when the people realize that the "hope of restoring a lost language is a vain one," they would experience a new and more intense hopelessness. He spoke up for the importance of improving roads and communications in order to destroy the monopolistic profiteering of local shopkeepers, and he emphasized the dangers inherent in continual emigration. Finally he stated that: "one feels that the only real remedy for emigration is the restoration of some national life to the people. It is this conviction that makes most Irish politicians scorn all merely economic or agricultural reforms, for if Home Rule would not of itself make a national life it would do more to make such a life possible than half a million creameries."

Synge was a sensible and shrewd observer of the life around him; his idealism, like that of Anatole France, was tempered by skepticism, and he was therefore unable to join any of the intemperately nationalist movements of his day. He saw social problems as stemming as much from the nature of man as from local conditions, and in his plays, feeling himself released from the necessity to be overtly nationalist or political, he presented themes whose political implications were, in fact, much more fundamental than perhaps he himself realized. It was after 1902, when he had suffered the attacks upon *In the Shadow of the Glen*, that Synge's plays began to deal with matters fundamental to the social and political problems of his times. In *The Tinker's Wedding*, he had praised, as in so many of his essays, the freedom of the vagrant, the vitality of the imagination unfettered by dogma or convention, and had attempted to show how the true energy of his country resided not in the bourgeois merchant or farmer nor in the priest, but in the peasant and tinker whose traditions enabled him to remain healthily instinctive and imaginative and to take joy from his vicissitudes.

With *The Well of the Saints*, however, the picture alters. The fable is ambiguous. On the one hand we may ridicule the blind Douls for preferring fantasy to reality and choosing rather to remain blind and poor than to join the world of sight and labor. We may regard them as defeatists, as obscurantists, as people lacking any sense of social responsibility. On the other hand, observing that the reality that they are required to face is destructive of all their beliefs in themselves, an enemy to their poetry, and an opponent to their sense of their individual richness, we may admire them for opting out of the "rat race." Similarly we may regard the saint as a fool, in that he obviously does not understand the world he attempts to cure, being blind himself to the nature of Molly Byrne and blind, too, to the way in which the Douls pursue an essentially spiritual vision in their poverty and are as devoted to the worship of eternal values as he. And yet he is a leader and perhaps wise in his attempt to substitute both the beauties and the harshnesses of reality for the pleasurable delusions of the beggars. The ambiguity which appears to be characteristic of the play at a first reading does not, however, survive a second. The fantasies of the Douls are so filled with poetry, and the near-mysticism of their attitudes towards the natural world is so radiant with the sense of beauty, that we cannot but accept their final decision as correct. Better is a dinner of herbs where love is, than a stalled ox and hatred therewith.

If we look at the message of the play in this way and realize that the figure of the Saint, travelling Ireland, curing ills, and preaching his truth, is also that of the political reformer, then *The Well of the Saints* can be regarded as politically loaded. The apathy of the Irish peasants when faced with talk of Home Rule and of politics is self-defensive; they do not wish for the kind of reality they are being offered, and they reject the rule of law. As Martin Doul says at the close of the play: "We're going surely, for if it's a right some of you have to be working and sweating the like of Timmy the Smith, and a right some of you have to be fasting and praying and talking holy talk the like of yourself, I'm thinking it's a good right ourselves have to be sitting blind, hearing a soft wind turning round the little leaves of the spring and feeling the sun, and we not tormenting our souls with the sight of the grey days, and the holy men, and the dirty feet is trampling the world." It is a complaint voiced also by Mary Byrne in an early draft of *The Tinker's Wedding*, when she tells the priest: "You and your marriage! Isn't generation and generations we are walking round under the Heavens and what is it we ever wanted with [your like]. Let you not be talking. We have the hot suns and the cold night and our bits to eat and sups to drink and a power of children and what more is it we want. Is it rings we want when the frost does catch on our fingers. Let you listen to this. When a man parts with copper to put rings in a pig's nose and you'ld like us to pay you with the time you'ld put an old ring on ourselves." It is also the complaint Synge himself makes when he observes an eviction on Aran:

> We were collected in two straggling bands on either side of the roadway, and a few moments later the body of magnificent armed men passed close to us, followed by a low rabble, who had been brought to act as drivers for the sheriff.
>
> After my weeks spent among primitive men this glimpse of the newer types of humanity was not reassuring. Yet these mechanical police, with the commonplace agents and sheriffs, and the rabble they had hired, represented aptly enough the civilization for which the homes of the island were to be desecrated.

One is reminded yet again of William Morris, who, in 1880, called on his audience:

> to face the latest danger which civilization is threatened with, a danger of her own breeding: that men in struggling towards the complete attainment of all the luxuries of life for the strongest portion of their race should deprive their whole race of all the beauty of life: a danger that the strongest and wisest of mankind, in striving to attain to a complete mastery over nature, should destroy her simplest and widest-spread gifts, and thereby enslave simple people to them, and themselves to themselves, and so at last drag the world into a second barbarism more hopeless than the first.

In that address Morris stated, quite simply, that: "modern civilization is on the road to trample out all the beauty of life, and to make us less than men."

Synge's detestation of modern capitalist society was as strong as his distrust of religious dogma. His essays are filled with references to the disadvantages of being born into the present time. In a notebook of 1907, after describing people met on the road, he said, "People like these, like the old woman and these two beautiful children, are a precious possession for any country. They console us, one moment at least, for the manifold and beautiful life we have all missed who have been born in modern Europe." In his essay on *A Landlord's Garden in County Wicklow*, published in 1907, he wrote with nostalgic affection of the "high-spirited and highly-cultivated aristocracy" of the eighteenth century and reflected that "where men used to collect fine editions of *Don Quixote* and Moliere, in Spanish and French, and luxuriantly bound copies of Juvenal, and Persius and Cicero, nothing is read now but Longfellow and Hall Caine and Miss Corelli. Where good and roomy houses were built a hundred years ago, poor and tawdry houses are built now; and bad bookbinding, bad pictures, and bad decorations are thought well of, where rich bindings, beautiful miniatures and finely-carved chimney-pieces were once prized by the old Irish landlords."

Synge, like Yeats, prized both the aristocracy of the primitive Aran islander and the culture and learning of the true aristocrat. He found the middle class abhorrent, and he spoke harshly, in his articles on the Congested Districts, of the greed and profiteering of the village shopkeepers, whom he saw allied with the priests in their support of an essentially disgusting social status quo. In a letter of 1905 to Stephen MacKenna, he wrote: "There are sides of all that western life, the groggy-patriot-publican-general-shop-man who is married to the priest's half sister and is second cousin once-removed of the dispensary doctor that are horrible and awful. This is the type that is running the present United Irish League anti-grazier campaign, while they're swindling the people themselves in a dozen ways and then buying out their holdings and packing off whole families to America." In a notebook of 1904, he said: "In Mayo one cannot forget that in spite of the beauty of the scenery the people in it are debased and nearly demoralized by bad housing and lodging and the endless misery of the rain." It was to Mayo that he turned for the setting of *The Playboy of the Western World*, even though much of the material he used for the play had been collected in West Kerry, for in Mayo he had found the society he wished to depict, and there he had seen how the natural, wild, intuitive life of the peasant had become demoralized and degraded by the influence equally of the church and the shopkeeper.

Much has been written about *The Playboy of the Western World*. It is a complex play and in many ways a savage one. We are treated to a portrayal of a society in which the teachings of the church have only served to add a further layer of superstition to those already present in the sensibility of the small farmers and shopkeepers who, while revering, half guiltily, the heroic rebels who have in the past defied law and morality, are now incapable of breaking free of social conventions in any other fashion than the purely verbal. To this confused community enters Christy Mahon, the man who has, in killing his father, rebelled against both church and state. He is lauded as a hero. He is treated as a Messiah—as Christ Messiah rather than Christy Mahon. The girls of the village bring him presents as in a parody of the Epiphany; the adulation of Palm Sunday is parodied in his triumph at the sports; when his pretensions are unmasked however, he is ridiculed; and when he does indeed murder his father—at least to all appearances—he is bound, burned in the leg, and offered up for sacrifice in a savage parody of the torture and crucifixion of Christ.

The play is filled with blasphemous epithets; it presents sexual degradation in its allusions to mercenary marriage and in its suggestions that the Widow Quinn might be a procuress for the Playboy if he wished to pay her price. There is adherence to neither old tradition nor new; the wakes for the dead are an occasion for drunkenness; the daughter of the house, Pegeen Mike, is spoken of as if she were a prize beast whom it was preferable to mate with a good sturdy stud the like of Christy Mahon rather than the puny Shawn Keogh. The whole play is, from the point of view of its portrayal of the society and attitudes, of western Mayo a black, though vigorously wild, presentation of degradation and ignorance and confusion.

That it is more than this, and, indeed, very much more, is now generally agreed, but its first audience saw only the savagery and the blasphemy and detected, quite reasonably, an attack upon the Irish character. They saw—or at least some of them saw—political implications. The *Evening Mail* reviewer said, "the parricide represents some kind of nation-killer, whom Irish men and Irish women hasten to lionize." David H. Greene in his biography of Synge wrote:

> The Playboy's self liberation from parental tyranny and from the loveless marriage imposed on him by peasant custom was a symbol of their own deep-seated urge to reject the tyranny in their own lives exemplified by Pegeen's forthcoming marriage to an oafish and spineless kinsman, dictated by her father and with the endorsement of Father Reilly's dispensation. The villagers in that Mayo shebeen could applaud Christy for his desperate act of emancipation because it was an embodiment of their own desires. But when it became a reality—suddenly and violently—and they were asked to stand up and be counted, they had only the courage of their dreams.

It is a fair summary of one aspect of the play. And it must have struck many that if Christy Mahon were to be considered, even for a moment, as a leader of the Irish people, as the father-killer praised for refusing to obey the injunctions of authority and bold to defy the patterns of social behavior imposed by the church, there was only one man in recent history who leapt to mind. Charles Stuart Parnell—praised for defying the English, for obstructing the procedures of Parliament, for supporting Land Agitation, for defying Landlordism—fell from power just as soon as that independence of mind, which before had seemed attached only to political matters, was publicly proved to have led him to take as mistress the wife of another man. What he had done privately had been the subject of a "gallous story" for some time, but it was now seen publicly and publicly admitted; it had become "a dirty deed."

I am not suggesting that Christy Mahon is intended as a direct allusion to Charles Stuart Parnell; I am only suggesting that to the Irish politicians the fall of the Playboy bore sufficiently close a resemblance to that of Parnell to make them uncomfortable. Dwelling upon the play could only disturb them further. The people who first glorified and then condemned Christy Mahon are more corrupt and more selfish than he. *His* dirty deed was the product of a passionate sense of outrage and of a desire for liberty of conscience; *their* deeds spring from self-interest, cowardice, and self-aggrandizement. The Nationalist movement rose up in fury at *The Playboy of the Western World*, and it is wholly intelligible that they should have done so.

Synge did not again touch, even thus obliquely, upon political matters. *Deirdre of the Sorrows* has few political implications and the later poems none. Synge was not, as Yeats suggested, "unfitted to think a political thought," but he was not a "party man." He was an observer, a recorder, a satirist, and, in many ways, a romantic. His political and social views were closely related to those of William Morris, but he did not have Morris's faith in socialism and the planned society. He observed the contraries in Irish society, and he displayed them faithfully, convinced that "lively and volcanic forces" were needed to make "earth's crust habitable" and deeply assured of the presence of these forces from the evidence supplied by his own life and family history. He worked for Ireland, for the cause of Irish freedom, by endeavoring to free it from the prison of its own self-delusions. Like Anatole France, he wrote with irony and skepticism. The Ireland he endeavored to heal by presenting it with an image of its own confusions, disorders, and dreams, in order that it might learn to move forward by a sensible manipulation and exploitation of these dynamic elements of society, may now have gone, but Synge's fundamental opposition to capitalist materialism remains with us, and even today his support and praise of the wild and energetic, of the nomad and of the lawbreaker, as essential ingredients in society would be echoed by very many of the disillusioned and outraged on both sides of the Atlantic.

4

Susan L. Mitchell

AIDE TO IMMORTALITY

Susan Mitchell was not a major writer, but she contributed much to the Dublin literary scene, becoming a jester extraordinary in a city where mockery has never been rare. She was well fitted for the position, for she was intimately acquainted with the Yeats family and with the AE circle, and her jokes at the expense of Irish men of letters were informed by a knowledge of character as well as of books.

She was born in 1866 in Carrick on Shannon. Her father dying in 1873, she was adopted by her three aunts, living first in Dublin and later at Birr. Later still she lived with the Yeats family in London, and just after the turn of the century she became a subeditor and chief assistant to AE on the *Irish Homestead.* She also worked with AE on the *Irish Statesman* until her death in 1926.

Her serious poetry is pleasing, sensitive, melancholy, and in its imagery and near-mystical tone often reminiscent of AE's verses. She achieves on occasion a simplicity which is moving and an economy of diction that qualifies sentiment with decisiveness. Her small poem "The Crib" is a good example of her simplest manner.

> Day closes in the cabin dim
> They light the Christmas candle tall,
> For Him who is the Light of all.
> They deck the little Crib for Him
> Whose cradle is earth's swinging ball.

This is a late poem. Her earlier work tends to be more elaborate and rhetorical. Her verse, however, is always well made, and perhaps because her vision was uncomplicated, it never suffers from those lapses of taste and sudden absurdities which mar AE's more ambitious writings. *The Living Chalice*, both in its first (1908) and in its expanded (1913) version, is a thoroughly pleasing collection of sensitive verses.

It was not, however, the sensitive and lyrical work which took Dublin by the ears; it was the tough-minded, deft, satirical work. *Aids to the Immortality of Certain Persons in Ireland: Charitably Administered by Susan L. Mitchell* was first published in 1908, and its cover bore a cartoon drawn by "Mac" in which the better-known Dublin literary folk are depicted in typical poses. The book opens with the author's review of her own work in which she quotes, about herself, Yeats's statement about Lady Gregory's *Cuchulain of Muirthemne*, "This is the best book that has come out of Ireland in my time," thus hinting her delighted disapproval of those who puff their friend's books. The collection closes with a page of mock publishers' announcements. The books listed are:

> *No Ideas Good or Bad*. By W. B. Yeats. A Sequel to *Ideas of Good and Evil*.
> *Supernatural Law in the Economic World*. A Treatise by AE.
> *The White Flower of a Blameless Life*. An Autobiography by George Moore.
> *Women of No Importance*. A Series of Sermons by Edward Martyn.

In between these two splendid gestures are the poems: "George Moore—A Ballad History" of rollicking allusiveness, "The Voice of One," a conversation piece in which the voices of Moore and Yeats can be distinctly heard, "The Ballad of Shawe Taylor and Hugh Lane," "The Irish Council Bill 1907," a bitter poem to which the author added another verse in April 1910. This later verse was never printed in a book but is an excellent demonstration of her most vigorous and downright manner:

> Home Rule is far off still
> Says the Shan Van Vocht
> And we've got an empty till
> Says the Shan Van Vocht
> Budgets four we've had since then
> And we still are asking—When?
> God Almighty, give us men
> Says the Shan Van Vocht

The book concludes with "Ode to the British Empire," which parodies Kipling's "Recessional." It is a small, but a gay volume. The second edition of 1913 is much larger, and ranges farther into politics as well as letters for its prey.

Susan Mitchell was a lampoonist rather than a satirist; her best jokes are both local and ephemeral, but on occasion she can wield the weapon of parody with some force. Her "Anti-Recruiting Song" concludes with two verses as direct and angry as one could hope for.

> He didn't see much glory, and he didn't get much good,
> In most unrighteous causes he bravely shed his blood;
> The best years of his manhood he spent across the foam,
> And when they'd no more use for him they took and sent
> him home.
>
> He'd bullets in his right arm, he'd bullets in his leg.
> He had no *gra* for working and he had no leave to beg;
> The peelers had an eye on him, twice he's been in quod,
> Now he's in Carrick Workhouse—Glory be to God!

This contrasts in both tone and intention with the gaiety of "George Moore Becomes High Sheriff of Mayo":

> We've some bright boys in Ireland, we've got our W. B.;
> Faith, Martyn, we have got yourself, we've also got AE.
> When Plunkett isn't writing books, he is our pride and joy,
> And though MacDonnell may be glum he's not a bad wee boy.
> We love our own O'Grady, we love our Douglas Hyde,
> And from this pleasant company there's one we won't divide;
> 'Tis yourself, Moore, you're the playboy, but you're faithful to
> the green.
> Though you're hangin' men and women down in Ballaghadereen.
> Down in Ballaghadereen, down in Ballaghadereen,
> Sending souls to instant glory down in Ballaghadereen.

The dexterity of Miss Mitchell's comic talent shows itself even more strikingly in *Leaguers and Peelers; or the Apple Cart*, a two-act musical farce, which was published in the *Irish Review* for October 1911, but has never been reprinted. This is Gilbertian in plot and in structure, owing a good deal to *Trial by Jury*. In it an apple vendor is brought into court for having disobeyed the law and followed the counsel of the Gaelic League in painting the owner's name on his cart in Gaelic. He is about to be sentenced when it is discovered that the cart belongs in fact to the judge's daughter. The judge is about to proceed stoically to sentence when it is pointed out that as his daughter is legally an infant, he is the guilty party. This situation is resolved by the nobility of the Hero who confesses to owning the cart, and who is willing to go to jail if he can marry the judge's daughter at the expiration of his sentence.

There are several splendid moments in this playlet, which makes ironic use of the tunes of both Irish and English patriotic songs. Thus the RIC sergeant sings, to the tune of *Rule Britannia*:

> When Dublin first at our command
> Arose up in the emerald pale,
> Upon this law we took our stand
> That Dublin Castle should prevail.
> Rule R.I.C. men, rule, rule these Irish knaves,
> Do your duty and they ever will be slaves.

Later in the play the foreman of the jury sing, to the tune of *God Save the King*,

> No Connaught Rangers we
> To bow the traitorous knee
>   Merely for gain
> What are we packed for here
> If not to close the ear
> To every fact we hear?
>   Down with Sinn Fein.
>
> My lord, we are agreed
> That Irish is his creed
>   Well may he swing.
> Who speaks a foreign tongue
> Good Irishmen among,
> Oh, let his neck be wrung.
>   God save the King.

While we, in the 1980s, may feel such satire to be merely amusing, to many people in the Dublin of 1911 it must have seemed an outrage. The parody of the national anthem would have seemed close to blasphemy, and Susan Mitchell did not avoid a similar accusation from Irish Nationalists, for her parodies of revered Irish songs are just as cruel, and her portrayal of the Irish is as comic as that of the British. *Leaguers and Peelers* may not be of the same stature as Swift, but it is written with a similar courage, and if it is, on the whole, cheeky and smart rather than subtly witty, it is the more efficient as a social weapon. Urbanity and subtlety are characteristic of only a few satirists. We have our Peter Pindars and John Skeltons as well as our Popes and Swifts. It is clear that Mitchell intended her lampoons to act with maximum efficiency in a particular situation, and did not expect them to interest posterity. As a consequence her work is now largely forgotten, but when rediscovered, it brings back the feel of her times more strongly than the work of many of her more distinguished contemporaries.

Susan Mitchell was not only a wit herself but also a source of wit in others. She marshalled many talents together in her anthology *Secret Springs of Dublin Song* (1918). Here, protected by anonymity, are parodies by Oliver Gogarty, AE, R. L. Tyrrell, Seumas O'Sullivan, Lord Dunsany, G. M. Redding, and "Michael Scott." Many of these squibs are hurled at no particular target, but simply thrown for the hell of it. Some are, however, dropped neatly at the heels of the unsuspecting Moore and the meditating Yeats. George Moore aroused amusement in Dublin much more frequently than W. B. Yeats; moreover, he also aroused anger. Susan Mitchell's one prose work was called *George Moore*. It was published in 1916 in Maunsel and Company's sober Irishmen of Today series. An idiosyncratic, witty, excoriating analysis of all Moore's works and foibles, it exposes, with relentless lucidity, his literary sophistication, his ruthless exploitation of friendship, his pretentiousness, his innocence, and his malice. It also presents us with an acutely sensitive portrait of the world of Irish Letters and lays bare, quite as amusingly as Moore's own *Hail and Farewell*, the confusions and absurdities of the Irish Renaissance. The book is filled with comments of Shavian pungency and concision. We are told that "'Impressions and Opinions' are very much Moore weighted with all his sincere and unreasonable personality." Moore, the self-confessed hedonist and womanizer, with the amoral man-of-the-world outlook, is neatly revealed as a poseur: "Perhaps the Latin races can sin gracefully, the Irish cannot. And Mr. Moore's sinning? He cannot escape from his birthright, Lough Cara set her seal on him, 'islands lying in misted water, faint as dreams.' As Silenus he is a poor thing. His leer is so much 'make-up,' and it is the more revolting because he is naturally sincere. He has no genius for the gross. It is a creed with him not to be ashamed, but here I catch him tripping for he is ashamed of being ashamed." Miss Mitchell makes very merry over Moore's conversion from a previously unstated Catholicism to an unconvincing Protestantism. She detects in him a zeal to appear zealous in a cause, and an ardor for the role of ardent believer in any available faith. Like many Irishmen, he found himself drawn towards "movements," but (also like many Irishmen) once involved in them he found his disputatious intelligence and thirst for drama only satisfied by comedy or rebellion.

Moore is regarded as being typically Irish also in his love of a public gesture, and in his natural talent for passionate buffoonery. His conversion to Protestantism we are told, "was conceived in the mood of light comedy." The prologue occurred when he

> wrote to the papers and announced his intended reception into the Protestant communion as a protest against the decoration of Maynooth with King Edward's racing colours. The chorus in Dublin, in a mood rightly related to the mind of the protagonist, commented gaily upon the spiritual state of one whose protest against a King took the surprising form of adopting the religion of that King against whom he protested . . . it was suggested by the chorus that Mr. Moore was trying to kill two birds with the one stone. He hoped to destroy one religion by explaining his reasons for leaving it and another by explaining his reasons for joining it.

This is hardly profound criticism, but it is distinctly illuminating of the religio-political confusions of Dublin in the Edwardian period.

Moore, indeed, served Ireland well, for he parodied in his own sincerities those which also afflicted his contemporaries and exposed, all unknowingly, the bland absurdities of much of the intellectual ferment of the Ireland of his time. Mitchell is fully aware of this and her book is as much a study of Dublin as of Moore, whose arrival in that city is presented with trenchant wit:

> We in Ireland are gifted beyond most peoples with a talent for acting, and in Dublin especially, while scorning culture, which indeed we have not got, we are possessed of a most futile and diverting cleverness. Mr. Moore's entrance on the stage in Dublin was marred by an audience having as much dramatic talent as he himself, and each so full of admiration for his own exercise of it that he had only

> a fierce criticism and no appreciation to give a rival player. We Irish are very much aware of our art as actors, we seldom lose ourselves in it, but Mr. Moore's dramatic concern with himself is so much interwoven in his nature that he can only be really himself in the various poses he assumes. He is absolutely sincere in each, and his Gaelic pose had for him a momentous importance that provoked the merriment of Dublin where no one really believes in anything and where nothing matters at all save as providing a subject for conversation, and where if by chance a noble aspiration arises in some heart, the effect of its utterance is exploded in the percussion of a drawing-room jest.

The candor of Moore's comments upon Ireland in *The Untilled Field, Parnell and his Island*, and in *Hail and Farewell*, is no more extreme than that of Susan Mitchell whose acerbity, however, is more frequently qualified by affection and dictated by principle. Nevertheless, her own version of the collaboration between Yeats and Moore in the writing of *Diarmuid* and *Grania* is just as funny as anything in Moore: "What an alliance! Literary Dublin sought in the play with intense interest for the footmarks of the writers and when it found God Angus described as 'A ragged old man wandering along the mountains prodding a boar,' it cried 'Lo Yeats' and behold it was Moore, and coming on the description of Conan scratching his head and complaining of lice it said 'Lo Moore' and behold it was Yeats. Yeats had come to the collaboration determined to be substantial and material like Moore. Moore had resolved to rise to the heaven of the picturesque and beautiful to meet Yeats. They had passed each other on the journey."

In spite of its rich comedy, Susan Mitchell's *George Moore* is more than "a collection of jokes against Moore, disguised as a biography" as Alan Denson has described it. It is a plea for freedom of discussion and for self-criticism by the Irish intellectuals. Moore's candors, though attacked for their malice, are praised for their courage. His naturalistic Zola-esque novels are admired for their insight into human necessities. Even his later religious stories, though regarded as perverse and willful, are complimented on their attempt to reexamine Christian belief and story. Moreover, throughout this book there are many occasions on which the author dares herself to discuss religious problems in Ireland and to examine critically all those articles of faith held so passionately by the leaders of the Irish Renaissance. In the last pages of the book, the whole situation of Irish culture is briefly examined and the conclusions stated there are as courageous—for this is 1916—as anything ever written by Moore. A few sentences from different parts of this last chapter make the point:

> There has always been a certain sterility in Irish ideals; we reach for a star or we scramble lower down for a terrestial bauble. In all their aims high and low Irishmen have a tragic alienation from life. They became peasant proprietors more because their fields were symbolic of the four fields of Kathleen ni Houlihan than because they might be sown and harvested and produce the food of man. They value their municipal privileges more for the sense of power these confer than from any serious intention of using these powers for simple human needs and comforts. Their political power has been treated as a game as diverting as musical chairs at a children's party, sitting, acting and voting to meaningless party tunes played at hazard and stopped at hazard. If this were not so, would we have our land in grass, our towns and cities in slums, and our country without a human hope to break down the barriers that our several quests have imposed upon us?

A little later in a passage written after the Easter Rebellion we read: "I often wonder what effect upon our normal constitution here in Ireland had all the movement of that febrile time that we call the Irish literary revival. Has any intellectuality at all emerged out of it, any public opinion, any essentially nationalistic flavour in our life? . . . our public life in Ireland is as barren of thinking as it ever was and there is no true cohesion amongst us, though there are many enforced unities." This view of the situation contrasts sharply with the blurred optimism and Nationalist enthusiasm of other writers of this time. Susan Mitchell was unable to find heroic majesty in muddle or to detect self-abnegatory mysticism in political ineptitude. In spite of her own firmly held and gracefully expressed religious faith, she was not one to suspect portent and miracle in every strange event; the gods that visited AE and sent symbols to Yeats were more inspired but less shrewd-eyed than hers. When she died in 1926, Ireland lost one of its most valuable citizens: a jester of strong moral principles and equally strong affections who had the courage to speak her mind and the wisdom to make it worth the speaking.

5

Division and Unity

AE and W. B. Yeats

George William Russell who chose to write under the initials AE was a second-rate writer, a third-rate painter, a politician of minor significance, but a phenomenon of major importance in the Ireland of his lifetime.

He was born in Armagh in 1867, and his early education was that of an art student. He attended, in the 1880s, evening art classes at the Metropolitan School of Art, Dublin, and at the Royal Hibernian Academy. He showed considerable ability as an artist but never pursued his talent to a conclusion; the majority of his paintings are technically unsatisfactory, and many of his oil paintings have grown dark and cracked. He gave up his art studies sometime before 1890. W. B. Yeats, whom he first met at this period, said in *Reveries over Childhood and Youth*, "One day he announced he was leaving the Art School because his will was so weak and the arts, or any other emotional pursuit, could but weaken it further." AE himself, however, while appearing to support this view in some of his autobiographical writings, once told Thomas Bodkin that, "though he had always desired to be a painter, he gave up painting because his lack of means forced him to enter into some more paying, if less congenial, business."

These two explanations indicate the extremes present in AE's character. On the one hand, he was a deeply religious, even mystical, thinker willing to subdue any of his personal desires or ambitions for the sake of the truth and the health of his soul. On the other hand, he was a highly efficient practical man, fully aware of economic realities, and determined to use his abilities as an organizer, writer, and economist to better the condition of rural Ireland.

It was the visionary AE who first attracted Yeats and who was most admired as a young man. Early he discovered a capacity for intense imaginative visualization bordering upon the hallucinatory. In *The Candle of Vision* (1918), he wrote: "I was aged about sixteen or seventeen years, when I . . . became aware of a mysterious life quickening within my life . . . I began to be astonished with myself, for, walking along country roads, intense and passionate imaginations of another world began to overpower me. They were like strangers who suddenly enter a house, who brush aside the doorkeeper, and who will not be denied. Soon I knew they were the rightful owners and heirs of the house of the body, and the doorkeeper was only one who was for a time in charge, who had neglected his duty, and who had pretended to ownership." He felt, at this time, that

> there were comrades who were speaking to me . . . They seemed to be saying to each other of us, "Soon they will awaken; soon they will come to us again," and for a moment I almost seemed to mix with their eternity. The tinted air glowed before me with intelligible significance like a face, a voice. The visible world became like a tapestry blown and stirred by winds behind it. If it would but raise for an instant I knew I would be in Paradise. Every form on that tapestry appeared to be the work of gods. Every flower was a word, a thought. The grass was speech; the trees were speech; the waters were speech; the winds were speech. They were the Army of the Voice marching on to conquest and dominion over the spirit; and I listened with my whole being.

Whether AE read at any time Richard Jefferies's *The Story of my Heart* (1883), we cannot now know, but there are similarities between Jefferies's nature-worship and idealism and AE's. To Jefferies, as to AE, the world of natural beauty is only an emanation of, and a veil across, Eternity. The "Sun Life" of Jefferies and the "Earth Breath" of AE are similar in more than their phraseology.

Whether or not AE knew Jefferies, he did admire Blake and shared this enthusiasm with W. B. Yeats. With Yeats he also discussed the work of the Theosophical Society with which they both became involved in the late eighties. With Yeats, too, he discussed in letters and in conversation many aspects of oriental mysticism, which also appear in the early poems of both writers. With all this in common, it may seem surprising that the two men did not work in closer harness. True, both were founder members of the Irish National Theatre Society, Yeats being its president; and the beginning of the Irish dramatic renaissance was, perhaps, the production of AE's *Deirdre* and Yeats's *Kathleen Ni Houlihan* by W. G. Fay's Irish National Dramatic Company in April 1902. Moreover, Yeats issued a book of AE's poems from the Dun Emer Press and, in 1932, invited him to draft the rules for the proposed Irish Academy of Letters. Nevertheless, the relationship was always a little uneasy, and the reason may lie partly in the two men's quite opposed approaches to the visionary.

The key to the difference may be seen in another passage from *The Candle of Vision*, where AE condemns the vanity of his early feeling that his visions were personal, and shows an aversion to any kind of self-dramatization or egoism. He says, "for some years my heart was proud, for as the beauty sank into memory it seemed to become a personal possession, and I said 'I imagined this' when I should humbly have said, 'The curtain was a little lifted that I might see.'" This contrasts sharply with the attitude expressed by Yeats towards the spiritual teachers who, he maintained, dictated the material of *A Vision*. In his dedication to the first edition of 1925, he says of the whole philosophical system, "I am longing to put it out of reach that I may write the poetry it seems to have made possible."

In the revised edition of 1937, Yeats describes how the spirit or daemon who was responsible for his wife's automatic writing responded to his offer to "spend what remained of life explaining and piecing together those scattered sentences. 'No,' was the answer, 'we have come to give you metaphors for poetry.'" Later in the same preface, Yeats jettisons the whole of the mystical element in his "system," which he says he now regards as "stylistic arrangements of experience comparable to the cubes in the drawing of Wyndham Lewis and to the ovoids in the sculpture of Brancusi."

Yeats's attitude towards the occult was at once more skeptical and more intellectually organized than AE's. Though, like Sir Thomas Browne, loving to pursue his reason to an "O Altitudo," he felt it always necessary to attempt rational investigation of psychic phenomena. Hence he tried "experiments," testing the power of arcane symbolism upon his friends and visitors; thus he questioned, indeed tried to cross-examine, his instructors. Finally, he qualified his "vision of eternal truth" with suggestions that it amounted to a psychological and historical system, rather than a religious one. This is even present in his early, and important, analysis of Blake's symbolic system, made at a period when he was more uncritically involved in the occult than he was in later years.

Thus the two men were, in this respect, opposed types. For Yeats, art and poetry had primacy over vision; whereas for AE, the vision might even make poetry and art an indulgence to be avoided. To Yeats the vision was one vouchsafed to the individual heroic seer; to AE it was common property and opposed to the vanities of the ego. Nevertheless, it sometimes seems as if Yeats was envious of AE's visionary experiences; he longed to see, but never saw, a ghost, and his own occult phenomena were restricted to strange sounds and scents, and to his wife's automatic writing. AE produced *A Candle of Vision* in October 1918. In the second edition of *A Vision*, Yeats states that his wife's visions began exactly a year earlier in October 1917; in the first edition he dates his meeting with the fictional Michael Robartes as "Spring 1917." *A Vision* was published in 1925. I cannot help suspecting the presence here of a degree of psychic "one-upmanship."

There are certainly similarities between the thought of Yeats in *A Vision* and in the poems arising from it and the thought of AE in another philosophical work, *The Interpreters* (1922). *The Interpreters* is a series of discussions between various characters who each represent one philosophic outlook. AE said in his preface, "*The Interpreters* may be taken as a symposium between scattered portions of one nature dramatically sundered as the soul is in dream." In this book there is a passage which is strongly reminiscent both of the basic contention in *A Vision* and of Yeats's description of Byzantium. "'The Earth spirit throws itself into innumerable forms of life,' answered Lavelle. 'Did you expect it to make its children all of one pattern? For every race its own culture. Every great civilization, I think, had a deity behind it, or a divine shepherd who guided it on some plan in the cosmic imagination. "Behold," said an ancient oracle, "how the Heavens glitter with intellectual sections." These are archetypcal images we follow dimly in our evolution.'"

This argument could easily serve as a preface to the whole of Yeats's account of the changing shapes of Western civilization in book 3 of *A Vision*. AE's book continues:

> "How do you conceive of these powers as affecting civilization?"
>
> "I believe they incarnate in the race: more in the group than in the individual; and they tend to bring about an orchestration of the genius of the race, to make manifest in time their portion of eternal beauty. So arises that unity of character which existed in the civilization of Egypt or Attica, where art, architecture, and literature were

> in such harmony that all that is best seems almost the creation of one myriad-minded artist."

Yeats, in *A Vision* (1925) wrote: "I think that in early Byzantium, and maybe never before or since in recorded history, religious, aesthetic and practical life were one, and that architect and artifers—though not, it may be, poets, for language had been the instrument of controversy and must have grown abstract—spoke to the multitude and the few alike. The painter and the mosaic worker, the worker in gold and silver, the illuminator of Sacred Books were almost impersonal, almost perhaps without the consciousness of individual design, absorbed in their subject matter and that the vision of a whole people." It would take more space than I have at my disposal to list the many other instances where *The Interpreters* and *A Vision* bear upon one another. In some cases it seems clear that both books have been influenced by common source material in theosophy and Neoplatonic philosophy. The descriptions of the characters in *The Interpreters* remind one of similar descriptions by Yeats of symbolic personages in books published both before and after 1922. The analyses of types of humanity in *The Interpreters* are similar to those used by Yeats though shorn of his special jargon.

In 1922, however, Yeats was, in other respects, moving farther away from AE. Since 1897 AE had been deeply concerned with the cooperative movement in Ireland. In that year he was appointed banks organizer for the Irish Agricultural Organization Society. In this capacity and later as editor of the *Irish Homestead*, he fought for the establishment of cheap credit facilities for farmers, in order to release them from the clutches of the commercial banks and the petty loan sharks or "gombeen men." He also, continually, supported the trade union movement and spoke at an Albert Hall meeting in support of the Irish Transport and General Workers Union Strike of 1913. In *The National Being* (1916) he spoke out on social and economic matters from a left-wing viewpoint, and with a trenchancy absent from his philosophical writings. His championship of freedom of speech and religious tolerance and his insistence that a narrow nationalism must be replaced by an international outlook met much opposition from many quarters. Yeats, writing to H. J. C. Grierson on 6 November 1922 gave his own view of the situation:

> We are preparing here, behind our screen of bombs and smoke, a return to conservative politics as elsewhere in Europe, or at least to a

> substitution of the historical sense for logic. The return will be painful and perhaps violent, but many educated men talk of it and must soon work for it and perhaps riot for it.
>
> A curious sign is that AE who was the most popular of men is now suffering some slight eclipse because of old democratic speeches —things of years ago. I on the other hand get hearers where I did not get them because I have been of the opposite party. AE has still however his great popularity in co-operative Ireland. The Ireland that reacts from the present disorder is turning its eyes towards individualist Italy.

This gives a false impression of AE whose democracy was less than complete. In *The National Being*, indeed, he makes many statements with which Yeats appears to agree. Far from substituting logic for historical sense, he says that a "powerful Irish character has begun to reassert itself in modern times." He sees the ancient Irish clan as "aristocratic in leadership and democratic in its economic basis," and sees this ancient character persisting in the work of "Swift, Berkeley, O'Grady, Shaw, Wilde, Parnell, Davitt" who were "intensely democratic in economic theory, adding that to an aristocratic freedom of thought." AE thinks this character still persists "in the mass" and that "it is by adopting a policy which will enable it to manifest once more that we will create an Irish civilization, which will fit our character as the glove fits the hand." He uses the word "individualism" pejoratively, however, saying, "we allowed individualism—the devilish doctrine of every man for himself—to be the keynote of our economic life; where above all things, the general good and not the enrichment of the individual should be considered." He states the necessity for leadership by the aristocracy, "not the aristocracy of birth, but the aristocracy of character, intellect, and will." And, like Yeats, he expresses his own and Ireland's love for the aristocratic character of Parnell. Moreover, like Yeats again, he believes in the Irish "respect for the aristocratic intellect, for freedom of thought, ideals, poetry, and imagination as the qualities to be looked for in our leaders."

The degree of agreement between Yeatsian "conservatism" and AE's vision of "democracy" is so considerable that it is hard to see why Yeats felt himself to be of "the opposite party." Partly, of course, Yeats feared the levelling process of even "economic democracy." In *On the Boiler* (1939) he wrote: "Instead of hierarchical society, where all men are different, came democracy; instead of a science which had re-discovered Anima Mundi, its experiments and observations confirming the speculations of Henry More, came materialism: all that whiggish world Swift stared on till he became a raging man." In passing, we might note that AE's version of Swift is a good deal closer to the author of *The Drapier's Letters* and *A Modest Proposal* than in Yeats's. We must also note that the same difference of temperament which made agreement upon the significance of visions impossible also made disagreement about politics inevitable, even though in both cases the two men based their thought upon mutually acceptable premises.

As in philosophy and politics, so in literature, AE was as much the guiding spirit of a group of writers and poets as Yeats. He edited *New Songs* in 1904, which included work by Padraic Column, Eva Gore-Booth, Thomas Koehler, Alice Milligan, Susan Mitchell, Seumas O'Sullivan, George Roberts, and Ella Young. None of these were perhaps very remarkable as poets, though there are lovely things in O'Sullivan, and Susan Mitchell's verse deserves more notice than it has yet received. When the *Irish Homestead* was merged with the new *Irish Statesman* with AE as its editor he became, says John Eglinton in *A Memoir of AE*, "the most noted disseminator of culture in Ireland," and "at his Sunday evening gatherings he acquired the ascendancy of a minor Dr. Johnson." At these gatherings, says C. P. Curran, "He made no difference of persons: the latest and youngest newcomer had his attention as if he were the long-awaited Avatar . . . A kindly wisdom throned over debate, comprehending and all-forgiving. The most divergent opinions found patient hearing, but the immoderate appeared a little ridiculous." Yeats contributed to the *Irish Statesman* under AE's editorship very few times. He contributed twice during his lifetime to the *Dublin Magazine* under the editorship of Seumas O'Sullivan. It seems that the membership of the AE circle was quite distinct from that of the Yeats circle, or was felt to be so by Dublin literary society. In fact, Gogarty, Frank O'Connor, and F. R. Higgins were common to both groups; these were all published by the Cuala Press and were also all published with prefatory material by AE.

It is hard to say whether Yeats felt AE's Sunday gatherings presented any rivalry to his own *At Homes*, though references in Yeats's letters to AE's Ely Place circle do suggest that he was aware of an element of faction in the situation, while being sure that AE was in no way creating faction deliberately. It is clear, too, that the lines of demarcation were partly drawn by talent. AE's acceptance of the most weakly fledgelings was in contrast to Yeats's preference for singing birds with a touch of the hawk about them. Yeats went out of his way to befriend, tutor, and derive excitement from the younger poets whose vigorous talent he admired; Dublin gossip even speaks of him on occasion, as setting out to "capture" young men from the circle of their acquaintance. AE was, as a social convener, less militaristic; friends and disciples happened to him; he did not seek them.

While gossip of this kind may seem out of place in an essay such as this, it does indicate, once again, the temperamental differences between the two men, and it emphasizes that Yeats's burning zeal for advancement of his own and others' poetic abilities was in opposition to AE's essentially less professional approach.

It is in the poetry and painting of AE that this difference shows most clearly. He was vain about his poetry, says John Eglinton, though he was vain about nothing else, and he could recite all his poems from memory, often with deep emotion. Yeats, on the other hand, could recall no poem without the aid of a manuscript and was much more open to suggested revisions. Indeed, he reworked his poems to an extent impossible to AE, showing in this an impersonal devotion to the art remarkable in a man otherwise so wedded to the notion of the importance of the individual voice. AE's poetry is imaginative, insubstantial, mellifluous; it does not alter very much from its beginnings to its end, and even though it sometimes relinquishes its gentle idealism for definite political statement, it never achieves the vigor and passion of Yeats. Clearly influenced by Pre-Raphaelitism and the brightly colored vocabularies of some of the poets of the nineties, it has a faintly defeated charm; the emotional depths may have been touched by the writer, but they are rarely plumbed by the poem. There are occasional Blakeian poems of tense symbolism, but these are often marred by outmoded or commonplace epithets. Behind them all there is obviously a vision of great power, but the execution blurs it; almost always a powerful opening is deprived of its effect by following weaknesses. Take "Fantasy," for example. It opens magnificently:

> Over all the dream-built margin, flushed with grey and
> hoary light,
> Glint the bubble planets tossing in the dead black
> sea of night.
> Immemorial face, how many faces look from out thy skies
> Now with ghostly eyes of wonder rimmed around with
> rainbow dyes.

The Vaughan-like power of the poem's opening two lines is destroyed by the two clumsy and near-comic lines that follow. The simpler poems are often more successful, but, here again, the poem rather demands the sympathy of the reader than creates it. Sympathy with and love of the man could transform the reader's resistance into assent, and for many people AE's poetry was as emotionally sensitive and as warmly human as its creator. The paintings are much the same. His swiftly executed drawings and watercolors are often radiant with light and filled with ideal presences. Frequently they portray divine beings, gods, spirits, and powers of the air; almost all were painted in the open air, either on his sketching holidays in Donegal or on his Sunday morning excursions. The composition is, however, frequently weak, and the forms are irresolutely disposed. In poetry and in painting AE remained, if we are to adopt acceptably high standards, a talented and sensitive amateur. In a letter to W. B. Yeats of 1900, he wrote about a suggested revision: "I don't agree with you about 'planets.' You can do as you like about excluding it from your selection—but change it I will not . . . I am obstinate about words which are a part of my idea and which cannot be altered without altering my meaning. I do not care whether another word is more beautiful if it does not convey the idea." This is the statement of a teacher rather than a poet.

I cannot, however, dismiss AE on such a note. He was, judged against the giant stature of Yeats, a minor figure. He was, however, enormously influential for good, both in politics and in literature. Not the least of his achievements was the way in which he continually, whether by accident or design, challenged, instructed, and disturbed his lifelong friend and occasional amicable opponent. W. B. Yeats.

6

W. B. Yeats as Master Poet

It is difficult for a poet of today to convince himself (or indeed anyone else) that he has the necessary authority to speak out on matters of importance. He may attempt to speak with an air of authority, but he has little real status in the social system. If his authority is questioned, he may point to his other work and suggest that, as a professor, or publisher, or businessman, or farmer, he is a person whose opinions should carry some weight. He cannot, however, derive the justification for his authoritative manner entirely from his poethood, unless his questioners are all members of the poetic fraternity.

In other times poets were able to speak with an authority born of their acknowledged position and function in society, as well as with the authority of those accepted as being divinely "possessed" or "inspired." In other cultures the poet was priest, historian, genealogist, philosopher, and medicine man. He both affected and recorded the history of his society. In the Middle Ages in Europe, the poet's functions were never in doubt, and his social position, which was psychologically if not financially secure, also gave him a certain freedom. Moreover, his various functions were so well understood that he could easily indicate which one he was, at a given time, engaged in performing by adopting a particular diction or verse form. It was accepted that certain forms and modes of speech were proper for serious and state affairs, that others were appropriate to verse and to entertain a popular audience, and that, in certain modes and genres, a number of conventional phrases, locutions, and devices were inevitable. This enabled the poet to indicate the area or genre in which his poem was operating, with great economy of means; it also enabled him to mix different dictions to more effect than is possible when there is no clear demarcation line between one diction and another. This state of affairs clearly existed in England up to the end of the sixteenth century.

When we look from the poets of the Middle Ages, and from Dunbar and Skelton, to the poetry of later periods, the problem of authority becomes clearer. One might even say that the poets of each decade had a slightly different answer to the question "What authority have you?" In the eighteenth century some pointed to sheer craftsmanship in verse, and some to sociological justifications. In the romantic period some elaborated notions of the poet as a pseudo-prophet, and some of the poet as *homo patiens*.

In the late nineteenth and early twentieth centuries the problem became acute. The followers of the romantics had worn out the notion of the poet as the embodiment of a transcendentally pure and suffering soul. Justification by subject matter was again replacing justification by sensibility. Henley and Davidson, in their different ways, began to present the poet as a critic of society. Browning's poet in his "scrutinizing hat," with his powerful psychological insights, began to be in vogue. The "Art for Art's Sake" movement—the aestheticism of the eighties, and the so-called fin-de-siècle decadence and sensationalism of the nineties—can be regarded as either a reactionary trend or the last fling of the believers in "Authority from Sensibility." By the end of the first decade of the twentieth century, the movement towards finding authority for the poet by subject matter had really taken over; moreover the subject matter had to be sociological in tendency.

One cannot, of course, present a general solution to this problem. Every poet will attempt to solve it in his own way and in terms of his own particular interests. Pound built his authority essentially upon the notion of "authority by subject matter," makeing his *Cantos* encyclopaedic in range and filling them with discussions of history, economics, and the rise and fall of civilizations. Nikos Kazantzakis created his great poem by basing it upon Homer and extending the Homeric epic. William Carlos Williams attempted to construct a universal myth of human society around a typical American city, which he called *Paterson*. The role of the Master Poet, however, demands more than the production of poetry. Almost all those who would generally be accepted as worthy of the title have written, in addition to their poems, books about the art of poetry; they have translated poetry from other languages and also created drama. Moreover, when fiction in prose became an important genre, they created fiction. They established their authority, indeed, as theorists as well as practitioners, and as writers in several of the genres of their time. Thus the list of European Master Poets must include the names of Dante, Chaucer, John Skelton, Ben Jonson, Milton, Goethe, Coleridge, Victor Hugo, Pound, Robert Graves, and W. B. Yeats.

The authority of the Master Poet, however, depends ultimately upon his poetry, and upon the voice in which it is spoken. Consciously or unconsciously W. B. Yeats set himself the task of solving the problem of how to become a Master Poet of the twentieth century.

W. B. Yeats began his writing career in the last years of the nineteenth century and in the shadow of late romanticism. A lonely, dreamy, rather frail child, whose brilliant artist father took a strongly Pre-Raphaelite view of literature; his natural tendency was to consider that the poet's sensibility need be his only justification. The splendor of his dreams justified his social arrogance

> When I was young,
> I had not given a penny for a song
> Did not the poet sing it with such airs
> That one believed he had a sword upstairs
> ("All Things Can Tempt Me")

Nevertheless, there was continually in his heart a hankering after a more solid justification. Perhaps on account of the Morris influence, perhaps because of his Irishness, he spent much time finding and founding small societies in which he could operate as a significant figure. Small societies of adepts tempted him greatly, as one can easily see from his attitude towards the Rhymers, the Society of the Golden Dawn, and his stories in *The Secret Rose*. Yeats also involved himself in the Nationalist movement and did yeoman service by editing and presenting folk stories and folk tales, thus establishing the fact that the Irish race had, indeed, a "Sword upstairs." When Lady Gregory's *Cuchulain of Muirthemne* appeared in 1904, he called it "the finest book that has come out of Ireland in my time." This was because it gave the community poet the store of material that traditionally was his; he could now celebrate the glories of the tribe, those glories having been rediscovered, and thus emulate the socially secure poet of earlier periods.

Tradition and the idea of tradition meant a great deal to Yeats. Indeed, a part of his answer to the authority problem was to indicate the poet's position in a number of traditions and his possession of a multiple-stranded heritage. One tradition was, of course, the Neoplatonic so exhaustively discussed by F. A. C. Wilson; it was not, however, the only one. The Dun Emer and Cuala Presses, of which Yeats acted as editor from their inception to his death, also reflected his sense of heritage; these, directly bequeathed him by William Morris, were part of that notion of the select audience and the court poet, the fine manuscript and the devoted scribe, which was important to his highly idealistic picture of the Middle Ages. Numerous other ways in which Yeats provided himself, and his role, with an ancestry can easily be listed: his genealogical concern with the Butlers, Pollexfens, Middletons; his pseudo-scholarly devotion to the idea of a great "line" of Irish scholars and orators—Swift, Burke, Grattan, Goldsmith; his own continual pretension to scholarship, and his love of an old book; his delight in the Samurai sword given him by Sato; and his passionate concern for the old Tower he could rebuild, are some of them. His discovery that one of his poems had become a popular "folk song," whose author's name had been forgotten, made him feel that he had become so much a part of the country that only his work remained; he had become one with the authors of Chevy Chase and Ichom of Irlonde, a poem which he used himself, extending it, becoming part of it, in order to feel himself one with the great voice of past singers.

Nevertheless, however assiduously Yeats contrived these bracing bulwarks of tradition for his none-too-ivory tower, the problem of authority is not answered for a poet by his beliefs about his role but by his performance of it, and it is here that Yeats reveals his greatness. No poet had adopted the stance Yeats felt proper for a great number of years. He was obliged to rewrite the whole script around a new character, the twentieth-century Master Poet.

It is here that the problem of diction again presents itself. What was the correct language for a Master Poet? Diction should, perhaps, indicate the social levels on which the poem is working, but in the late nineteenth and early twentieth centuries the language of most poetry seemed entirely divorced from the language used for other purposes. Moreover, there was no clear pattern of conventional usage to enable a poet to imply, by means of his vocabulary or tone, the nature of his poetic stance. This problem—the consequence of the breakup of the medieval pattern, and, later, of the romantic revolution against the eighteenth-century neoclassical conventions which had, in part, replaced it—had become even more severe with the years. It had become so severe, indeed, that Browning had been obliged to invent an individual diction of his own, which he could lard with social pointers. Hardy had also created an inimitable manner, as had Davidson. These poets, however, had the actual personality of the *makar* less in the forefront of their subject matter than Yeats. Yeats, who had seen the artist as hero (and the hero as some kind of artist) from his earliest days, had the poet as one of his central themes. In Yeats's lyrical work from its beginning to 1910, one can see a tension between his growing concept of the Master Poet persona and his inherited post-romantic phrases, words, and locutions. Yeats's revision of them was often an attempt to harden the diction and thus alter the persona.

Nevertheless, even in the first versions of the poems published before 1910, one can see the hard, bare, colloquial diction rubbing shoulders with the decadent romantic style and cadence. Specific Irishisms ("When I was a boy with never a crack in my heart") exist alongside pastoral affectations ("The woods of Arcady are dead," "the hapless faun") in *The Wanderings of Oisin* (1889). Attempts at folk ballads jostle attempts at eclogue. In *The Countess Cathleen* (1892) some attempt is made to create a single persona who could be both court and folk poet. In "Apologia addressed to Ireland in the coming days," there are references to the speaker as part of a tradition which is at once nationalist and druidic:

> Know that I would accounted be
> True brother of that company
> Who sang to sweeten Ireland's wrong,
> Ballad and story, rann and song;
> Nor be I any less of them
> Because the red rose bordered hem
> Of her whose history began
> Before God made the angelic clan,
> Trails all about the written page,
> ....
> Nor may I less be counted one
> With David, Mangan, Ferguson,
> Because to him who ponders well,
> My rhymes more than their rhymings tell

In the poem there is also a reference to Ireland as a "Druid Land." Now all this can be seen as the product of a bad conscience; Yeats felt he should be writing political and folk poetry, but found himself writing mystical poetry. This may be partly true, but I think it would be more true to say that Yeats, venturing for the first time upon any kind of extended "public" statement of his own function as a poet, was really more interested in making the speaker of the poem a successful fiction than in defending his own attitudes. Certainly, in the next volume, *The Wind Among the Reeds,* we get the persona of the speaker presented carefully in the third person. Thus we have poems in which a lover-poet speaks: "Aedh tells of the Rose in His Heart," "Aedh to Dectora," "Michael Robartes remembers" and so forth. These titles were revised later to read: "The Lover tells of the Rose in his heart," "The Lover mourns for the Loss of Love," and "He remembers Forgotten Beauty"; these later titles deliberately recall the stance of the medieval courtly poet, and remind us of the titling used by Synge in his translations from Petrarch. The first titles were supported by notes on the personalities mentioned and by a whole scenario of story and allusion. The last named poem, indeed, started off its life as "O'Sullivan Rua to Mary Lavell," but Robartes proved a more satisfactory notion.

Thus Yeats has done what he so often did—created a drama in which certain songs could be made, certain debates conducted—in order to provide himself with a perspective conducive to poetry. Later the scenario can be shelved and the songs remembered. This is, of course, largely what he did with *A Vision*; it was an enabling device. Such devices allowed Yeats to hide his own personal involvement in the attitudes he was presenting or to leave unanswered, even by himself, the question of the extent to which he agreed with the statements made. This is often wise for a poet; if all his statements are made in the first person he may begin to worry over whether he believes in the opinions his poems express and forget to worry over whether or not he fully assents to their structures. Yeats certainly worked frequently in this way, and one often finds a character anticipating views and attitudes of a speaker who is later presented as if he were the poet himself.

I say "as if he were" because it is my contention that "Yeats" is as much of an invention as the fictional speakers he labelled as Michael Robartes and Crazy Jane. I would even say that the creation of a significant and highly individual "Poet-as-Speaker" is Yeats's most important single dramatic and poetic achievement. Others have, of course, manufactured similar personae: Donne is an obvious example as also is the Byron of *Don Juan*. Yeats's invention, however, is more complex than theirs, and it developed additional complexities over the years.

One can easily see this development taking place. In revising *The Wind Among the Reeds*, Yeats not only removed the references to Aedh and O'Sullivan Rua and Michael Robartes, but rearranged the poems of which they had, originally, been the speakers into two groups, one spoken by "the Lover," and one by "the Poet." This later recasting makes a second look at the poems spoken by "the Poet" advisable. They are slight, and include references to "passionate rhyme," to the working at "poor rhymes" "day out, day in," and to the poets (it is implied) as both courageous and proud. They are called a "lonely, proud, winged multitude" in "To his Heart, bidding it have no Fear" which was first published under another title in 1896. From 1899 to 1921 it was called "To My heart bidding it have no Fear." It was altered to the present title in the collection of *Later Poems* in 1922.

In the next collection of lyrics, *In the Seven Woods* (1903), the persona has begun to emerge more clearly. Though the poems are described as "chiefly of the Irish Heroic Age" only two of the thirteen poems involved a fictive speaker in their first printings—Red Hanrahan and Echtge—and in the book itself only Red Hanrahan remained. In this book, too, there is the poem "Adam's Curse," which, though in dialogue form, is Yeats's second attempt at explicit lyrical statement upon his role as poet. The first version of 1902 contains the lines:

> I said "a line will take us hours maybe,
> Yet if it does not seem a moment's thought
> Our stitching and unstitching has been naught.
> Better go down upon your marrow bones
> And scrub a kitchen pavement or break stones
> Like an old pauper in all kinds of weather;
> for to articulate sweet sounds together
> Is to work harder than all these and yet
> Be thought an idler by the noisy set
> Of bankers, schoolmasters, and clergymen
> The martyrs call the world."

This poem, emphasizing that

> It's certain there is no fine thing
> Since Adam's fall but needs much labouring.

also emphasizes the poet's opposition to the machinery of commerce, education, and religion, and allies him with the "martyrs." It is clear, too, that the poet's craft is supposed to result in "sweet sounds" that must appear occasional, spontaneous, impromptu.

This is, of course, a lyric stance. In the same collection, however, we get the ceremonial "The Players Ask for a Blessing on the Psalteries and Themselves" which ends

> The proud and careless notes live on
> But bless our hands that ebb away.

It appears as if the poet must somehow combine deliberate labor, and even ceremonious speech making, with impromptu lyric utterance. The diction of "Adam's Curse" is tougher than that of many previous poems, however. The speaker has observed scullery maids as well as mystical roses and is capable of an almost vulgar directness of speech.

The next important collection of short poems that Yeats produced is *The Green Helmet of 1910*. Between 1903 and 1910, he had published several plays and had rearranged, selected, collected, revised, and reshaped his earlier poems in several ways. *The Green Helmet* is a most important collection, for in it Yeats moves forward towards the vigor of language which is typical of his later work, and which is central to the understanding of his fully achieved persona.

I have argued elsewhere that much of this shift in tone, and this new directness and harshness may be due to Yeats having read the unpublished poems of Synge in 1908. Whether or not this is true, there is certainly a great change here. The book in its first, Cuala Press, edition is divided into three sections. The first is headed "Raymond Lully and his Wife Pernella" and contains poems which stem directly from Yeats's love for Maud Gonne. They are some of his most obviously personal poems, and it is interesting that Yeats thought it necessary to disguise them thus. He may (though it does not seem likely) have wished to avoid embarrassing Maud Gonne. But I feel that, though this may be part of it, the fundamental cause was his intense need to have even his most personal poems spoken by a created person distinct from himself. Poetry must be spoken through a mask, by an invented persona.

The second section of the book was originally called "Momentary Thoughts," and in this section Yeats takes up his notion of creating apparently impromptu lyrics. The section opens with yet another poem about the poet's role and craft:

> The fascination of what's difficult
> Has dried the sap out of my veins, and rent

Spontaneous joy and natural content
Out of my heart

This, however, is followed, after two epigrams, by the un-Petrarchan poem with the Petrarchan title, "To a Poet who would have me Praise certain Bad Poets, Imitators of His and Mine." And after another five poems, in the penultimate poem of the section, we read:

All things can tempt me from this craft of verse:
One time it was a woman's face, or worse—
The seeming needs of my fool-driven land

This contrasts sharply with both the tone and the sentiment of the first section. The voice is harsh, and the note direct. The poet is not a martyr now, but a fighter, a man on the move. Now the poet is justifying himself by his opposition, by his individual strength, but also by his new understanding of the multiple nature of his tradition.

The poems published in 1914 and thereafter can usefully be regarded as forming a kind of unity. I do not mean that they all make use of the same persona, or that they all deal with similar subjects, but that their variety, and their apparent inconsistency can be regarded as forming part of one overmastering intention. This intention can be summarized in the words of Synge, often quoted by Yeats, who said that the poet should make "the whole of life" his subject matter. It can also be summarized as a deliberate attempt at syncretism: the discovery of antinomies and oppositions and the combining of them into one whole which could be represented by a single persona. This persona reveals itself in terms of both the poet's canon and in terms of the speaker of a small number of key poems which openly attempt syncretism in either personal or objective terms.

The first poem, "The Grey Rock," of *Responsibilities* (1914) is itself an attempt to identify the multiple traditions in which the poet should work; it includes these significant lines addressed to the members of The Rhymers Club:

You kept the Muses' sterner laws,
And unrepenting faced your ends,
And therefore earned the right—and yet
Dowson and Johnson Most I praise—

To troop with those the world's forgot,
And copy their proud steady gaze.

The book itself places poems about the heroic past alongside poems of the present, but the latter are always related to the past. Thus we get in one poem the challenging colloquialism of

You gave but will not give again
Until enough of Paudeen's pence
By Biddy's halfpennies have lain
To be "some sort of evidence,"
Before you'll put your guineas down

Though the word "lain" has a slightly formal and archaic air, and "guineas" and "pence" are not part of a completely vulgar diction, the passage is dominated by the wish to speak in forceful everyday tones. Later on, however, we get

What cared Duke Ercole, that bid
His mummers to the market-place,
What th'onion-sellers thought or did
So that his Plautus set the pace
For the Italian comedies?
And Guidabaldo, when he made
That grammar school of courtesies
Where wit and beauty learned their trade
Upon Urbino's windy hill,
Had sent no runners to and fro
That he might learn the shepherds' will.

Here the references and the diction are far from vulgar in their overall effect. Nevertheless, there are colloquial elements, such as the commonplace "learned their trade" and "set the pace" and the deliberately anachronistic "grammar school." In the diction of this poem, as in that of the majority of Yeats's later poems, the formal and archaic is set beside the colloquial and contemporary; vulgarisms are juxtaposed with pedanticisms; slang and ceremony coexist. Yeats was fully aware of this aspect of his diction and commented upon it, both directly and obliquely, several times. It is one aspect of his syncretic method, and one way in which he attempted to fuse the "dream of the noble" with that of the "beggar man"—the poet as scholar fusing with the poet as street singer or vulgar minstrel.

In *The Wild Swans at Coole* (1919), Yeats developed his syncretic approach further. "In Memory of Robert Gregory" not only presents the speaker as partaking of the insights of both scholar and common man by mixing dictions, but the poem attempts to group together disparate and conflicting attitudes by celebrating the memory of friends who embodied them. Robert Gregory himself portrayed as "Our Sidney and our perfect man." He was a countryman and a lover of the countryside. He was a painter, who

> understood
> All work in metal or in wood,
> In moulded plaster or in carven stone
> ....
> Soldier, scholar, horseman, he,
> And all he did done perfectly
> As though he had but that one trade alone.

By being this twentieth-century version of the complete Renaissance gentleman, Robert Gregory was "all life's epitome." Thus we can see that "the whole of life" to Yeats means the whole of life as presented in one personality, who fuses the present with the past, and combines all the arts in one allmastering genius.

If we take Robert Gregory as a pattern of excellence, we can see most of the parts of that pattern reflected in the other poems in *The Wild Swans at Coole* which present love of the countryside, the attitude of the soldier and horseman, and the viewpoint of the classical scholar and of the artist.

Alongside the use of unifying personalities in Yeats's work, however, we must recognize a similar use of divisive characters. Michael Robartes and Owen Aherne are two of these. Another two, in "Ego Dominus Tuus," are simply labelled "Hic" and "Ille." A third pair are "the Saint" and "the Hunchback" in the poem of that name. This was, of course, the period during which Yeats was working on *A Vision* (1925) which he described, in its 1937 edition, as being "stylistic arrangements of experience comparable to the cubes in the drawing of Wyndham Lewis and to the ovoids in the sculpture of Brancusi." *A Vision* arranges history and presents both the movements of history and the nature of human personality in a number of categories, which relate to each other in a complex manner. The final intention, however, is not to present variety, but unity. There may be many "phases of the moon" but, Yeats points out in the 1956 edition of *A Vision*, "The ultimate reality because neither one nor many concord nor discord, is symbolized by a phaseless sphere." Later, in the same work, "I have now described many symbols which seem mechanical because united in a single structure, and of which the greater number, precisely because they tell always the same story, may seem unneccessary. Yet every symbol, except where it lies in vast periods of time and so beyond our experience, has evoked for me some form of human destiny, and that form, once evoked, has appeared everywhere, as if there were but one destiny, as my own form might appear in a room full of mirrors." Again, now referring to the "Phaseless sphere" or "Thirteenth Cone," he says, "It becomes even conscious of itself as so seen, like some great dancer, the perfect flower of modern culture, dancing some primitive dance and conscious of his or her own life and the dance. . . . Only one symbol exists, though the reflecting mirrors make many appear and all different." The one symbol that Yeats postulates is thus an image of syncretic unity. Apparent variety and apparent inconsistency are the result of different perspectives upon this one central reality.

Much of Yeats's work in *Michael Robartes and the Dancer* (1921) and *The Tower* (1928) is devoted to the discovery of this one symbol which will sum up, somehow or other, all phases of human experience, and therefore, all the different stances of poetry. Both the city of Byzantium and the Tower at Thoor Ballylee are investigated as candidates for the position. Byzantium, however, seems meaningful only in the context of a Neoplatonic tradition. It is in the title poem of *The Tower* that the one symbol begins to emerge. Looking down from the battlements, the speaker recalls the history of his country and the poets who have been involved in it and have celebrated it. Having done this and perceived the way in which the poet is both a vehicle of the great memory and a celebrant of passing beauty, a part of the passing scene, he moves on to consider his own position. He refers to the pride of his countrymen, to Burke and to Grattan, and then declares his faith:

> I mock Plotinus' thought
> And cry in Plato's teeth,
> Death and life were not
> Till man made up the whole,
> Made lock, stock and barrel

Out of his bitter soul,
Aye, sun and moon and star, all,
And further add to that
That, being dead, we rise,
Dream and so create
Translunar Paradise.
I have prepared my peace
With learned Italian things
And the proud stones of Greece,
Poet's imaginings
And memories of love,
Memories of the words of women,
All those things whereof
Man makes a superhuman
Mirror-resembling dream.

Thus man is now seen as the true creator of his universe. Man as poet creates a dream which, like a mirror or like many mirrors, reflects back different versions of the one face.

In *Meditations in Time of Civil War* which, significantly (for Yeats took pains over the arranging of his collections), is the next poem in *The Tower*, we are presented with the poet in the act of creating the mirrors. These reflect back to him ancient Greece, ancestral houses, Milton's *Il Penseroso*, Irish soldiers of the Civil War, Japanese art and tradition, the countryside, unicorns, hawks, and Babylonian prophecies—to name but a few of the themes and images occurring to the speaker's mind. This activity of the poet, however, does not appear to solve the problem of his role in society, for the last stanza of the last section reads:

I turn away and shut the door, and on the stair
Wonder how many times I could have proved my worth
In something that all others understand or share;
But O! Ambitious heart, had such a proof drawn forth
A company of friends, a conscience set at ease,
It had but made us pine the more. The abstract joy,
The half-read wisdom of daemonic images
Suffice the aging man as once the growing boy.

It could be argued that it is in the following poem, "Nineteen Hundred and Nineteen," that Yeats first brings all his concerns together and discovers a structure exactly suited to his endeavor. Let us give it a more detailed examination.

Nineteen Hundred and Nineteen

I

Many ingenious lovely things are gone
That seemed sheer miracle to the multitude,
Protected from the circle of the moon
That pitches common things about. There stood
Amid the ornamental bronze and stone
An ancient image made of olive wood—
And gone are Phidias' famous ivories
And all the golden grasshoppers and bees.

We too had many pretty toys when young:
A law indifferent to blame or praise,
To bribe or threat; habits that made old wrong
Melt down, as it were wax in the sun's rays;
Public opinion ripening for so long
We thought it would outlive all future days.
O what fine thought we had because we thought
That the worst rogues and rascals had died out.

All teeth were drawn, all ancient tricks unlearned,
And a great army but a showy thing;
What matter that no cannon had been turned
Into a ploughshare? Parliament and king
Thought that unless a little powder burned
The trumpeters might burst with trumpeting
And yet it lack all glory; and perchance
The guardsmen's drowsy chargers would not prance.

Now days are dragon-ridden, the nightmare
Rides upon sleep: a drunken soldiery
Can leave the mother, murdered at her door,
To crawl in her own blood, and go scot-free;
The night can sweat with terror as before
We pieced our thoughts into philosophy,
And planned to bring the world under a rule,
Who are but weasels fighting in a hole.

He who can read the signs nor sink unmanned
Into the half-deceit of some intoxicant
From shallow wits; who knows no work can stand,
Whether health, wealth or peace of mind were spent

On master-work of intellect or hand,
No honour leave its mighty monument,
Has but one comfort left: all triumph would
But break upon his ghostly solitude.

But is there any comfort to be found?
Man is in love and loves what vanishes,
What more is there to say? That country round
None dared admit, if such a thought were his,
Incendiary or bigot could be found
To burn that stump on the Acropolis,
Or break in bits the famous ivories
Or traffic in the grasshoppers or bees.

II

When Loie Fuller's Chinese dancers enwound
A shining web, a floating ribbon of cloth,
It seemed that a dragon of air
Had fallen among dancers, had whirled them round
Or hurried them off on its own furious path;
So the Platonic Year
Whirls out new right and wrong,
Whirls in the old instead;
All men are dancers and their tread
Goes to the barbarous clangour of a gong.

III

Some moralist or mythological poet
Compares the solitary soul to a swan;
I am satisfied with that,
Satisfied if a troubled mirror show it,
Before that brief gleam of its life be gone,
An image of its state;
The wings half spread for flight,
The breast thrust out in pride
Whether to play, or to ride
Those winds that clamour of approaching night.

A man in his own secret meditation
Is lost amid the labyrinth that he has made
In art or politics;
Some Platonist affirms that in the station
Where we should cast off body and trade

The ancient habit sticks,
And that if our works could
But vanish without breath
That were a lucky death,
For triumph can but mar our solitude.

The swan has leaped into the desolate heaven:
That image can bring wildness, bring a rage
To end all things, to end
What my laborious life imagined, even
The half-imagined, the half-written page;
O but we dreamed to mend
Whatever mischief seemed
To afflict mankind, but now
That winds of winter blow
Learn that we were cracked-pated when we dreamed.

IV

We, who seven years ago
Talked of honour and of truth,
Shriek with pleasure if we show
The weasel's twist, the weasel's tooth.

V

Come let us mock at the great
That had such burdens on the mind
And toiled so hard and late
To leave some monument behind,
Nor thought of the levelling wind.

Come let us mock at the wise;
With all those calendars whereon
They fixed old aching eyes,
They never saw how seasons run,
And now but gape at the sun.

Come let us mock at the good
That fancied goodness might be gay,
And sick of solitude
Might proclaim a holiday:
Wind shrieked—and where are they?

Mock mockers after that
That would not lift a hand maybe
To help good, wise or great
To bar that foul storm out, for we
Traffic in mockery.

VI

Violence upon the roads: violence of horses;
Some few have handsome riders, are garlanded
On delicate sensitive ear or tossing mane,
But wearied running round and round in their courses
All break and vanish, and evil gathers head:
Herodias' daughters have returned again,
A sudden blast of dusty wind and after
Thunder of feet, tumult of images,
Their purpose in the labyrinth of the wind;
And should some crazy hand dare touch a daughter
All turn with amorous cries, or angry cries,
According to the wind, for all are blind.
But now wind drops, dust settles; thereupon
There lurches past, his great eyes without thought
Under the shadow of stupid straw-pale locks,
That insolent fiend Robert Artisson
To whom the love-lorn Lady Kyteler brought
Bronzed peacock feathers, red combs of her cocks.

When Yeats first published this poem in the *Dial* of September 1921, he called it "Thoughts upon the Present State of the World," and it does attempt to outline the state of European culture and civilization in 1919. In that year Europe was reeling under the effects of the First World War, and Ireland was suffering from the persecutions of the Black and Tans, a militia drawn from the ranks of disillusioned British ex-servicemen, which was intended to combat the activities of the Irish rebels but which indulged in many acts of looting and terrorism.

The situation was perilous, and Yeats relates it in the first stanza of his poem to the downfall of Greek civilization; the reverence of the people for true religion (symbolized by the image of olive wood) and for the masterworks of art (symbolized by the ivories of Phidias and the golden grasshoppers and bees) has been destroyed. The poem progresses in terms of many such references. It is as if the speaker's richly endowed mind were ranging over the whole tangled complex of the social scene and finding images and echoes from the past that complement and explain the present and that lead him towards philosophic certainties.

The speaker's "voice" is also an important element of the poem. It contains both scholarly and vulgar cadences, and it includes the marketplace rhetoric of swinging iambs as well as the brusquer rhythms of the scholar forced into antirhetorical accuracies and also includes the more careless clumsiness of the honest speaker suspicious of an overeasy smoothness. Thus the persona is one who convinces us of his right to speak in all available tones of all available things.

The overall structure of the poem is that of a catena, a series of separate wise or crypto-religious statements strung together to form a pattern. The first section presents us with the ambiguity of a double perspective. The opening places us in Athens at the end of Greek civilization, and there are no references in the remainder of the section that explicitly contradict this placing, although it is clear that the descriptions of the false glories of war, of ideals betrayed, and of the brutal soldiery, refer to the ideals of earlier Irish nationalism and the current troubles as well as to the Athenian situation. The return to Greece at the end of the section makes it clear to us that a description of the one is also that of the other; the Greeks facing ruin and the Irish struggling for freedom are at the same point of the same dance.

I use the image of the dance because it is the next one to take our attention. Loie Fuller's Chinese dancers were an attraction of the Folies-Bergère in the nineties; the main feature of their performance was the colored silks they whirled and manipulated under the electric light, thus presenting (to Yeats's mind) the very essence, the Platonic idea of dance, for the individual bodies were less important than the colored webs and scarves that, in their swathings and circlings, suggested the possession of the dancers by some overmastering impulse subduing and cancelling their subjective personalities in the service of a greater rhythm. This image, therefore, relates the poem yet again to the rhythmic and cyclic nature of history in which we are all involved and by which we are all possessed.

It is not entirely illogical for the poem to move next to the presentation of the swan symbol, for the swan in Greek mythology must remind us of the myth of Leda and of her possession by the spirit of Zeus that led both to the creation of the ideal beauty of Helen and to the complete destruction of a civilization. Just as the swan created Helen, so the lonely soul possessed though even briefly by a god, may, with one last song before its sexual or absolute death, commit destruction in a rage of purity. We, however, more usually busy ourselves in constructing imprisoning labyrinths by which we may possibly continue to be troubled after death. Contemplating the surge of the swan into the desolate sky, we realize that we were deluded when we imagined that our laborious subtleties could mend anything. Our dreams—whether of triumphant Troy, a perpetual Athens, or a noble Dublin—were mere folly.

Explication of this kind is hardly adequate, for Yeats was not composing an allegory and his symbolism is capable of many complexities of interpretation. Nevertheless, such explication does indicate the tightly knitted intellectual pattern of the poem and its world-encompassing rhetoric. The poem itself indulges in cyclic repetitions, as do the civilizations to which it refers. The weasels fighting in a hole, which image the civil strife in Ireland and its animal pettiness, recur in the fourth section, where much that has already been implied or stated is gathered together in one exact and passionate quatrain. This breaks the comparatively gentle, meditative flow of the poem with an outburst of anger, just as its short-lined epigrammatic form breaks the rhetorical flow of all that has preceded it.

Out of anger emerges mockery, and the speaker wakes from his meditative soliloquies and directly addresses an audience. He ridicules, one by one, the labors of the idealists; and then, reaching total nihilism, he condemns also the act of ridicule and curses those mockers who refuse to make any effort to bar out "the foul storm."

In the final section, the "foul storm" itself has arrived and is described. There is violence upon the roads of Ireland and Europe. The daughers of Herodias, those far-from-ideal dancers, who bring death to all prophets and all idealism, have returned. They are blindly caught up in the labyrinths of their own schemings, as are we with our petty considerations as described in the third section of the poem. They contrast, in their disorder, tumult, and dust, with the Chinese dancers—whose shining clothes suggested possession by a "dragon of air" rather than the dragon of nightmare described in the first section or the fiend to be described in this. As their dance fades the final draconic, grotesque image appears, that of the spirit, Robert Artisson, who in fourteenth-century Kilkenny tormented and obsessed the Lady Kyteler. The names matter little, but the gesture is important. For the peacock feathers and cocks' combs (there is a play here upon the notion of coxcomb) that she sacrifices to her demon lover are a parody of true religious ritual, and they contrast with the opening reference to the image of olive wood and with all the other images of spiritual passion and intellectual purity. Here, again, we are given a double perspective by means of ambiguity, for the horses are at once those of the warring factions in Ireland and those of the apocalyptic riders foretelling the end of the world.

Such creatures as the daughters of Herodias and Robert Artisson are, however, all part of the cyclic movement of history, and Yeats himself related them to his own growing philosophic system as presented in *A Vision* (1925) and, later, saw them as significant in terms of Spengler's view in *The Decline of the West*. Indeed, the whole of Yeats's poem is part of a completely systematized politico-philosophical view of the nature of the growth and fall of civilizations. It is also a dramatically personal poem.

In speaking of "Nineteen Hundred and Nineteen" as personal, I am not thinking of the autobiographical element, though this is clearly present in the first two sections. Nor do I mean the personal anguish, though this, too, is clear enough from the intensity of language and the sudden compulsive shifts in emotional level. I mean the voice—which is Yeats and Yeats alone. It is not the voice of a ventriloquial figure that has been given a valuably wide range of verbal characteristics: it is an individual man who speaks with an idiosyncractic style that may be comprehensively oracular but is also human. Here are all Yeats's tricks of speech. We have the blandly unself-conscious oddity of such archaisms as "perchance." We have sentences balanced weightily upon ponderous conditional clauses and upon the gesticulatory use of "some" and "that." We have the swift, easy, almost Marlovian swing of one line countered by the deliberate, near-pedantic clumsiness of the next. We have scholarly diction and literary image juxtaposed with vernacular directness and commonplace reference. These make up—in part, at least—the voice of Yeats. It is an individual voice, as "Nineteen Hundred and Nineteen" is an individual vision, but the individual is representative of the race, embodying the dream both of noble and of beggarman, fusing the subjective and the objective, the ideal and the pragmatic. In "Nineteen Hundred and Nineteen," W. B. Yeats contrived a poem "upon the present state of the world" as relevant to its time as Milton's "Areopagitica" and as timeless in its significance. This he must have realized when he altered his title, for the poem is not about the "present state" of the world, but about the world itself, and 1919 is simply the vantage point from which it is viewed.

Although "Nineteen Hundred and Nineteen" comes across as a deeply personal poem it is not autobiographical; it is a structure of meditations and reflections and contains no personal anecdotes. "Among School Children" takes a different tack, and its use of personal memory and its philosophical attitudes have been commented upon by many critics. I do not need, therefore, to add to their commentary here. I am concerned to point out only one aspect of the poem. This is the nature and range of its references. In the first stanza we are in a twentieth-century Catholic school, where the children are being taught by nuns. In the second stanza we are referred to the myth of Leda and the Swan, a myth which explains the downfall of one civilization and the foundation of another. We are also referred to Plato, who is one of the founders of our way of thinking. The third stanza fuses the image of Helen of Troy with that of Maud Gonne and a child in the schoolroom. The fourth stanza moves us briefly into another period and another civilization with its reference to the "quattrocento." The fifth and sixth stanzas move between the speaker's present and the past of Porphyry, Aristotle, Plato, and Pythagoras. In the seventh stanza the Greek and the Christian myths are brought together with additional references to timeless maternal emotions. The poem concludes with the stanza which appears to resolve all these conflicts and similarities into the one symbol.

> Labour is blossoming or dancing where
> The body is not bruised to pleasure soul,
> Nor beauty born out of its own despair,
> Nor blear-eyed wisdom out of midnight oil.
> O chestnut tree, great-rooted blossomer,
> are you the leaf, the blossom, or the bole?
> O body swayed to music, O brightening glance,
> How can we know the dancer from the dance?

Thus "Among School Children" presents references to myths and beliefs that are basic to two great civilizations, perceives similarity and dissimilarity, and discovers one symbol which brings all things into unity.

The interpretation of this one symbol has caused a good deal of head scratching, and I am happy not to have to go into it at all thoroughly. I wish only to relate it, and the poem in which it appears, to the series of other autobiographical meditations which Yeats composed, and this but briefly. The poem "All Souls' Night" is one of this series and again presents many images which the poet wishes to contemplate, "Till meditation master all its parts." In *The Winding Stair and Other Poems*

(1933), "A Dialogue of Self and Soul" performs the same maneuver. Here the speaker states,

> I am content to follow to its source
> Every event in action or in thought;
> Measure the lot

In "Blood and the Moon," the speaker sees his "ancestral stair" as one travelled by Goldsmith, Berkeley, Burke, and Swift and then relates it to the dead civilizations of Alexandria and Babylon. The nonautobiographical "The Seven Sages" deals also with the Irish tradition and makes use of the same characters. "Coole Park, 1929" and "Coole Park and Ballylee, 1931," again autobiographical meditations, discuss the traditions of poetry and scholarship, and their "Traditional sanctity and loveliness." "Vacillation" relates philosophies of different cultures and focuses them through the lens of the one inquiring contemplative mind. In *A Full Moon in March* (1935), "Parnell's Funeral" relates present-day Ireland to the Ireland of Swift and to images of ancient Sicily and Crete. In the *Last Poems and Two Plays* (1939), the syncretic tendency is observable in numerous poems—"An Acre of Grass" places Shakespeare and Blake alongside Michelangelo; "The Municipal Gallery Revisited" repeats the maneuvers of the Coole Park poems. "The Statues" develops its theme with reference to Greek civilization, the Middle Ages, Shakespeare, Irish legend, and the Easter Rising of 1916. "Long-Legged Fly" sees Julius Caesar, Helen of Troy, a child in a street, and Michelangelo experiencing the same kind of entranced inspiration. "The Circus Animals' Desertion," more narrowly autobiographical than many, nevertheless is in the same series as the Coole poems.

It is in "Lapis Lazuli" however, that the syncretic or synoptic method reaches a new clarity. The first paragraph refers to the poets as being "gay" and contrives to mention both King Billy and the zeppelin raids of the First World War. The second paragraph deals with Shakespearean tragedy and maintains that "Hamlet and Lear are gay," suggesting that there is a triumphant gaiety in the way the poet has mastered and understood his themes of human agony. The third paragraph presents us with an image of the fall of civilizations under the attack of wandering hordes and points out that Callimachus's sculpture is now totally lost. Here however we are made to see the poet's gaiety in a new light:

No handiwork of Callimachus,
Who handled marble as if it were bronze,
Made draperies that seemed to rise
When sea-wind swept the corner, stands;
His long lamp-chimney shaped like the stem
Of a slender palm, stood but a day;
All things fall and are built again,
And those that build them again are gay.

This is the poet's duty and justification. He is not simply the self-reflecting creator of a hall of mirrors but a continual renewer of past achievements, a living embodiment of tradition. Tradition, in the last verse paragraph of the poem, is presented to us by way of three Chinamen carved in lapis lazuli, who stare "on all the tragic scene":

One asks for mournful melodies;
Accomplished fingers begin to play.
Their eyes mid many wrinkles, their eyes,
Their ancient, glittering eyes, are gay.

The role of the poet, therefore, is twofold. He must bring all things into unity, the past into unity with the present, the classical with the Christian, the nationalist with the cosmic, the local with the general; and he must remake what has fallen, thus becoming at once the worker in many traditions and the unifier of all.

This view of the poet's function successfully answers the problem of authority posed at the beginning of this chapter. It does not, however, solve the question of the means towards this end. The means Yeats chose were as various as the task demanded. He wrote ballads in which his sense of the vulgar tradition was fused with this appreciation of its essential dignity. His mixed diction gave his ballads the same balance of formality and freedom which one finds in the Scottish border ballads, without in any way imitating them. He adopted the tone of the lyric poet desired by Synge, making poems which were simultaneously earthy and controlled. He developed the eclogue form and the poetic sequence. Where his own central persona (that of the all-combining maker) was too myriad-minded for his matter, he took on the mask of Crazy Jane or Tom of Cruachan, or of an anonymous man or woman, or of a saint or ballad singer. In each poem he presented sharp conflicts, dramatic assertions, vivid paradoxes that can all be found restated, and resolved in the great series of meditations where the brooding mind of the Master Poet, the "great dancer," shows itself conscious of its "own life and the dance." As a consequence, the viewpoints expressed in the different poems are not consistent with one another. Judicious selection will result in one's tracing Yeats's debt to this or that tradition; one can make him out as essentially a Neoplatonist, or a sophisticated folk poet, or a fascist, or a solipsist, or almost what one wishes. Much, of course, can be made to fit with Neoplatonism for that is a philosophic system which is itself syncretic, bringing many strangers into companionship with an Elizabethan dexterity and capacity for doublethink.

There is, however, one central symbol, one unifying force, and this is the fully achieved persona of the Master Poet which contains all human attitudes and passions. Yeats's autobiographical meditations are so contrived as to relate together in personal terms many widely differing attitudes, with each of which he shows sympathy for one reason or another. Lady Gregory, Synge, Horton, the Middletons, Pollexfens, Dowson, Johnson, Robert Gregory, Hugh Lane, Daniel O'Leary would probably agree with one another on no single point were they to be placed in the same room. Grattan, Swift, Burke, Goldsmith, and Berkeley would make a somewhat lively committee. Blake and Plotinus might agree on occasion but what of Aristotle, Michelangelo, Sato, Landor, Donne, and that fisherman in Connemara tweeds? The only conceivable meeting place is in the mind of Yeats, a mind of Shakespearean capacity.

It is not its capacity, however, which is its most astonishing characteristic: it is its ability to so order its contents as to give us the impression that it is an embodiment of a whole culture. The references combine to remind us that the Master Poet is a man representative of all European cultural history. Sometimes they indicate, more narrowly, his being representative of the culture and history of Ireland. But even when this is the case, the masterful references to Irish phenomena as being significant of universal principles and traditions make us see Ireland as itself a summary of human experience and human history. References to Greek philosophy and to medieval art both unify and universalize his meditations by relating them to cultural fundamentals of Western civilization.

In this Yeats is doing neither more nor less than the Master Poets who preceded him. If we look at the work of Dante, Chaucer, Spenser, Ben Jonson, and Milton, we see that each attempted to fuse together different traditions—to marry the "classical" with his national inheritance, to comment upon the role of the poet even as he performed it, and to produce work which could be viewed as emanating from a mind and sensibility representative of the central beliefs and concerns of Western civilization. Later poets did much the same, though, as it became increasingly more difficult and finally impossible for one man to have even a smattering of all existing knowledge in history, philosophy, and literature, the masterworks became more limited in range. Thus, in the romantic period, Wordsworth's major work was an autobiographical investigation of poetry and the mind of the poet, Byron's masterpiece was wider ranging but avoided the darker depths, and Tennyson's *Idylls of the King* was a narrowly national epic. Whitman in his *Leaves of Grass* chose to characterize and embody a national sensibility and to suggest that it was central to all humanity and Browning chose to create in terms of a version of medieval Italy which gave him the opportunity to explore what he clearly felt to be a significant cultural crux and matrix. Pound, a follower of both Browning and Whitman, attempted the larger scope of a truly international poem, a universal contemplation of the lot of man. All these poets, however, like Yeats, took synopsis, syncresis, and synthesis as their three guiding principles, and all, for better or worse, gave poetry a new authority in their time.

7

THE VISION OF JACK B. YEATS

"BUT ALL WILD sights appealed to Synge, he did not care whether they were typical of anything else or had any symbolical meaning at all. If he had lived in the days of piracy he would have been the fiddler in a pirate-schooner, him they called 'the music—' 'The music' looked on at everything with dancing eyes but drew no sword, and when the schooner was taken and the pirates hung at Cape Corso Castle or the Island of Saint Christopher's, 'the music' was spared because he *was* 'the music'." This comment upon Synge by Jack B. Yeats reveals as much about its author as its subject and hints at attitudes which persisted throughout Yeats's paintings, writings, and life. Jack Yeats, like Synge, was—to use my own words—"an observer, a recorder, a satirist and in many ways a romantic." Like Synge, he was passionately interested in the life of the people and viewed planned societies with skepticism, even while objecting to capitalist materialism. Like Synge, he relished the wild and the odd, and he perceived and commented, both affectionately and sardonically, upon the contrary nature of humankind and upon the conflicts in human society. He was, like his brother, W. B. Yeats, concerned not merely to work in one medium but in several, and he was, like both W. B. Yeats and Synge, an innovator. Moreover, once one surveys all his work—the drawings, the paintings, the prose works, the plays—one discovers an overmastering unity, a bringing together, not only of "beggar and nobleman" but even of the media themselves. For the prose works frequently include minidramas and the plays, stories; and both are supported, and sometimes accompanied, by sketches and paintings.

A thorough survey of all Jack B. Yeats's work is not possible within the confines of this book, but a relatively brief one may serve to show

how he, like his brother, managed to bring into dynamic unity all the contraries he observed, and in so doing became not only Ireland's greatest painter but also one of her most original and rewarding writers.

Students and lovers of twentieth-century art are already well aware of the importance of Jack B. Yeats as a painter, but readers interested primarily in literature may not be familiar with his life or his writings. It seems sensible therefore to begin with a few biographical facts.

Jack Butler Yeats was born on 29 August, 1871 and was the youngest of John Butler Yeats's children, W. B. Yeats being the eldest. He spent the greater part of his childhood in Sligo, where early he showed his fascination with both drawing and the theater, writing and illustrating childish plays and acting them out in a toy theater. He studied art at Westminster School, and before the turn of the century, first in London then in Manchester and later at Dartmouth, he had established himself as a cartoonist and illustrator. His work of this early period is bold in line and dramatic in concept, the drama often approaching in mood the melodramatic directness of folktale or of those pirate stories he delighted in reading.

His childhood experiences and enthusiasms clearly colored his imagination. He showed a love of the fantastic and of the savage innocence of Irish peasantry. His delight in dreams of far lands and strange countries was one he shared with the poet John Masefield, who contributed verses to his early plays for children and who clearly intensified his interest in things piratical. Indeed, in old age when told that there was a rumor that, as a youth, he had fallen out with his brother and gone to sea for seven years, after commenting, "I was never at sea in my life," he explained the influence of the sea upon his work with the single name "John Masefield."

The rumor, however false, indicates the apparent lack of sympathy between the two brothers, but it must be remembered that the younger continually contributed to the Cuala Press broadsides of which W. B. was an editor. Both were admirers and friends of J. M. Synge (though the younger was more his intimate). Each has recorded his admiration of the work of the other. And both were interested in folk anecdotes, ballads, and the supernatural, though they expressed their interest in different ways.

It was in the first decade of the century that Jack Yeats began to show his paces most clearly. In 1902, with Pamela Colman Smith, he produced a series of broadsheets, each of which contained verse and two illustrations, one at least of which was hand-colored. This clearly emanated from a feeling which he shared with his brother that art could be "taken to the people" in this way and reflected the strong influence of the thought of William Morris upon the Yeats family generally. These broadsides led W. B. Yeats and his sisters to issue a similar monthly series from the Cuala Press from 1908 to 1915, and a later series in 1935 and 1937. W. B. Yeats contributed poems to the broadsheets, just as Jack Yeats's drawings appeared in the broadsides. Moreover, it was these broadsides which led W. B. Yeats, especially in his later years, to develop his earlier ballad style and to write songs for which music was often specially composed, with the wish expressed in *On the Boiler* to become himself part of a folk tradition.

In 1905, Jack Yeats first began to paint consistently in oils. His work in this medium between 1905 and 1924 still made use of the heavy outlines he had used as a book illustrator, and he took his subject matter frequently from his memories of the peasants, beggars, and tinkers of western Ireland whom he knew so well, and whom he also portrayed in his illustrations to Synge's *Aran Islands* and to the articles on the Congested Districts which Synge wrote for the *Manchester Guardian*. He also, however, made great use of the circus, which he used to visit with Masefield. These circus and peasant paintings have a solidity reminiscent of Millet; the paint is applied with heavy insistence, and the color is much more drab than in his later work. His work of this period has been associated with that of the London group, and, in its strange combination of anecodotal realism and symbolic distortion has been compared with that of Sickert. Even though realism seems a part of his work at this time, he never painted from actuality but always from memory; the distortions are less the product of a fallible memory than of an intention to transform, dignify, dramatize, and elucidate the actual and to cast over it "a colouring of the imagination." Moreover, in even the most serious or pathetic of these works there is a quirkishness, a flicker of humor, a fascination with and a delight in oddity. This is particularly evident in his picture book, *Life in the West of Ireland*, which was published in 1912.

This delight shows itself even more openly in his writings of this period. Jack Yeats was the author of a number of plays for children with hand-colored illustrations. Their titles are indicative of their contents: *James Flaunty: or, The Terror of the Western Seas; The Scourge of the Gulph; The Treasure of the Garden: A Play in the Old Manner*. This last is advertised by Elkin Matthews, who published a whole series of *Jack Yeats's Chap Books* with the note: "Stages with Prosceniums designed by the Author, Footlights, Slides, and Scenes, can be had, price 5s net each." Apart from these plays he wrote a story, *The Bosun and the Bob-Tailed Comet*, and an account of the toy boats made by himself and his friends as children, with the title *A Little Fleet*.

Setting aside the exuberant drawings with their superbly rhythmical use of line and their masterly compositions, the plays themselves include, for all their manipulation of the clichés of childhood adventure, a disturbing juxtaposition of the ebullient and the macabre. The plot of *The Scourge of the Gulph* is as follows:

Captain Carricknagat, a black-bearded pirate, aboard his ship off the Isle of Plumes, learns that his wife has been captured and eaten by cannibals. The message is brought by Bosun Broad, who has lost an arm in the fight but has escaped with a letter from the unfortunate woman. This letter asks the Captain to find her body, remove her skull, place it in a black box with silver hinges, and bury it on the round hill on the Island of Plumes. The Bosun and the Captain find the skull, but the Bosun dies of "the black thirst" before the Captain is able to dig a grave with his sword to bury what he calls "This sad piece of ivory." At that point Joe Miles, a sailor who has earlier been marooned, comes upon the Captain and, believing the box contains treasure, kills the Captain. On opening the box he discovers the skull and brings the play to an end with the words: "An empty skull, a black box, a dead skipper! Have I done anything or nothing?"

This curtain recalls similar moods at the close of some of W. B. Yeats's plays for the most adult audiences, in which, after all the agony, the question is again put. *The Herne's Egg* (1938) ends with Corney commenting: "All that trouble and nothing to show for it, Nothing but just another donkey." This is, indeed that dying fall, that weary or appalled asking of the cosmic riddle with which much poetic tragedy ends. The note of soliloquy is necessarily frequent in these plays, for the nature of the cardboard theater, with its figures held perpetually in the pose in which they have been painted, requires a somewhat static drama. Thus Jack Yeats's plays for children have the same restricted or formal pattern of movements as that provided by W. B. Yeats for his plays, though for a different reason. Ernest Marriott in his small monograph on the work of Jack Yeats makes the point:

> It seems to me that these diminutive dramas show something of the fanciful simplicity and directness of phrase which we find in the work of the better-known dramatists of the Irish movement. . . .

> Bosun Hardbite addressing McGowan who is seated on a mooring post on the quay says, "Sit there on yer old iron mushyroom till the seaweed grows you." An Emigrant replies, "The poor captain is feeling sad in his heart. The poor man, like the rest of us, doesn't like leaving the dear silk of the kine." At the beginning of [*The Treasure of the Garden*] the captain ruminates, "What a roaring life it is too, chasing the rich ships—the big fat pigeons with crops full of gold. But it's the other thing that sickens—fighting two great ugly frigates in a little ditch of a creek . . . they fall across you and lie on you like a dead horse." The impressive scene where he makes this speech is a battered deck with bullet-riddled pirates hanging from the shrouds in the last horror of bodily death.

If Jack Yeats took the role of "the Music" in his pirate drama, he also took it in many of his drawings and prints of this period. The series of hand-colored prints by him which were issued by the Cuala Press almost all belong to his earlier manner. In them one can see certain themes emerging over and over again—the solitary watcher, caught up in reflective nostalgia; the sailor, with his eyes full of strange places, walking alone through the city street; the ballad singer, a vehicle for songs even odder and older than himself; the peasant inextricably a part of the rude barren landscape. These are often accompanied by images of physical exuberance and energy, even of a kind of brutality, as they are also accompanied in the work of his friend Synge and in much of the work of Masefield. In these prints, he makes use of the bright colors and bold forms of an art both emanating from and directed at popular tastes and notions.

Sometimes this leads him into an overcrude simplicity as in the print of St. Patrick where interpretation and reinvigoration have been replaced by hagiography; on the whole, however, his prints are superior to those of the majority of his contemporaries. Their "Gaelic" quality attracted AE who wrote in 1909, "We have had abundance of Irish folklore, but we knew nothing of folk art until the figures of Jack Yeats first romped into our imagination a few years ago. It was the folk feeling, lit up by genius and interpreted by love. It was not the patronage bestowed by the intellectual artist on the evidently picturesque forms of a life below his own. I suspect Jack Yeats thinks the life of a Sligo fisherman as good as any, and that he could share it for a long time without being in the least desirous of a return to the more comfortable life of convention." The folk art quality which AE detects not only emerges from the use of themes which excite the common "folk"—races, hurling matches, circuses, outlaws of the land or sea—but also from a curious wonderment and rhythmic stridency. His colored prints and drawings frequently use large areas of bold color and contrast them simply. His greens and blues are more intense than natural, just as his figures are also exaggerated in shape and gesture. In the black and white drawings, he uses a multitude of lines, covering earth, sky, and clothing with closely packed ripples, so that the whole picture is often throbbing with rhythm. The heavy outlines are not, thus, imposed upon the figures but are developed from the pressure of life within them. This is, for all the apparent calm of many of the resting or idly talking figures, a tumultuous art.

It was not until 1924 that a similar turbulent quality emerged in his oil painting and in his writing. Perhaps his best prose work is *Sligo*, first published in 1930. This is a helter-skelter of freely associated memories, reflections, fantasies, and jokes. There is no shape to it; its form is that of the rhythms of the mind alone, and in this it occasionally reminds one of Joyce's *Ulysses* and *Finnegans Wake*. Yeats, however, is an original, not a disciple. His high jinks are like nobody else's, though his methods in this, and in his later *The Amaranthers*, do seem to anticipate many of those used by Flann O'Brien in *At Swim Two Birds* (so praised by Joyce) and by T. H. White (especially in *The Elephant and the Kangaroo*). His particular vein in *Sligo* emerges clearly from his account of the reason for the title. It is given after forty pages.

> About a name for this book. I was making some notes one day while travelling in a train through a boggy country in Ireland when a melodeon player opposite me asked me if I wouldn't stop and "give out a tune" and he handed the melodeon towards me. "I have no ear," I said. "Ah, to hell with ears," he said "I play it with my body. Are you writing a book?" he said. "Well I am making notes for one," I said. "What are you going to call it?" he said. "I don't know yet," I said. "Call it Sligo. It's the name of a town," he said, "the only town in Ireland I never was in. I was near it once but I stopped on the brink and took the long car with a unicorn yoked to it for a town called Ballina. Call it Sligo, it ought to be a lucky name." So Sligo it is. When he asked me to play a tune he pronounced it Chune, a very good way too. If they give me music to my grave I will sooner they will call it a Chune than a Toon: there is a want of dignity about the word "Toon" and I would not look forward to it.

This, in its inconsequence and dry humor, is reminiscent of Sterne. In other passages, however, we find a satirical absurdity that is Swift without Swift's anger.

> But why tow, why not let others tow as they like it. There are more up-lifters in the world than subjects of uplift. Let them uplift us, shoulder high. Then we will be able to see over their heads to the several promised lands, from which we have come, and to which we trust to go. When the uplifters are wedged and milling together, and we are tired of sitting, we can stroll about on their solid heads, and view these lands. There will be very few of us and so, like weeks of Sundays, the time will pass pleasantly, each in turn doing the honours of each's own promised land. I suppose walking on heads will be a little like walking on cobble stones. Of course all Uplifting heads are exactly the same size and Uplifted come to the same level, the skulls are thick and we will be wearing pampooties, so they will not mind our strolling over the tops.

An even more Swiftian quality emerges in the passages about the Ropes family and its ancestors in which the evolution of a society is parodied. Jack Yeats, however, unlike Swift, wrote from affection and believed in the basic goodness of humanity. One need only compare Swift's accounts of sectarian conflicts, political and religious, with Jack Yeats's account of how the Ropes family explained the nature of the tides: "They all sat in a ring on the warm sand and settled about it. Not all at once. But after a good many days they reduced the idea to two parties. Those who held that the sun drew the water up and down and those who held that the water was working the sun. The usual thing. And there was very little hope of anything being settled, until a small wedge party got up an idea that the whole place was pulsing any way it liked if you were satisfied. So they all agreed on that." The lighthearted, but in no way trivial satire of *Sligo* is attached to a pseudo-autobiographical thread of narrative and reflection, as it is also in later works, the most notable of which is *And To You Also* (1944). This book is even more exuberant than *Sligo*, and its prose is even more carefully slapdash. Here Jack Yeats expresses yet again his strong feeling of the limitations of language as a medium of expression and attempts to expand its boundaries in a number of ways. One of these is the use of the incantatory and absurd list—as practiced by Rabelais. His introduction to one magnificent list is as follows:

> Now—thinking of you also I would like to give you from my store a really full-waved chapter heading, and we are in luck for I have under my hand a list of suggestions for the contents of a chapter which I will not write. But I will not waste the list so here it comes, and as you have been standing up to breast the gravelly storm as far as this without a breather, I'll call it

Chapter Two,

and here goes:

> J. Toole, and Cook, and James Sullivan, and his great poster. Swede turnips, Weight-lifting, man in his walking clothes grunting. Swan song, heard record and refused to die. Vale of Aylesbury and all the falls. Waterfalls everywhere—Jem Mac. Jem Smith. The Lord Mayor's coachman. Paintings outside booths at the Fairs. The private performance of the little play called Hand Knocks. Bob Habbijams. The M.C. Harris. Pictures on walls of Inns, and of the Lambeth School of Arms. Shapes the bus conductor. Rain. Glissade. House Boats. Walking by Seashores. Song Book Shops.

And so it continues for four pages, showing a dexterity in free association, a verbal music, a capacity for pattern making that are truly astonishing.

Jack Yeats is, in fact, a prose artist of real importance, and an innovator. His prose contrasts sharply with his brother's hieratic and stately periods and has far more flexibility and range. It is, perhaps, less sonorous; it is certainly less solemn. It is as capable of epigram but incapable of pretension. It is not, however, less profound, only less earnest. Jack Yeats's novels and stories are as original as his memoirs. His first full-length novel, *The Amaranthers*, divides itself into two parts. In the first one the members of the club are introduced to us and are shown to be (among other things) devoted to the making of toy boats behind the sober facade of the island's only (small) skyscraper. The remainder of the book chronicles the adventures of James Gilfoyle who finally reaches the island and befriends the Amaranthers, who have suffered the effects of an earthquake.

In *The Amaranthers*, as in *Sligo*, digression is frequent and amusing. We have a full description of the performance of a play which sounds, in some respects, like a drama concocted by a combination of Anouilh, Ionesco, and Jean Genet, with Robert Louis Stevenson supervising. We have the life stories of several bizarre characters. There is a sudden death, banditry, high finance—it is a gallimaufry of a book. Some parts of Gilfoyle's adventures are distinctly reminiscent of the adventures told by Masefield, especially in *Odtaa*, but they are odder and parody the adventure story rather than exploit it seriously. The book is also, however, filled with radiance, gaiety, and intense enjoyment of physical beauty, so that even while the reader is laughing, he is also being charmed.

In *On the Boiler*, W. B. Yeats wrote of his brother's *The Charmed Life* (1938), "He does not care that few will read it, still fewer recognize its genius; it is his book, his 'Faust,' his pursuit of all that through its unpredictable, unarrangeable reality least resembles knowledge. His style fits his purpose for every sentence has its own taste, tint and smell." This is true also of *The Amaranthers*. It is one of the most original of books, though it clearly relates to the Irish tradition, having Swiftian passages, as well as passages that remind us of the broad and magical comedy and adventure of Irish epic. Moreover, as in Irish epic the magical adventure often approaches farce but is countered and qualified by an underlying romantic seriousness, so that the grave and the gay remain in tension and give the book a fundamental ambiguity of outlook as they do so often in Joyce. It is perhaps this balance of the grave and gay, this combination of the tragic and comic, that is characteristic of much of the best Irish writing. It is notable in Synge, O'Casey, Joyce; it is present, though to a muted degree, in Goldsmith; it is characteristic of the best of Wilde and Congreve, and it appears in heroic proportions in Swift.

It is also present in Jack Yeats last, energetic, prose work, *The Careless Flower* which was published in 1947, when he was 76 years old, and which contains, yet again, a wealth of shrewd observation, a perpetual dance of language, and the same romantic-skeptical view of human affairs that animates the earlier work.

The energy which is so remarkable a feature of Jack Yeats's writings of his old age is also characteristic of his paintings of the same period. In these the color has become hectic, challenging, expressionist. The rhythmic vitality of line in his earlier drawings has now been transformed into thick oil color, so that the landscapes and figures are all trembling with the same gay vitality, even though the total symbolism of the pictures may be tragic or pathetic. Moreover, just as in the earlier drawings the rhythm of the figures takes up that of the landscape, so in the later paintings man and environment are possessed by the same vitality and animated by the same force. The force which animates the later paintings of Jack Yeats, however, is stronger and more deeply passionate than that which suffuses the earlier. Indeed it is easy to see Jack Yeats's work as falling into two periods. It is difficult to regard the painter of *The Scene Painters Rose* (1927) and the author of *Sligo* (1930) as being the same man as the creator of *The Dwarf of the Circus* (1912), *Life in the West of Ireland* (1912), and *A Little Fleet* (1909). Though his paintings had been included in the New York Armory Show of 1913 and hung alongside work by Picasso, Matisse, Cezanne, Duchamp, and Picabia, it was not the painter of these works but the creator of such later masterpieces as *Helen* (1937) and *Grief* (1951) whom Oskar Kokoschka addressed as "Jack Yeats, the Last of the Great Masters of the World."

Jack Yeats was not only an innovator as both painter and novelist, however. He was also a formidable playwright, and the plays he created in the period from 1933 to 1949 are as different from his early drama for the toy theater as are his last oils from his drawings for the sporting magazine *Paddock Life* in the 1890s.

It is not easy to sum up the character of these plays without lapsing into dangerous generalizations, but it seems clear that Jack Yeats used them even more than he used his novels to present his philosophy of life, which was as riddling, as lively, as romantic, and as satirical as one might expect. There are a number of recurrent themes. In every play there is talk of death and in seven of them a death, or a presumed death, is central to the pattern the play makes. In half of them a central character is a much travelled stranger whose arrival on the scene sets off a chain of events that appears to have its own interior logic rather than to be caused wittingly by any of the characters. In most of them we are given the strong impression that the characters are caught up in a pattern of destiny which they recognize only dimly, if at all. Human intentions are pointless: we are prisoners of a will greater than our own: we can only, if we are wise, accept what life brings us and live as much by chance as by choice.

This last contention is particularly obvious in *The Deathly Terrace*, which seems to be the first play of this series. Andy, a film producer, and Sheila, an actress, land by boat at a terrace on which they intend to film a scene of "the dead man by the sea." They find the corpse of Nardock who appears to have killed himself and they make the film. However, when the film is given its premiere, Nardock appears in the theater alive. In the next act Andy catches up with Nardock, and they exchange stories of their experiences. When Sheila appears in a boat they both fake suicide and leave her to think they died of love for her and so to regard herself as a goddess who can "dance in and out of the hearts of men." The play is ill proportioned, the greater part of it being taken up by the conversation between Andy and Nardock, but, in fact, this conversation is the heart of the play's vision. Nardock tells Andy: "Time has no meaning to me, I am embedded in time and floating in eternity. I have seen the Peruvians in pigtails and the Chinese in kilts. I have gone down into the heart of the volcano, and placed my hand where the pulse should be and called on it to shake. And I have stepped from the fragment of one star to the nucleary fragment of another, and I have looked at myself so doing. . . . I am an Egoist steeped in generosity and seethed in affection."[1] He describes his travels and tells how he invited the circle, fire, and the "sinking of the stone in the pond." He invented "continuosity" and everywhere he went he left a blessing behind him and everywhere he showed himself to be a joker, a leg-puller:

> A poet has shown us the sadness of the last man, the hangman with no one in the world left to pull his legs. But I can see another picture of the last man looking with desolated eyes searching for the last leg but two, just to pull it, and his mind will be brimming with splendid schemes for leg-pulling—too late, and he could not stoop to pull his own leg. . . . Too late, that is a sad word, never say it, say too soon, perhaps. But never say too anything, there is no such thing as redundancy to those who are imbedded, as you and I are, in continuosity, because if there is too much of anything at any moment, we only hold it over in the heel of the fist and later link it up with the coming event, and so linked together we get continuosity, impetuosity and exuberance.

If Nardock is the prophet of a new, or a very old, creed, Andy is his fitting disciple. Andy tells Nardock the following story about his father: "[he] decided that I must be dedicated to luck, that chance should rule my life, not premeditation. So when at the age of five years, my·education having got beyond my mother's powers, I chanced to spell out the word 'school' without having any idea what it stood for, I was taken to board school but on the way I lost my little shoe in the mud opposite a small house which had a notice in the window DOWTON COLLEGE, I went there. It had style, that College. There were eleven pupils. I made up the dozen and we wore mortar boards. The school caught fire and was burnt out, when I was ten years of age. So my father came to the conclusion that my school days were over."

Andy's life story continues, fantastic in invention, witty in implication, and exuberant in feeling. The inventiveness and exuberance of his tale may remind us of the tales of Baron Munchausen. Jack Yeats certainly read Munchausen, for his wife Cottie gave him a paper-covered edition. Nardock and Andy, however, are not derived creatures; their combined philosophy is central to Jack Yeats's own vision. In his prose works he utilizes that very continuosity Nardock claims to have discovered and with an appropriate "impetuosity and exuberance." In such

1. All quotations from Robin Skelton, ed. *The Collected Plays of Jack B. Yeats* (London: Secker & Warburg, 1971).

great pictures as in *The Blood of Abel* (1942), the figures appear to be caught up in the rhythm of life itself and to be formed of the same pulsating and exuberant material as the earth upon which they stand and the sky beneath and towards which they make their human gestures. "The egotist steeped in generosity and seethed in affection" appears over and over again in the prose romances, and if one looks at the painting *The Two Travellers* of 1942, one might well feel, from the loquacious stance of the figures and their relationship to the moving and changing landscape, that the travellers represented portraits of Nardock and Andy contemplating another venture into the magnificently absurd.

The word *absurd* had to crop up sooner or later; and, perhaps, it is as well that it should do so here, for the theater of the absurd as practiced in some of the works of Beckett, Genet, and Ionesco is not infrequently Nardockian, and the spirit of continuosity, of flux, and the theme of man ridiculously embedded in time yet floating in eternity, is present in Beckett's novels as well as in those of Flann O'Brien. I am not, at this point, attempting to make out a case that Jack Yeats was the teacher, directly or indirectly of these later writers (none, in any case, could have read *The Deathly Terrace)*, but I am concerned to show that Nardockian viewpoint is much more than a whimsical piece of ingenuity; it is one statement of an attitude which pervades an enormous amount of European literature of the last forty years. One can understand why *The Deathly Terrace* was never performed or published. It is structurally ill balanced, and it demands an audience that was not available at the time it was written. To move from that play to the first three plays that were published is to be initially a little disappointed. *Apparitions* is no more than a folk anecdote of a practical joke, and its main interest is the fact that Yeats used the practical joker once again as a central character and did so in such a way as to portray the folly of self-importance and vanity. On the other hand, *The Old Sea Road*, the second play published under the general heading *Apparitions*, is a different matter.

The Old Sea Road, like the *Camino Real* of Tennessee Williams, is a highly metaphysical entity and the play is a parable. It opens with two laborers, Nolan and Dolan, spreading stones on the road. They are dully clad, and throughout the play, we are told, "The sky, sea and land are brighter than the people." Nolan tells Dolan—and the chiming names suggests, deliberately, a cross-talk act: "it's time I retired, but the times we live in won't let me. Fancy me, let alone yourself, spending the whole blessed day laying stones on the Old Sea Road. We spread them here, and in the fullness of time they roll down the hill until they reach the charming village of Cahirmahone, where they lie night and day to trip up the feet of the ancient warriors of the place." Along this road walk many people, the schoolteacher and her favorite pupil, the student of mathematics, the policeman, the ballad singer, the postman, the publican, and an old peasant man and woman. Along the road too comes Michael of the Song, a wanderer, and he meets Ambrose Oldbury, a practical joker of whom there has already been much talk. Michael, despite his poverty and hunger, is excited by life. He tells the mathematics student, "the whole world's exciting. If it was the least tint more exciting the unfortunate inhabitants would be exploding into fragments making star sparks of themselves." He is very much his own man, saying, "To Hell with the departmental store all under one roof. I'm under my own roof, and I don't want yours. Every man under his own thatch and the ladies under their own, if you like." When he meets Ambrose he asks him why he is a practical joker. Ambrose tells him:

If I could bring off a solid joke with four dimensions I'd be satisfied. But I never saw one that had more than two, here and there. All I ask is reasonable fun and that's denied me by a benighted people.

MICHAEL: That's because you are not able to consume your own amusement as it comes, and carbonize it for further use, if you did . . .

AMBROSE: Pardon me, If I did I wouldn't be sitting out on an old bank talking to you at this time of evening. I'd be sitting in lonely study regaling myself on my own regalia and chuckling to myself.

MICHAEL: You've had your last chuckle long ago. You've lost the instinct, you common omadhaun.

AMBROSE: I've lost nothing, everything is sticking to me. I'm smothered with it. I tell you I'm the fella with the grand piano legs that carries the world on his back. I'm the feller that's full to the brim. I'm the brim myself in fact, I'm the end of everything.

MICHAEL: You flatter yourself, you've just come on the wrong pitch and now you're all het up about it. What you want is a good sleep, and a think it over.

AMBROSE: I'll think nothing over again. I'm done with thinking things over either before or after the event. I'll open my mouth and swallow the wave.

Ambrose's last practical joke is to burn all his money, tell Michael, "from now on I'm a living joker starting in on the ground floor" and to offer him a drink from his flask. The drink kills them both.

Ambrose's surname, "Oldbury," is an obvious indication of his character as a death bringer, but he is not really the medieval figure of Death walking the roads. He is one who challenges, by means of his jokes, the validity of life itself. He tells Michael: "I'll show you something you've never seen before, I'll warrant you. I'll show you Man upright defying the slings and arrows and getting away with it. I'll show you how the rich can dissolve in their own essence in the twinkling of an eye." The essence of the practical joke is the way it makes its victim feel insecure and unable to trust his own eyes or own ears. It peoples his world with delusions; it takes his realities and proves them illusion. Thus it might be said that Death is the greatest practical joker of all. In the midst of life we are in death; in the midst of reality we are insubstantial. We are, to quote Nardock, "embedded in time and floating in eternity."

The deaths of Ambrose and Michael do not have the same miraculous effect as those of Nardock and Andy; they alter no one's lives. Ambrose's practical jokes, unlike Nardock's, leave no blessings in their wake. Nevertheless both Nardock and Ambrose, like Jimmy in *Apparitions*, take pleasure in challenging the supposed stability of the day-to-day world.

Rattle, the last of three plays published in 1933, is equally concerned to present a disruption of the norm. The firm of Gardeyne and Golback is on the point of collapsing. Those involved in it are trying to decide what to do with the wharf and warehouses, and it is thought that the site might be sold for a cinema. While these discussions are going on Ted Golback receives a letter telling him that he has inherited "property in mines, lands, forests and lakes" in the South American country of Pakawana. In due course the Pakawanian representatives arrive, and a presentation of the deeds is made. The final movement of the play shows us Ted in Pakawana, where he is told about the country and its ways by the philosopher Dr. Canty. Unfortunately there is an apparently rather token rebellion in progress, and Ted is shot and killed before ever reaching the capital.

This is an unfair summary of the play, for it leaves out the exuberant speculations and dreams of many of the characters; it omits all the wit of the conversations and the humor of the Pakawanian speeches and the fantastic description of Pakawanian society by Dr. Canty. Nevertheless, this bald account does indicate that the play deals both with hope and with death, and that its structure is rather that of an adventure narrative than of the usual drama of tension and confrontation. It appears to flow along as if the characters were borne upon a tide they could not control or even clearly recognize. The image of the wave is, in fact, central to the drama. When the plan for building the cinema falls through, Alec Gardeyne tells his brother William: "My disappointment about the Picture House has depleted me for the time being. But no doubt, if I had a long rest somewhere, I could lay out a plan of some sort. But of course I see that something must be done almost at once." William replies:

> That's it. It's this "almost at once" business that bothers me. There's something in this "almost at once" which grits against. . . . No, grits is not the word. But there's something that stems the flow and ebb. Can you be said to stem an ebb? There is something which is the exact opposite of the steady ebb and flow, flow and ebb, of the tide up and down this river, just at our doorstep, as we might say. Why yesterday (*He gets up and walks to river door and looks out*). Ah, and there it is still! Why, yesterday there was a piece of broken wood, off a packing case with some letters on it, P.E.A.C., I think—and then it was broken off. It may have been for peach or peaches, perhaps tinned peaches. But there's the bit of wood again. Yesterday I watched it go up with the tide, and again come down with the tide. And then I saw it get caught in an eddy just beside our wharf where there were some other things floating. There it stayed caught up. It seemed to me as if it was symbolical of something. It was specially odd that I should see it because, if I hadn't got the day for our meeting wrong, I wouldn't have been here at all yesterday, and so I would not have seen the peach on the deep (*He laughs*) going up and down. But there is some symbol there. Perhaps this vagrant wood is to show that the rhythm that cannot be mastered can be enjoyed until it laps you gently into a state of static bliss with a number of other pieces of drift.

It is certainly no coincidence that when the Pakawanian deputation arrives Dr. Canty tells Ted: "we do now with the hand of General Golmozo, assisted by the hand of Dr. Canty, we make you Edward Golback, a brother of the Golden Wave, and do wrap you in the cloak of waves." When Ted is dying in Pakawana, he asks to have the decoration, the Wave, placed around his neck.

"The rhythm that cannot be mastered can be enjoyed," said William Gardeyne and his words remind us of Nardock's notion of continuosity and Andy's adherance to chance. It is, however, necessary to forgive the rhythm its mastery. Dr. Canty, when asked where the General is, tells Ted: "Oh, in Vino Veritas at first, later, Golden Slithers on a new moon with appropriate music. In Vino Veritas the wondering questioning alcoves of the brain get filled with activity and the victim wants to know, O Jehovah, why? To know all is to forgive all. To forgive all is not to want to know all." The theme is repeated when Ted is dying.

> TED: To know all is to forgive all, and doesn't that cut both ways?
>
> CANTY: Yes, yes. To forgive all is to know all.

It is with solicitude for the dying man rather than with any sense of personal guilt that the leader of the rebels, Gossgocock, bends over Ted and asks Canty, "Can he give forgiveness?" Canty tells him, "His forgiveness flows from him in a straight line to you."

Life acceptance must finally include death acceptance. It must also include a capacity to be carried along by the rhythms of apparently chance events and to enjoy the hope or dream as much as the substance, the joys of speculation as much as those of realization. Thus Ted dies contented with his experience of the dream of Pakawana and does not resent the loss of the reality; thus the Gardeyne brothers enjoy their plans for the wharf's destiny as much as they would the success of those plans, and perhaps more. The commonplace and the dull only exist if we allow them to do so; we can always defeat them by an exercise of the imagination and by the contriving of happy speculations.

It must have been with some such thoughts as these in mind that Jack Yeats wrote *Harlequin's Positions*. As in *Rattle*, we are presented with a disruption of ordinary events by the arrival of someone from overseas. In this instance it is a relative from abroad who visits a small group of people in a little Irish town. He tells his new friends:

> I discovered that those positions the harlequin takes with the wand in his hands all have names. I don't know if his were peculiar to himself. He turned always from one to the other to complete the series, five in number:—
>
> Admiration
> Pas de Basque
> Thought

> Defiance
> Determination
>
> I committed them to memory—Harlequin positions—and have made them my order of—order of existence, if I may put it that way.

This speech gives us a clue to the intentions of the playwright, a clue which is badly needed, for *Harlequin's Positions* flows easily along from conversation to conversation and very little happens that could be called obviously dramatic. Annie, the orphan friend of the family, sells a piece of land and decides to take everyone on a voyage round the world on the proceeds; the voyage never takes place, however, for there are rumors of war and it is decided not to venture. As the talk of war grows more widespread the police suspect Alfred Clonboise, the visitor, of being some kind of spy. The war rumors prove false, and he is not arrested. There is, one might well say, nothing very much to it all.

And yet there is something in it. As Clonboise says, "There is something in everything." He goes on to say:

> There was a group of young men in Buenos Aires when I was there who tried to found a religion on that—something in everything. One of them, the Secretary of the Society, picked up a horseshoe nail, walking with me one day near the Market and he began, on that nail, expounding, expounding. At first I was dizzied, but after a little I was completely bored, and so was he. If I could have constructed the ambling pad, the horse, Aunt Claire, from the horseshoe nail, I would have mounted it and ridden away from the Secretary, leaving him nothing but my dust. I would have taken a taxi, and pushed him away as I pushed in, but at the moment, I was embarrassed to the point of not having a taxi fare. It was just before my fortunes took a sudden upward turn. You know, "the darkest hour" and that kind of thing.

It was Walt Whitman who once said, "All truths lie waiting in all things." Alfred Clonboise tells the young man, Johnnie, as they talk on the hill overlooking the little harbor: "Everything's symbolical if you look at it in the right way."

It is not easy to look at *Harlequin's Positions* in the "right way" for the talk of which it is largely constructed is inconsequential, highly anecdotal, and seems rather aimless. Nevertheless, what does emerge finally is a picture of the different stances the characters adopt towards passing events and an affectionate, ironic attitude towards those stances. Whether or not all that is said and done can be labelled as one or more of the Harlequin's positions is hard to determine; what is clear though is that Jack Yeats was engaged in presenting us with a picture of a group of characters caught up in life's rhythm, each of them important to themselves and each of them uncertain of their proper roles. To the perceptive eye, everything is symbolical, for every moment links up with other moments and implies beliefs, values, and a history. One has only to watch the world around one to see drama and poetry. It is this demand which *Harlequin's Positions* makes on its audience, as also does the later drama of Samuel Beckett where a single simple event, two people upon a bench exchanging half-a-dozen words perhaps, is given symbolic intensity by forcing us to label it as "theater" and to scrutinize it narrowly.

This is of course a partial truth. There are moments of melodrama, as when the Guard discovers Alfred Clonboise's revolver and when we are told of the way Johnnie's father and Mr. Bosanquet died. There are also passages of grotesquerie such as that in which the second Pilot describes the draper's assistant who broke his neck and who cannot be seen behind the counter "with his head on his shoulders": "It's a sin to laugh at him, but it's a fact he don't mind. He's a bit of a curiosity for everyone. It was the drink did it, and it didn't stop him drinking either. It costs him nothing. All the travellers that come to the town like to take him out and buy the stuff for him, anything he fancies. They like to see him pour it as if he was going to pour it in his ear." Nevertheless, *Harlequin's Positions* on the whole represents the farthest Jack Yeats went towards antidrama and the nearest he got to anticipating the methods of such later playwrights as Pinter and Mortimer. We are more entertained by the play than we may be by observing life itself, but we are equally unable to sum up the total implications of what we have seen, and the play does not end with any grandiose curtain to help us pretend a conviction. It is part of that continuity, that continuum which is life, and its rhythms are natural rather than theatrical. I am reminded of that picture by René Magritte in which a painting on a easel records that exact part of the landscape which the canvas hides from view; the painting is no more than a segment of the actual given significance by its utilization of an artistic medium.

What I have said about *Harlequin's Positions* applies also in part to *La La Noo* and *In Sand*, where we are also presented with elements of antitheater. It does not apply to *The Silencer*, which is similar to *The Deathly Terrace* in its use of melodrama and in its verbal exuberance. *The Silencer* opens in a pub where a group of businessmen are engaged in chatting idly about the weather and discussing life in general. Marshall enters with Hartigan whom he introduces to the company. Hartigan immediately reveals himself as a compulsive talker, a teller of tall tales and a spellbinder. One of the businessmen is so attracted by his zestful and curious view of life that he gives him a job but Hartigan's love of talk causes an appointment to be missed and business to be lost. Employed by another man, he pauses en route to the bank to give a stranger exact and lengthy instructions and is robbed of the money he is carrying. Thieves planning to rob a jeweller's then set Hartigan to distract the attention of the policeman with his stories and chatter while they carry out the operation. The scheme does not work, however, and all the would-be-thieves but Sam and Hill are captured. Hill revenges himself on Hartigan, shooting him down while he is talking to a man on the street and killing him instantly.

Hartigan's last speech before his death clarifies his role for us:

> All deaths are game deaths; death sees to that. It's the penultimate moment that shakes the brave. Chinamen in all parts of the world where I have seen them, appear to me to be neither waiting, nor watching, nor regretting. And you are doing the whole three this moment I know; I know it in my bones. And you can't deny it; and you don't want to deny it. . . . You are afraid and ashamed of what you cannot help. You are saying to yourself that I'm one of these dud inspirational philosophers given away with a penny paper and you think I am holding you against your will, and you have no will. You are listening to me because you have nothing to say yourself. You are not going away because you have nowhere to go. You have forgotten you have a home. You have forgotten you have a tongue. The bell has forgotten it has a clapper. Anyway, you have no one to pull the bell rope for you and the bell can't get outside itself and pull its own bell rope, now can it? Speak me fair! You cannot speak me fair or unfair! You're held with a basilisktic stare. A basilisk of your own creation. You love the sound of me and you hate the sense. You love time and hate the clock. You wade in stars and hate the ocean seas that lap over you like a sinking tent. . . . Look at your boots; they're all smeared with stars.
>
> And you don't know it, and could not say what street, what city you are in. You left a desk and you could not say where you left

> it. You are speechless because I talk for you. You think you speak yourself. You think I echo your thoughts. You have no thoughts; you never had thoughts. Those things that straggled across your brain were not thoughts, they were wheel tracks in the dust, it will make no difference to you. You have never existed in your own right. You exist now in mine. As the waves of the wind ripple the flag flying from its flag-pole, so you move and exist. As one ripple disappears on the flag's flying tail, another is beginning at the rope making its journey from the hoist to the fly. By my lips you live; by their stillness you pass away or back again into your solidity of a poised dust mote. You could wish yourself alive but you will never do it.
>
> The song says:
>
> "Even the dear little fish,
> Though they can't think they can wish."

Here again is the "Egotist," though he seems in his speech to be less "steeped in generosity and seethed in affection" than was Nardock. Like Nardock, however, he rejoices in life and perhaps even embodies all life's vitality. Hill, while visiting a séance later in the play, in order to ask forgiveness of Hartigan's ghost, is told by that ghost:

> Stars pass in the sky, forgetting the sky they plough, and forgotten seed stars are sown in forgotten furrows, and a harrow comes a-harrowing, a harrow that is nothing but the breath of the memory of the breaths of all the birds; like the oranges, all thoughts here are fruit and flowers on the same stem. As the basket is woven on the uprights, which are the good thoughts, and the weaving osiers the bitter thoughts, so I know that one day by forgetting here and there we will arrive at but one thought—one thought to satisfy all needs, if needs there will be for the thinker. But not yet is that one thought set for me. I cannot in the twinkling of a star be forgetting the grey beards of the seas. In comfort of body I recall dreadful days of old, fighting odds too heavy, far too heavy. But then I was held in a body which has neither fear nor ache, unless the misty vapour of the lake can ache. Do the clouds ache in their hearts because the lake distorts their reflections? Not they! They say if there were no clouds there'd be no lakes. And what are lakes but puddles grown up? And what are little puddles but little drops of water, and little grains of sand too; they make the mighty ocean and the pleasant land too. A song of innocence; little drops of water and little grains of sand are

> innocent because they are little. But why not big lakes and roomy mountains innocent too? Is a little innocence better than a big innocence? No, a thousand times, no! Ten thousand times ten thousand innocences are just that and nothing more, and what a lot that is. Oh, dear heart, be glad; dear heart that had to be constantly screamed at. Screamed at your ear to keep you up to your best, if it did keep you so up, which I forget. But now, dear Heart, be glad! Is a taking-notice-of a heart necessary to make it glad! But is there a point where the glad heart is so glad it doesn't know it's glad? But glad eyes, I think, always knew when they were glad. But that's a-going back; no, not a-going back exactly but a-going out sideways into the realms of the days that are no more. Not so much, no more, as forgotten . . . or forgotten from their order. So that where we leave down one gangway, we come aboard skipping up the next. Ever ashore, ever a-floating; before the wind and in the wind's eyes, in the trough and on the crest, forgetting where the foaming stars come down and the twinkling waters rush up.

This speech so irritates Hill that he puts a bullet into the dictaphone from which the voice comes but the specter of Hartigan is not damaged; it continues to dance in mockery and delight. Policemen enter and arrest Hill for creating a disturbance, but it turns out that they are not real policemen, only partygoers in fancy dress. Truth and justice, which Hill, paradoxically, saw as his principles when he killed Hartigan, and which are for him stable notions, are shown to be as illusory as everything else.

The Silencer is perhaps Jack Yeats's most complex play and the one which presents his philosophy most explicitly. In the two climactic speeches, the first coming just before Hartigan's death and the second just before his spectral voice is silenced by a bullet from Hill's gun (or 'silencer'), we are given the essence of his beliefs. We are told not to blind ourselves to the experience of life by waiting, watching, and regretting. We are accused of failing to notice the nature of the life we live, of ignoring the eternity upon which we are afloat. We are advised to see the unity of life, to perceive how the good thoughts and the bitter ones, the happiness and the pain are woven together into unity and are necessary complements to each other. We are warned against self-regard and self-pity; we must see ourselves as part of a total pattern and learn to forget the unimportant details of living and even, finally, our own identities, our own self-consciousness in order that we may become part of that "one thought" which, Blake tells us, "fills immensity." Hartigan's ghost, however, is not yet ready to become one with the spirit of the universe.

His spirit is still chained to earth by memories; it is even possible that it may return to earth; having left down "one gangway," it may return by another one. Clearly, for Jack Yeats death is not a conclusion but a continuance and a change of perspective and brings an understanding and recognition of the overall rhythm of the universe.

Possibly it is necessary to see this philosophy as a background to the two other plays I must discuss, *La La Noo* and *In Sand*. It is also necessary to realize that the same philosophy imbues the paintings and the prose works. If we look at one of his last paintings, *Glory* (1953), we see, in T. G. Rosenthal's words, "youth, maturity and old age all talking and rejoicing in the glory of life." They are standing in a landscape so organized as to remind us of the rhythms of the sea, of the flow and ebb, of the rise and fall of waves; and we see that the turbulence of the figures is at one with the turbulence of their setting. We see their individual glory as part of universal glory. So it is also with the other paintings of the forties and fifties, and so it is with the prose memoirs and novels. There is an intense and zestful presentation of the way in which sensation follows sensation as man is borne along in continuosity; there are marvellous wishes and fantasies, but there is always also a mingling of the pathetic with the exuberant, and a unifying theme of delight in evanescence. We must delight in the transient because it is transient, because it leads on always to the new, to something else. The hero is always the wanderer, the man who does not attempt to impose fixity upon a restlessly unfixed universe, who does not fear the clock, but embraces the passing of time and accepts death with a sigh for what has gone and with a trusting gladness at what is to come. Jack Yeats's portrayal of people in his books is enormously sympathetic but his sympathy extends beyond the individual to the life process itself. He loves the living human creature, but he is in love with life itself and with the rhythm of the universe that contains and comprehends both life and death.

This may seem too weighty a series of considerations to be applied to *La La Noo*, and yet, if it is kept in mind while reading the play, it sharpens the edge of the irony. *La La Noo* is set in a lonely Irish pub. The Publican and a Stranger are talking together when they are interrupted by seven women who have been to a nearby fair and who now wish shelter from the rain until it is time to catch the bus on the road some little distance away. The stranger is much travelled, somewhat loquacious and filled with interest in life. The women are a mixed bunch; they all talk together and their talk is of love and death as the talk of country people so often is. The First Woman says:

I would hate to see any man die. I didn't see my father die. He was away from me when he died. I have no brother or sister and my mother died when I don't remember her. And I thought I was going to see the Jockey boy die there on the Strand today. I was sick at it. I didn't want to see it. I am glad now, not only for him, but for myself. But surely I cannot expect to live all my life and see no man die. 'Tis too much to expect.

FOURTH WOMAN: I never seen them die. I seen them wither and when my back was turned they died on me. Wouldn't they put the life across you? They like to with their tricky ways. They're in hands with death the whole time, the dirty twisters.

FIFTH WOMAN: I don't care what you say, I'll see a man die and then I'll die myself and it won't be long either.

Shortly after this exchange the women decide to leave the pub and walk to the road to wait for the bus. They are drenched by a sudden shower and return. The Stranger put them in another room, and they take off their wet things and hand them to him round the edge of the door so that they can be dried at the Smith's forge nearby. When the clothes are dry and they are dressed again, they realize that it is nearly time to catch the bus. The Fourth Woman runs for it. The rest wait for the Stranger to drive them in the Smith's lorry. The Stranger has never driven a lorry before, and he runs it into a tree and is killed. It is only then that the Seventh woman reveals that she is able to drive a truck and so the women leave the Landlord alone with the body of the Stranger.

Although the play builds up steadily towards the catastrophe of the Stranger's death and the Fourth woman's prophesy is fulfilled in that she turns her back on the company and runs off before the disaster occurs, *La La Noo* is more than a macabre anecdote. The talk circles around themes of universal significance. The Sixth Woman asks rhetorically, "Are there not enough wounds on the creation of the earth?" The stranger tells the Publican he ought to thank God for living in a quiet place and adds: "What do you want with heavy death and destruction, doing no good to anyone only cataracts of harm to man made in the image of God." There is trivia in the talk too, talk of superstitions, of clothes, of the weather, and almost all the talk is speculative. The Publican frequently refers to myths of the heroes that had fought in the near countryside, and he tells the Stranger: "The world away from us this day is full of terrible cruel things. There was vampires and dragons in the old days, long ago, if you could believe the old tales, and I could believe them, for there are raging vampires eating at the hearts of the people all over the world this evening, while you and me here in the quiet, are just talking a little encouragement to ourselves." *La La Noo* was first performed in 1942, and this speech is an obvious allusion to the Second World War. The Publican is a fearful man and afraid to wander. The Stranger is a travelled man full of talk of wonders. The women are all questioning and speculative. Indeed, the drama of *La La Noo*, though it seems at first sight to be a presentation of the theme that death lies in wait for us all and is always both awaited and unexpected, is something more. It is a portrait of a questioning, fearful, speculative mankind. Its dramatic technique is almost that of antidrama. The talk is unforced, natural, wayward. It is, one might say, a slice of life—and a slice of death. In its casual, fluid manner it anticipates once again the conversational mode of later theater.

Nevertheless, behind it there lies something else. The women's nakedness, their stripping off their clothes, is clearly symbolic. But of what? We are reminded of Lear's "unaccommodated man." We are forced to recognize that all our trappings and our dignities are transient. We may even recall, thinking of the Publican's reference to the war, that in the chapter of Revelation which announces the coming of Armageddon we have seven angels, and we have the words: "Behold I come as a thief. Blessed is he that watcheth and keepeth his garments lest he walk naked and they see his shame." That Jack Yeats might have had this verse of Revelation in his mind and have wished to set his small country play against the backcloth of that terrific prophecy may seem improbable. And yet, when he painted a tinkers' encampment in 1941 (the year before *La La Noo* was produced), he called it "The Blood of Abel" and thus referred the spectator directly to a specific chapter of Genesis.

Jack Yeats was not an allegorical but a symbolist writer. He dealt not in precise references but in allusions and echoes. The meaning of his work is the meaning we find in it, and he gives us many meanings to choose from. This is one of the points made very clear by *The Green Wave*, a conversation piece which he intended as a prologue to *In Sand*. This consists only of a conversation between two elderly men about a painting. The heart of the question is displayed in one exchange:

2ND ELDERLY: What is it?

1ST ELDERLY: It is a wave.

2ND ELDERLY: I know that, but what sort of a wave?

> 1ST ELDERLY: A green wave—well—a rather green wave.
>
> 2ND ELDERLY: What does it mean?
>
> 1ST ELDERLY: I think it means just to be a wave.
>
> 2ND ELDERLY: I like things to mean something, and I like to know what they mean, and I like to know it at once. After all, time is important, the most important thing we know of, and why waste it in trying to find out what something means, when if stated its meaning clearly itself we would know at once.
>
> 1ST ELDERLY: If that wave could speak it might say: "I'm an Irish wave and the Irish are generally supposed to answer questions by asking questions," and the wave might ask you what was the meaning of yourself!

At the close of the conversation the 1st Elderly Man tells his friend teasingly, "I see it's beginning to worry you again, so next time, before you come, I'll get some artistic friend of mine to paint some buttercups and daisies on the side of my green wave and turn it into a green hillside, and then it won't worry you any more." This is a very double-edged remark. Why should a hill be less disturbing than a wave? Is it the instability, the fluidity, the unfixedness of the wave that disturbs us? Or is it that we see in the wave that we are too blind to see in the land, the restless rhythm of life and its mystery? We know of course from Ambrose Oldbury's boast that he will swallow the wave from the "Order of the Wave" in *Rattle*, from the talk of tides and gangways in *The Silencer*, and from the speeches of Nardock in *The Deathly Terrace* that the wave is for Jack Yeats an image of great significance and suggests the flux and rhythm not only of this mortal life but of the eternity upon which we are afloat. The picture of *The Green Wave* itself appears in number 4 of the Cuala Press Broadsides (new series) in 1937,[2] and it may be that it was the making or the publication of this print that gave rise to the writing of the play. The wave as presented in the broadside is not, however, simply green. It has red in it also and thus contrives to suggest the current of life itself, the tide of the blood. Naturally, the sea is a central character in Jack Yeats's drama as in his novels: it certainly figures importantly in *In Sand*.

2. I am indebted to Professor Norman Mackenzie for drawing my attention to the existence of this picture.

The theme of *In Sand* is, I suspect, taken from a poem by Walter Savage Landor which was once very well known and which was published in many anthologies including Palgrave's *Golden Treasury*. The poem goes:

> Well I remember how you smiled
> To see me write your name upon
> The soft sea-sand . . . . O! *what a child*!
> *You think you're writing upon stone*!
> I have since written what no tide
> Shall ever wash away, what men
> Unborn shall read o'er ocean wide
> And find Ianthe's name again.

The story which the play tells is simple enough. Anthony Larcson, who regards himself as a "joker" and an "egotist," is dying, and he tells his lawyer to arrange that after his death a young girl should write upon the sand at low tide the words, "Tony, we have the good thought for you still." This is done and the girl, who was chosen by lot, also receives a bequest which enables her, when she comes of age, to go on a holiday and thus to meet the man she marries. The couple travel all over the world and on every beach she visits, the girl Alice writes the words, "Tony, we have the good thought for you still," though she has no recollection of Larcson himself at all. While visiting a tropical island her husband, Maurice, receives a cable which tells him he is ruined, and he dies within the same day. Alice remains on the island, living on the charity of the proprietor of the hotel. After her death a new Governor thinks to make the island a republic and he and a Visitor discuss plans to develop the island and even begin to put some of them into practice, though they are delayed by the early beginning of the tourist season. The play ends with two young people writing upon the sand the words, "Tony, we have the good thought for you still," not understanding them, but knowing that they bring good fortune.

The play is in three acts, each one presenting a different aspect of the main themes. In the first we are given Larcson's last words and the writing of the name on the sand by the young girl. His friend and confidant, Oldgrove, tells Larcson: "You always, in the past, had grand ideas. Indeed, you often told me ideas and plans that would have shaken up all the Bank Managers of this place, retired, and in active service. But you never put any of your plans into operation—you had too kind a heart to want to upset anyone." Nevertheless, the last plan of Larcson does upset people somewhat. The Mayor, after reading a part of his formal speech on the seashore, stops reading and reflects on the society of the town:

> it is only the hard who have survived in the last generation in our town. Whatever may have gone on in other places, you know, as I know, here it has been tooth and nail. Get a good hold and never shift it till you get a better. It has been down, or be downed. . . . Maybe it would have been better if this man, whose wishes we are following out today, had never decided to leave these wishes which are in a sense a criticism of our bad old ways, and a criticism I say of even the best of our ways. . . . The ways of men, and especially men on their deathbeds, are strange ways, and can not be understood by those who stand in their full health, not thinking of their last hours, but of the hours which keep coming towards them like waves of the sea, some with crests of glistening foam on them and some dark as blood, no two waves alike.

In the second act we find Alice and Maurice "not thinking of their last hours" though Alice has written Larcson's message with its reminder of human transcience everywhere she has been. Maurice, however, just before he receives the fatal telegram, says: "We're fancy free, nothing to stop us except misfortune—other people's misfortune—or our own. We can keep moving like the finger on the wall but we don't write anything on the wall—only the sand of the sea-shore." All these images and thoughts come together in the last act of the play when we are told by the old sailor of the island's past, and the Visitor and the new Governor make their plans to create an autonomous republic.

It is in this act that Jack Yeats makes use of that theme of utopia which appears so frequently in his novels and which is also touched on in the last act of *Rattle*.The old sailor tells the Visitor of the island's days of innocence. He was cast away there as a young man, and says: "The people on the Island thought a lot of me. For three years I never did a stroke of work. The people brought me anything I wanted, they thought I could work miracles. . . . When they were tired of feeding me for nothing, they gave me a little canoe and I went fishing and by and by I got a little patch, and I found I was able to grow a few sweet potatoes and, one thing and another I made out." He describes the development of the island society, and how they were some "Supression Governors" eager to cut down trees and to ban pleasure, and some "Earthly Paradise Governors" who attempted to build roads which were washed away by the rains and to make improvements which never lasted. It seems that the island insists on retaining its own dreamy gentle identity and that no governor can alter it.

This account prepares us for the new Governor who wishes to modernize the island. The Visitor tells him that the island needs a motor-road (there are no motors), a picture gallery, a race course, and a swimming pool (everyone swims in the sea). He suggests the formation of an army and the creation of a prison. All these necessary attributes of modern society can only be created symbolically. The motor-road must be simply a track marked out on the sands and the swimming pool a sea pool labelled in blue paint. What matters is not, it seems, the thing itself but the idea of the thing. Whether or not the army is needed it must exist for dignity's sake; whether or not a flag is required it must be created for the sake of show. It is curiously like a child's game. The Governor is particularly insistent that the islanders must be prohibited from writing the wrong kind of slogans on the seashore, and he draws up a list permitted slogans. When at the close of the play the tourist season begins and occupies the attention of the hotel people so that they have no time to spare for creating a revolution, a brown boy and his girl friend write upon the sand, "Tony, we have the good thought for you still." The Governor, told that the slogan brings luck, then writes the words himself and realizes that he has broken his own law.

> What have I done, I who was given these Three Stars (*he touches them with his fingers*) each for seven years obedience and for causing others to obey, I have disobeyed my own ukase.
>
> But I have obeyed alone.
> I have disobeyed alone.
> I will die alone.
>
> (*He pulls revolver from holster and raises muzzle to his chin*)

The brown girl and boy and the Visitor prevent the Governor from committing suicide and then the brown girl says: "Don't be fretting yourself, Governor, look . . . look at the sea's edge! The tide is coming in now fast, look, look, the waters are covering up and washing away everything that we have written."

Anthony Larcson's joke has worked. He has managed by means of his words to prevent the island losing its innocence and turning into the ruthless modern society he disliked and accused. He has also reminded us that all mortal dignities and hopes are ephemeral and that having "the good thought" is more important than having the materially successful life. The island that his words preserve from progress is like the sea in the ebb and flow of its governors, its changes from supression to amelioration. Alice and the Old Sailor have submitted themselves without resentment to the tide and achieve not merely resignation to coming death but also contentment. *In Sand* lacks the fiery exuberance of *The Silencer*, and the bareness and directness of *La La Noo*, but it has its own quality of lyric melancholy and easy philosophy. It is, perhaps, an old man's play, but it is not a play of defeat—for at the end one puts the book down with a feeling for human warmth, affection, simplicity, and a faith in the mysterious good life can give if it is trusted.

Jack Yeats's drama was inimitable. There are no other plays quite like his. He anticipated in his plays many later fashions and the work of other playwrights. In *The Deathly Terrace* there is a use of what we now call "high camp" that anticipates much later theater, including some scenes by Beckett and Ionesco. In his antidramatic talk-plays he anticipated Pinter and Beckett. His work fits more easily, it might be said, into modern European literature of our time than does that of his brother. It may be some time before his work is properly appreciated and evaluated. His prose works are still unavailable to all but wealthy and assiduous collectors. But I believe that, once the whole of his writing does become available, he will be recognized as being one of the most original and important of twentieth-century writers and as towering a figure in literature as he is in painting. Moreover, once the complete writings are set alongside the drawings and paintings, it will become apparent that there is, in all Jack Yeats's work, an extraordinary unity. Not only do paintings illustrate and extend themes of the writings, but the writings explore and investigate symbols and scenes presented in the painting. Jack Yeats, like his friend Synge, tackled "the whole of life" and, like his brother, brought all things into unity.

8

A State O' Chassis

The Early Plays of Sean O'Casey

In 1926 Sean O'Casey was awarded the Hawthornden Prize for Literature. Interviewed by the *Daily Sketch*, he said:

> I started as a baby; a very weak baby; a very irritable baby; and a very hungry baby. And I remained a very hungry child.
>
> And still as a very hungry child, I got my first job as errand boy to an ironmonger at 4s a week. You see, my father died when I was three or four years old, and so my older brothers, who had all been fed and educated, came off better than I did.
>
> And now I suppose you'll be wanting to hear what I was doing after that. Working, sleeping, eating, drinking, cursing, starving, fighting, courting, going on strike, reading, educating myself in my leisure moments, and learning the Irish language.
>
> Or was it perhaps how I started playwriting that you were after knowing? I started by accident. I had joined a sort of club in Dublin, where they taught you Irish, and dancing, and all that, and we used to act and produce plays. Awful plays.
>
> So one day I said: "I'll write you a play worth acting." So I sat down and wrote "The Frost and the Flower" (good title isn't it? I like good titles for me plays!). But the committee wouldn't have it. It wasn't good enough.
>
> But it was, and I knew it was, and so I sent it up to the Abbey Theatre. They sent it back with a letter, a kind letter, beginning "Almost a good play, but not quite," pointing out the faults. I wrote two more, but each one the Abbey sent me back. So I burned them and wrote my first success, "The Shadow of a Gunman."

The Shadow of a Gunman, which O'Casey later described as his worst play, still has a flavor of the amateur about it. The central figure of the young poet who allows himself to be thought a member of the outlawed Irish Republican Army because he enjoys being flattered and admired, is a very unconvincing character. He speaks as the young O'Casey must have thought young poets should speak, and not as he had heard them speak in actuality. He cries out in soliloquy: "Oh, Donal Og O'Davoren, you way's a thorny way. Your late state is worse than your first. Ah me, alas! Pain pain ever, for ever. Like thee, Prometheus, no change, no pause, no hope. As, life, life, life!" This kind of talk is, of course, intended to show that the young poet, Davoren, is himself playing a part, and regarding himself as a romantic idealist, but it is overdone; this would not matter so much if the other characters in the play were not so superbly authentic.

The conflict between dream and reality which is at the heart of all O'Casey's work is presented so violently that the play almost disintegrates. Contrast Davoren's speech, with its affected cadences, with the vital rhythm of the speeches of Mrs. Henderson when she tries to get the supposed Gunman to help Mr. Gallicker deal with his troublesome neighbors. "Well, Mr. Davoren, the residents in the back drawin'-room, as I aforesaid, is nothin' but a gang o' tramps that oughtn't be allowed to associate with honest, decent, quiet, respectable people. Mr. Gallicker has tried to reason with them, and make them behave themselves—which in my opinion they never will—however, that's only an opinion an' not legal—ever since they have made Mr. Gallicker's life a HELL! Mr. Gallicker, am I right or am I wrong?" The irony of the situation is brought out beautifully by Mr. Gallicker's letter to the Irish Republican Army, for it is a legalistic letter, applying for social justice, to an organization outlawed by the Government. It is also a trivial, selfish letter, having no shade of that idealism which we must suppose to animate these rebels against the established order; self-sacrifice for a cause is the last thing that Mr. Gallicker would think of.

Davoren himself realizes this but is incapable of translating his own idealism into action. It is only the girl, Minnie, who is capable of action: she saves Davoren from the British soldiers by carrying off the bag of mills bombs left in Davoren's room by the real gunman and is herself killed as a result. She, however, has not died for a political but for a personal passion; her love of Davoren destroys her and not her love of Ireland. It is she who, as representative of the ordinary people, contradicts Davoren's low estimation of the common folk. When Seumas tells

Davoren that he thinks "a poet's claim to greatness depends upon his power to put passion in the common people," Davoren replies:

> Ay, passion to howl for his destruction. The People! Damn the people! They live in the abyss, the poet lives on the mountain-top; to the people there is no mystery of colour: it is simply the scarlet coat of the soldier; the purple vestments of a priest; the green banner of a party; the brown or blue overalls of industry. To them the might of design is a three-roomed house or a capacious bed. To them beauty is for sale in a butcher's shop. To the people the end of life is the life created for them; to the poet the end of life is the life that he creates for himself; life has a stifling grip upon the people's throat—it is the poet's musician. The poet ever strives to save the people; the people ever strive to destroy the poet. The people view life through creeds, through customs, and through necessities; the poet views creeds, customs, and necessities through life.

It is Minnie, not Davoren, however, who attempts to play the savior; it is Minnie who challenges life and says to herself: "She's had to push her way through life up to this without help from anyone, an' she's not goin' to ask their leave, now, to do what she wants to do."

Minnis is only the first of a number of strong-minded courageous women in O'Casey's drama. She is also typical of many characters who, caught up in events beyond their power to understand or control, die unheroic, pointless deaths.

It is not surprising that O'Casey should take up such themes for his drama. He lived through the Irish Rebellion of 1916 and the troubled years following as one of the Dublin poor. He saw firsthand the confusion, waste, and humanity of ordinary folk trapped by the idealism and stupidity of their leaders. Even though he viewed the results of political idealism with a jaundiced eye, he tended to see the fault as being in the people, not the ideal; his drama moved steadily towards the expression of outright socialist, even Marxist, doctrine; his characters are ridiculed not for believing in a faith but for completely misunderstanding the faith they profess. This misunderstanding is productive of both comedy and tragedy; in the early drama, the didactic intention is subordinate to the interest in the rich complexities of human behavior, so that we are left, at the final curtain, less with a political message than with a sense of the splendid variability of the human animal. Indeed, in *Juno and the Paycock*, O'Casey's second play for the Abbey Theatre, we tend to be more fascinated by the knaves and fools than by the reasonable people, and even the magnificent long-suffering Juno Boyle pales somewhat beside the ne'er-do-well "Captain Jack Boyle" and his crony Joxer. Moreover, the personal tragedy of Johnny Boyle, who spends the whole play in terror of the firing squad that eventually overtakes him, seems somehow less significant than the tragedy of his mother, who remains alive to cope with her husband's fecklessness.

Captain Jack Boyle and his crony Joxer are two of O'Casey's most remarkable characterizations. Boyle lives in a world of fantasy; he pretends to illness in order to avoid work; he lies about an inheritance in order to get credit from the shopkeepers; he refers frequently to an entirely imaginary career at sea; and he blusters, sobs, sings, orates, and boasts his way through life with an enjoyment of his own performance that is truly astonishing. His main audience is his crony Joxer, who admires his every word and echoes him with the fidelity of the born parasite. Boyle's fantasy about his sea-goin days is a great comfort to him; it is more real to him than reality, and much more dignified: "Them was days, Joxer, them was days. Nothin' was too hot or too heavy for me then. Sailin' from the Gulf o'Mexico to the Antanartic Ocean. I seen things, I seen things, Joxer, that no mortal man should speak about that knows his Catechism. Often, an' often, when I was fixed to the wheel with a marlinspike, an' the wins blowin' fierce an' the waves lashin' an' lashin', till you'd think every minute was goin' to be your last, an' it blowed, an' blowed—blew is the right word, Joxer, but blowed is what the sailors use."

> JOXER: Aw, it's a darlin' word, a daarlin' word.
>
> BOYLE: An', as it blowed an' blowed, I often looked up at the sky an' assed meself the question—what is the stars, what is the stars?
>
> JOXER: Ah, that's the question, that's the question—what is the stars?
>
> BOYLE: An' then I'd have another look, an' I'd ass meself—what is the moon?
>
> JOXER: Ah, that's the question—what is the moon, what is the moon?

This is indeed one of the main questions of the play. All the characters but Juno are trapped by a dream. Johnny fought for the Irish Republican

Army, filled with idealism, then, for what cause we do not know, turned informer, and now faces death. His sister, Mary, fell for the blandishments of the lawyer's clerk, who brought news of their inheritance, and ends up pregnant and deserted. Captain Boyle longs for the dignity and position of wealth, and, when news of the inheritance comes, he plays the Peacock, until his neighbors and creditors discover that the money is not going to arrive. Even Jerry is unable to face reality; he will not take Mary back when her pregnancy is discovered.

Only Juno Boyle can face reality and can show an unselfish feeling. At the end of the play when Mary is frightened to go to the morgue to see the body of her dead brother, she says:

> I forgot, Mary, I forgot; your poor oul' selfish mother, was only thinking of herself. No, no, you mustn't come—it wouldn't be good for you. You go on to me sisther's an' I'll face th' ordeal meself. Maybe I didn't feel sorry enough for Mrs. Tancred when her poor son was found as Johnny's been found now—because he was a Diehard! Ah, why didn't I remember then that he wasn't a Diehard or a Stater but only a poor dead son! It's well I remember all that she said—an' it's my turn to say it now: What was the pain I suffered, Johnny, bringin' you into the world to carry you to your cradle, to bring you to your grave! Mother o' God, Mother o' God, have pity on us all! Blessed Virgin, where were you when me darlin' son was riddled with bullets, when me darlin' son was riddled with bullets? Sacred Heart o' Jesus, take away our hearts o' stone, and give us hearts o' flesh! Take away this murtherin' hate an' give us Thine own eternal love!

There is tragic dignity in this speech, but O'Casey does not bring his curtain down on this note. Though Juno may be able to see the need for a change of heart in the country, she is in a minority. Soon after she has left the house her husband and Joxer return to it, drunk. The comedy of their drunken conversation ends the play—and makes it, paradoxically, more a tragedy. There is hope to be gained from Juno's sorrow; there is no hope in the Paycock and his crony, whose drunken talk is a savage parody of all the fine words of Irish patriots.

> BOYLE: The counthry'll have to steady itself . . . it's goin' to hell . . . Where're all . . . the chairs . . . gone to . . . steady itself, Joxer . . . Chairs'll . . . have to . . . steady themselves . . . No matther . . . what anyone may . . . say . . . Irelan' sober . . . is Irelan' . . . free.

JOXER: Chains . . . an' . . . slaveree . . . that's a darlin' motto . . . a darlin' motto!

BOYLE: If th' worst comes . . . to th' worst . . . I can join a . . . flyin' . . . column . . . I done . . . me bit . . . in Easther Week . . . had no business . . . to . . . be . . . there . . . but Captain Boyle's Captain Boyle!

JOXER: Breathes there a man with soul . . . so . . . de . . . ad . . . this me . . . o . . . wn, me nat . . . ive . . . l . . . an'!

BOYLE: Commandant Kelly died . . . in them . . . arms . . . Joxer . . . Tell me Volunteer Butties . . . says he . . . that . . .

JOXER: D'jever rade Willie . . . Reilly . . . an' his own . . . Colleen . . . Bawn? It's a darlin' story, a darlin' story

BOYLE: I'm telling you . . . Joxer . . . th' whole worl's . . . in a terr . . . ible state o' . . . chassis!

The same combination of the farcical and the poignant occurs in *The Plough and the Stars*, which roused the Abbey Theatre audience to riot and which was the last play of O'Casey's career as an Abbey Theatre Dramatist. The rioting was not unexpected; O'Casey prophesied that the Abbey audience would be disturbed by his new play; like Synge, however, he was undismayed by the trouble it caused, and, like Synge, he felt that art, to be successful, must include violence. He told the *Daily Sketch* in 1926:

> you can't sever yourself from humanity, for there's nothing else that counts. Didn't Synge say, "Although his head may be in the stars his roots must be in the earth"?
>
> And that's my idea of Art. There must be blood in all things that are written, in all pictures that are painted, in all songs that are sung. There must be the cry of humanity; it may be a ferocious cry, a bitter cry, an angry cry; but if it isn't a human cry it isn't Art. For life is the primary fact . . .
>
> I'm publishing my play over here. "The Plough and the Stars," and I'm dedicating it to my mother. My mother had a wonderful laugh, a beautiful laugh, and I heard her laugh a quarter of an hour before she died. And I am dedicating my play "To the laugh of my mother at the Gate of the Grave".

This is a most appropriate dedication, for *The Plough and the Stars* uses its comedy for tragic purposes. At the very opening of the play, before we are introduced to the Clitheroe family which is to be tragically disrupted by the Irish Rebellion of Easter week 1916, Mrs. Gogan makes the nervous Fluther Good even more nervous by saying: "there's many a man this minute lowerin' a pint, thinkin' of a woman, or pickin' out a winner, or doin' work as you're doin', while th' hearse dhrawn be th' horses with the black plumes is dhrivin' up to his own hall door, an' a voice that he doesn't hear is muttherin' in his ear, "Earth to earth, an' ashes t' ashes, an dust to dust" . . . It always gives meself a kind o' thresspassin' joy to feel meself movin' along in a mournin' coach, an' me thinkin' that, maybe, th' next funeral 'll be me own, an' glad, in a quiet way, that this is somebody elses." Mrs. Gogan represents those people who regard politics, art, idealism, and sentiment as folly and who are entirely caught up in the simple business of survival. Her forebodings are delivered with relish and with a sturdy conviction of her own survival. The other characters each present us with a different reaction to the social and political situation. Nora Clitheroe places her love for her husband before everything else, and it is the intensity of his love which destroys her when he is killed. Her uncle Peter thinks himself a patriot but is really only in love with the uniforms, the processions, and the speeches. He deeply resents the Covey who is the only person in the play who attempts to analyze and understand the predicament in which Ireland finds herself. It is typical of O'Casey's technique, however, that the Covey's Marxism is garbled, and his scientific explanations are more glib than accurate. Moreover, he is an unpleasant, contentious character, without loyalties of affections. Consequently, even though he presents us with an example of the kind of intelligence that the other characters lack and need, he is no hero. He lacks the humanity of the more simple characters. On the other hand, his cynicism enables us to see the idealism of the rebels as ignorant and naïve. This naïveté is exposed over and over again.

There is a sharp contrast between the rebels' attitude towards the Irish cause and the attitudes of the common people for whom they suppose themselves to be fighting. After the processing and speechmaking in the second act, Captain Brennan, Lieutenant Langon, and Jack Clitheroe speak excitedly in the tones of a boy's adventure story:

> BRENNAN: We won't have long to wait now.
>
> LANGON: Th' time is rotten ripe for revolution.
>
> CLITHEROE: You have a mother, Langon.

LANGON: Ireland is greater than a mother.

BRENNAN: You have a wife, Clitheroe.

CLITHEROE: Ireland is greater than a wife.

When the revolution does occur, however, not all the characters are as selfless. Mrs. Grogan and Mrs. Burgess delightedly join in the looting. The English soldiers, nervous and confused, shoot at shadows and kill the innocent. The enemy turns out to be quite as incapable of understanding what is happening as are the rebels. O'Cassey, in fact, deliberately allows the English soldiers to be somewhat sympathetic towards the people they must oppose. The consequence of all the idealism is "a terrible state o' chassis," and it is surveyed with compassion for the bewildered suffering and absurd pretensions of the human animal.

The Plough and the Stars is perhaps O'Casey's greatest play. It may lack the didactic power of some of his later work, but it expresses so much compassion, so much human warmth, without a single moment of false sentiment, that one can only marvel at it. O'Casey has the ability which only great playwrights possess, of combining intellectual condemnation of folly with passionate sympathy for the fools. His hypocrites may outline for us all that is rotten in the state of Ireland, but they also present us with the individual's pathetic need of dignity and self-justification. It is often the confusion of the fools that gives us the central insight into the drama, as when Peter rages against the teasing of Fluther and the Covey, "As long as I'm a livin' man, responsible for me thoughts, words, an' deeds to th' Man above, I'll feel meself instituted to fight again' th' sliddherin' ways of a pair o' picaroons, whisperin', concurrin', concoctin', an' conspirin' together to rendher me unconscious of th' life I'm thryin' to live!" This is more than the cry of a silly old man being tormented by the jibes of his companions. It is an accusation against all the forces that combine to make ordinary life impossible; it is the simple man's objection to idealists, intellectuals, politicians, and disturbers of his comfortable apathy. Nora Clitheroe is the tragic, as Peter is the comic, victim of these forces, and her accusation, before complete breakdown overtakes her, is more graphic: "Oh, I saw it, I saw it, Mrs. Cogan . . . At th' barricade in North King Street I saw fear glowin' in all their eyes. . . . An' in th' middle o' th' sthreet was somethin' huddled up in a horrible tangled heap. . . . His face was jammed again th' stones, an' his arms was twisted round his back. . . . An' every twist of his body was a cry against th' terrible thing that had happened to him . . . An' I saw they were afraid to look at it."

O'Casey was not afraid to look at it. In *The Shadow of a Gunman*, *Juno and the Paycock*, and *The Plough and the Stars*, he looked steadfastly at the absurdity and pathos of his countrymen. He saw their heroes as incompetent idealists, unaware of the certain consequences of their actions. He saw the heroic impulse itself as egotistical, a denial of human warmth, and an escape from confused reality into a world of fantasy where everything could be seen as black or white. He saw the Irish people as greedy, ignorant, feckless, and their boasted national feeling as just one more expression of that instinct for theatrical sentiment which is basic to the Irish character. He did not stop short of ridiculing the most sacred emblems of the national mystique—the uniforms, the songs, and the banners. It is not very surprising that numbers of his countrymen were less than grateful for the light he shed upon them in the sight of the world.

O'Casey was, however, more than an Irish dramatist. Though his three important early plays are all concerned with specifically Irish themes and derive enormous strength from his portrayal of the Irish poor, they have universal implications. In that fascinating interview with the *Daily Sketch*, in response to the question: "When you go back to Dublin, now that you're successful, will you live among the best people?" he did not reply with a paean of praise for the Dublin working class but answered: "I have *always* lived among the best people. And I have chosen them myself. I have always had as my friends Billy Shakespeare and Goya and Balzac and Anatole France and Shelley, and many others." Like Shakespeare, Goya, and Balzac, O'Casey dramatized, with mockery and compassion, particular occasions and vivid individuals, in such a way as to illuminate the predicament of the whole human race. While the Irish Republic may now be free of political and religious violence, Ulster is still in the situation O'Casey described, and in the Middle East and in Latin America, idealism and hypocricy, romanticism and pragmatism, tragedy and farce continue to create torment, for fools, hypocrities, and politicians are still with us, and O'Casey's plays will always remain relevant in a world that appears to be fairly continually in "a terrible state o' chassis."

9

The Workshop of W. B. Yeats

W. B. Yeats, like Wilde and like Synge, inherited a tradition of romanticism and also a divided culture. He was, as a young man, keenly aware of the Irish past and felt compelled to revive interest in it, and to renew and re-create Irish story and myth. He was equally aware of the English Romantic tradition, devoted to the work of William Morris and the Pre-Raphaelites, and passionate about William Blake. Indeed, perhaps his earliest and clumsiest attempt, outside his poetry, to bring the two halves of his inheritance together was his attempt to prove that William Blake was an Irishman. His interest in Blake led him far beyond the confines of conventional literature and philosophy, obliging him to become involved in Hermetic philosophy, and therefore in classical literature and myth. He was, indeed, supremely and centrally aware of the conflicts and contraries in his cultural inheritance, and it is one of the glories of his later poetry that he contrived to unify them into an overmastering world view of astonishing profundity and power.

The mind of Yeats was one of Shakespearean capacity and the greater part of the critical works concerning him are devoted to exploring and explicating his symbolism and his philosophy. Neither symbolism nor philosophy, however, would have been effective had Yeats not also been a master craftsman and yet this aspect of his work has received very little attention from the critics, partly because the fascination of his thought has proved so intense as to make concentration upon these aspects inescapable and partly because the current critical fashion is rather to discuss meaning than structure. Nevertheless, when one does begin to examine the verse techniques of Yeats one soon discovers that the way he constructs his poems tells us a good deal about his philosophy and his symbolism, for the form and the content in Yeats's lyrics are invariably fused into unity, and to discuss the one is therefore also to discuss the other.

There are several ways of approaching the study of a poet's verse craftsmanship. One is to get hold of his manuscripts and examine the way in which succeeding drafts are altered, cut, enlarged, rearranged, until the poem is perfected. Another is to examine the way in which published poems are revised from time to time and to discuss the reasons for each alteration. The trouble with both these approaches is that any one revision may occur for a number of quite distinct reasons, and what looks like an attempt to change the cadence may be an attempt to clarify the message. I have chosen a third method, therefore. I want to look at a small selection of the final versions of the poems of Yeats's maturity, picking those poems which seem to me to reveal most clearly those techniques which have given his verse its individual, unique character.

William Blake once said, "Without contraries is no progression," and Yeats, who was a devotee of Blake, constructed both his philosophy and his technique in terms of oppositions. His themes are often developed in the form of explicit or implied dialogue. His analysis of history and human personality was based upon a search for the dynamic relationship of opposed forces. His plays were based, as all plays must be, upon the establishment and exploration of conflicts. It is not surprising therefore that when one turns to the mature verse of the period between 1914 and 1939, one immediately discovers a verse dynamic based upon a conflict of styles and manners within the poem.

This is most obvious in those poems where a refrain is used not merely to echo the meaning or manner of the individual stanzas but to counter it, as if the refrain were spoken by some other voice insisting perpetually upon a different point of view, and a different perspective. In "The Apparitions" the refrain is couched in concrete, particular terms and refers to an image from everyday experience; whereas the stanzas are abstract and general in diction and inclined to become grandly rhetorical. Thus the philosophical, rhetorical, and heroic exploration of the theme is, each time the refrain occurs, suddenly and dramatically related to ordinary individual experience. This results in a bathos which at first seems almost to ridicule the pretentions of the speaker. As the poem proceeds, however, comic bathos becomes ironic counterpoint, and at the close of the poem, it is the down-to-earth refrain and not the rhetorical flourish which has the greatest emotional intensity. Thus the poem is not based upon an opposition which remains static, but upon the dynamic development of a relationship between two different modes of perception.

Because there is safety in derision
I talked about an apparition,
I took no trouble to convince,
Or seem plausible to a man of sense,
Distrustful of that popular eye,
Whether it be bold or sly.
Fifteen apparitions have I seen;
The worst a coat upon a coat-hanger.

I have found nothing half so good
As my long-planned half solitude,
Where I can sit up half the night
With some friend that has the wit
Not to allow his looks to tell
When I am unintelligible.
Fifteen apparitions have I seen;
The worst a coat upon a coat-hanger.

When a man grows old his joy
Grows more deep day after day,
His empty heart is full at length,
But he has need of all that strength
Because of the increasing Night
That opens her mystery and fright.
Fifteen apparitions have I seen;
The worst a coat upon a coat-hanger.

Here, although the body of the verse is always abstract, the contrast in tone between verse and refrain increases as the poem proceeds, for only gradually do we move from the colloquial ease of "I took no trouble to convince" with its careful avoidance of affirming energy, to the "increasing Night / that opens her mystery and fright" with its positive and almost heroic tone. We therefore arrive at the conclusion that when the refrain becomes most meaningful the contrast between refrain and stanza is at its most extreme.

This contrast between refrain and stanza is also helped by the manipulation of the rhyme scheme. The refrain lines do not rhyme, and yet the stanzas are in couplets. In the first stanza the rhymes are not particularly emphatic: Derision/apparition, convince/sense, eye/sly; only the last one is at all forceful and that comes just before the unrhyming refrain in order to emphasize the change in tone. In the second stanza we have good/solitude, night/wit, tell/unintelligible; the rhyming is played down, and thus the contrast between refrain and stanza is less extreme than in the previous stanza. In the last stanza, however, the rhymes: joy/day, length/strength, Night/fright, increase, one by one, in richness and force, thus making the nonrhyming seen/coat-hanger far more of a contrast than ever before in the poem.

In "The Apparitions," therefore, we can see two aspects of Yeats's verse-dynamic in the use of refrain. In "Three Songs to the One Burden," we can discover the same technique used in the opposite manner; here the refrain is heroic and the body of the stanza commonplace, concrete, particular:

> My name is Henry Middleton,
> I have a small demesne,
> A small forgotten house that's set
> On a storm-bitten green.
> I scrub its floors and make my bed,
> I cook and change my plate,
> The post and garden-boy alone
> Have keys to my old gate.
> *From mountain to mountain ride the fierce horsemen.*

Here the contrast in terms of rhythm is even more obvious than it was in "The Apparitions." The body of the stanza is constructed in terms of a free handling of alternate lines of iambic tetrameter and iambic trimeter, an established ballad measure. The refrain, however, is quite differently constructed. The first half of the line—for the sense and syntax of it demand a small pause after the word *mountain* and therefore we can divide the line reasonably enough—goes "From MOUNTain to MOUNTain," which is a pair of amphibrachs. The second half, "RIDE the FIERCE HORSEmen," is a syllable shorter, but places its heavy stresses in the places where the first half had weak stresses, and is weak where the first half is strong. If one were to add a heavily stressed syllable at the end of the line, one would have a line whose first half was rhythmically the exact opposite of its second half, a pair of amphibrachs countered by a pair of amphimacers.

I devote attention to the details here because I think it's important to realize that Yeats kept up the principle of dynamic contrast within the refrain line itself, and important also to realize that just as the tetrameter lines are rhythmically countered by the trimeter lines, so the refrain keeps up this movement from long to short units by making the second part of its line shorter than the first.

I have, perhaps, become wearisomely technical in my attempt to explain the structure of the Henry Middleton poem, but it must be remembered that Yeats himself was a most laborious and careful worker, intent upon seeing that every detail of his verse structure was in keeping with the overall character of the poem. This we know from many passages in his letters and from his manuscripts, and it is by the detailed examination of apparent happy accidents that we can most clearly see the fantastic technical expertise of Yeats's verse.

Of course the contrast between refrain and stanza varies in intensity, and there are many poems in which it forms only a minor part of the poem's structure. Most usually, whether or not contrast is an important part of the relationship, the refrain is used so as to increase in significance as the poem proceeds; it is as if the refrain were an object which, each time it is examined, reveals further beauties or meanings. Thus the poem itself presents an increasing intensity of vision and the refrain, always being the same, acts as a standard, a yardstick, by which this intensity may be measured. A good example of this and of the use of the refrain as a voice coming from "outside" the poem is "*What Then*?"

His chosen comrades thought at school
He must grow a famous man;
He thought the same and lived by rule,
All his twenties crammed with toil;
"*What then*?" *sang Plato's ghost.* "*What then*?"

Everything he wrote was read,
After certain years he won
Sufficient money for his need,
Friends that have been friends indeed;
"*What then*?" *sang Plato's ghost.* "*What then?*"

All his happier dreams came true—
A small old house, wife, daughter, son,
Grounds where plum and cabbage grew,
Poets and Wits about him drew;
"*What then?*" *sang Plato's ghost.* "*What then?*"

"The work is done," grown old he thought,
"According to my boyish plan;
Let the fools rage, I swerved in naught,
Something to perfection brought";
But louder sang that ghost, "*What then?*"

This poem, of course, attaches the refrain to the body of the stanza at the close of the poem, by altering it a little, and providing a link with the word "but." It also gives us a small dramatic shock by altering the refrain at a point when we had grown used to it. In this poem, however, the climax of the life story appears to be a success which only increases the questioning of the ghost. The ghost, indeed, is louder and nearer to the speaker at his life's end, when he feels that the meaning of existence must be scrutinized even more intensely. Thus the linking of refrain with the body of the last stanza is not only a trick of verse but also an expression of the poem's meaning. The ghost is, in verse-structure, brought nearer to the speaker, just as it is in the story that the poem tells. Form and content, in Yeats's mature verse, always work together, and form unity.

I have spent a good deal of time on what might be called the ballad style because in these the verse-dynamic is fairly simple to observe, and because the techniques used are basic to Yeats's method. If we move on from this kind of poem to what appears to be a totally different kind of poem, we find other techniques being used, but, it seems, for similar reasons.

From 1914 onwards Yeats spent a good deal of time on writing autobiographical, meditative poems in which he looked back upon his own experiences, celebrated the memory of his friends, and pondered the philosophical implications of it all. In these poems he obviously needed to find a style which would combine imaginative intensity with colloquial ease, so that it should appear as if the speaker were thinking aloud, and yet so intent upon his thoughts that every now and then the language of reflection would become the language of passion or rise into the decisiveness of confident rhetoric. This meant that, when the meditation began, he could not afford to give his poem an obvious thumping rhythm but must let it appear rhythmically casual, unforced. Still he had also to provide it with enough discipline to prevent it slithering into prosaic nevertheless. Consider the opening of one of the most famous of these poems, "The Municipal Gallery Revisited":

Around me the images of thirty years:
An ambush; pilgrims at the water-side;
Casement upon trial, half hidden by the bars,
Guarded; Griffith staring in hysterical pride;
Kevin O'Higgins' countenance that wears
A gentle questioning look that cannot hide
A soul incapable of remorse or rest;
A revolutionary soldier kneeling to be blessed;

One does not need to analyze the meter to see that this verse is metrically awkward, deliberately clumsy. The lines are broken up by long pauses. The sentences rove over from one line to another without any apparent attempt at smoothness or symmetry. The rhyme gives one a feeling that the whole thing is controlled to some extent, but, because the rhythm is not smooth, we cannot easily anticipate the occurrence of rhyming words. It seems almost as if the rhymes and the line endings occur arbitrarily, when the speaker's fancy decides and not according to any rule. Nevertheless, there does seem to be some disciplined organization involved; we can hear it, but we cannot at first identify it.

If we read "The Municipal Gallery" once again, it becomes clear that the rhymes are used so as to give us the impression of casual speech, while the alliteration and assonance within the lines give us, without our at first realizing it, a strong impression of disciplined unity. Listen to the *m* sounds in the first three lines. *M* is not a very emphatic sound, and that is why it is the right one; it links the lines together unobtrusively:

> Around Me the iMages of thirty years:
> An aMbush; pilgriMs at the water-side;
> CaseMent upon trial

There are other links here, too. The first two lines begin "Around ME," and "An Ambush," thus repeating the combination of *A* and *M*. In the following lines the trick becomes a little more obvious:

> Casement upon trial, half hidden by the bars,
> Guarded; Griffith staring in hysterical pride

"Bars" at the end of one line is caught up by "Guarded" at the beginning of the next, and "Guarded" is followed immediately by "Griffith." The *i* sound of "Griffith" is taken up in "hysterical," which also links up with the *H* sound of "Half-Hidden" that occurred a little earlier. When the stanza comes to its end, and therefore to a minor climax, the alliteration becomes more obtrusive because more tightly arranged:

> A soul incapable of remorse or rest;
> A revolutionary soldier kneeling to be blessed.

The main links here are the repetition of *a* in the body of each line followed by *est* at the end, the *re* sound occurring twice in the first line and once in the second. The *ble* of "incapable" in one line is repeated in the "Blessed" of the next. Even the *N* of "incapable" is echoed in "kneeling." In fact, if we look at these two lines, we find that every consonantal sound in the first line is repeated in the second, with the exception of *P*, which reappears in its more emphatic form as *B*.

This use of alliteration and assonance runs throughout the poem, as a kind of undercurrent. As the poem becomes less colloquial, and less casual, and as the speaker's thoughts, which at first were random, become more ordered and begin to take on passion and decision, the meter becomes more regular and the syntax easier. As a consequence, the rhyming becomes more predictable, and in the last stanza, though we still have a marked use of alliteration and assonance, we find that the poem's formal structure has become much clearer.

> And here's John Synge himself, that rooted man,
> "Forgetting human words," a grave deep face.
> You that would judge me, do not judge alone
> This book or that, come to this hallowed place
> Where my friends' portraits hang and look thereon;
> Ireland's history in their lineaments trace;
> Think where man's glory most begins and ends,
> And say my glory was I had such friends.

Here the repetition of sounds has been made even more emphatic by repeating whole words—"judge," "friends," "glory"—but the lines are much smoother so that the rhythm and the rhyme also have a powerful effect. In "The Municipal Gallery Revisited," Yeats used consonance and alliteration to provide discipline under the apparently casual and clumsy surface until such time as the meditation itself became decisive, and therefore ordered meter and orthodox rhyme-placing became possible; at this point he did not drop his alliterative method but intensified it by repeating whole words, not merely sounds. Thus here, the verse-dynamic is expressive of the changing tone of the poem, and not only unifies the whole but also develops as the poem's theme develops.

Sometimes the assonantal and consonantal devices are used to add another dimension to a lyric, rather than to give unity and progression to a meditation. In "Those Images" the third line of each of the four stanzas uses internal consonance or assonance:

What if I bade you leave
The cavern of the mind?
There's b*e*tter *e*xercise
In the sunlight and wind.

I never bade you go
To Moscow or Rome.
*R*enounce that d*r*udge*r*y,
Call the Muses home.

Seek those images
That constitute the wild,
The lio*n* and the virgi*n*,
The harlot and the child.

Find in middle air
An eagle on the wing,
Recogn*iz*e the f*i*ve
That make the Muses sing.

Here the last verse uses the assonantal and consonantal technique more emphatically than the earlier ones so that the progressive dynamic of the verse once again corresponds with the thematic development of the poem.

I said earlier that Yeats's verse-technique was based upon the use of contraries, and his use of assonantal and consonantal devices fits well with this general statement. Much of the native poetry of Ireland, Gaelic poetry, is not metrical and does not rhyme. It is syllabic and uses assonance and consonance in highly elaborate patterns. Yeats was probably aware of this, and at the time when he was writing his later poems, he was collaborating in a number of projects with F. R. Higgins who was consciously attempting to make use of Gaelic techniques in his verse. It is therefore not unreasonable to suggest that Yeats, in fusing a highly controlled assonantal/consonantal technique with the orthodox rhyming and metrical techniques of the English tradition, was playing one verse tradition against another. Conflict certainly does occur; the consonance is often so emphatic as to make the rhyming appear secondary, and quite frequently an apparently metrical poem shifts gears and becomes syllabic in structure rather than metrical. It was a part of Yeats's genius as a poet to combine traditions of craftsmanship, just as he was able, in his subject matter, to combine explorations of Christian and pagan tradition and to speak in the same poem, and with the same intensity, of Phidias and Michaelangelo.

It is, however, the diction of Yeats that combined different viewpoints most obviously. We have already seen how, in his balladlike poems, he can juxtapose rhetoric and vulgarity, the concrete and the abstract. Yeats's poems are often characterized by this kind of contrast. Most usually we find a diction that reminds us, in its vocabulary and syntax, of epic, or of sentimental romanticism in the Pre-Raphaelite manner, placed alongside a downright colloquial, even carelessly casual, diction that is not so much nonliterary as antiliterary in feeling. Often even quite a short poem will involve this diction conflict. In "An Acre of Grass," for example, we find the first stanza speaking casually, in conversational, faintly slapdash, syntax. The second stanza becomes more formal in its syntax, and the images are part literary and part vulgar. The third stanza is formal, rhetorical, passionate. And the last stanza is constructed entirely in a series of inversions, so that it is about as far in style from the first stanza as could possibly be imagined:

Picture and book remain,
An acre of green grass
For air and exercise,
Now strength of body goes;
Midnight, an old house
Where nothing stirs but a mouse.

My temptation is quiet.
Here at life's end
Neither loose imagination
Nor the mill of the mind
Consuming its rag and bone,
Can make the truth known.

Grant me an old man's frenzy,
Myself must I remake
Till I am Timon and Lear
Or that William Blake
Who beat upon the wall
Till Truth obeyed his call;

A mind Michael Angelo knew
That can pierce the clouds,
Or inspired by frenzy

Shake the dead in their shrouds;
Forgotten else by mankind,
An old man's eagle mind.

In the first stanza there are two or three thoughts placed together so casually as to seem random reflections. In the last stanza, however, there is only one thought, and the vocabulary, diction, and theme are all heroic, even magnificent.

Here, again the changing diction echoes the theme and even adds to the stated meaning of the poem. The "Picture and book," dismissed as simply pastimes for leisure moments in stanza one, become, once the poem has thought further, Blake and Michelangelo, expressions of the greatest intensity of which man is capable. Moreover, this summit of human experience is expressed in highly literary, even slightly archaic language. The language of human excellence is the formal wrought language of literature; the most intense life is the life of art.

The diction of Yeats is a complex subject which demands further attention. In this essay I only wish to suggest that Yeats deliberately played literary and antiliterary, rhetorical and vulgar, ways of speech off against one another. The result was often a poem that seemed to be spoken by a man who was at once an aristocrat and a peasant, a high priest and the man next door, a man, in other words, capable of many viewpoints many perspectives. It is clear from the subject matter of the poems that this is the case; the language supports this impression and intensifies it.

The myriad-minded quality of Yeats's poetry has been commented upon by many writers, and so I do not need to elaborate upon it here. I ought, however, to make one further point about the kind of craftsmanship which I have been discussing, for it is important to see that it is in no way an oddity in twentieth-century Irish writing and is, indeed, itself in some ways an expression of ancient tradition.

The medieval poets of Ireland and Wales were very much technicians, and the techniques they invented and developed frequently involve an interweaving of different devices, in the same ways as the petroglyphs and early celtic designs in gold and upon illuminated manuscripts involve them. The twenty-four official meters of Wales, first set down in codified form in the fourteenth century, contain structures of dazzling complexity, and readers of Kuno Meyer and Gerard Murphy will know that Irish poetry is scarcely less complex. It is, perhaps, dangerous to generalize about national characteristics, but it is my view that the Celtic literary tradition is one of deliberate and studied elaboration, and that this elaboration as often as not results in cyclic forms and in frequent counterpoint. Twentieth-century Irish writers, having been given back their inheritance by the generation of Yeats, reveal this kind of complexity in many ways. One has only to summon up the names of James Joyce, Samuel Beckett, and Flann O'Brien to see this aspect of Celtic tradition in full flower, and the complexities and elaborate interweavings in the plays and novels of Jack B. Yeats, the symbolism of the later drama of Sean O'Casey and George FitzMaurice, the technical sleight of hand of the later poems of Austin Clarke, and the riddling elegance of the poetry of Denis Devlin could all serve to support my view, as could, from Wales, the poetry of Dylan Thomas, the work of David Jones, and that of the Powys brothers.

I am not concerned here to make a case, but rather to suggest the possibility of making one, and therefore of seeing the laborious craftsmanship of Yeats and of Synge (particularly in his Petrarch translations) as being within a particular Celtic tradition. "The fascination of what's difficult" (to use Yeats's line) has been felt by many Irish artists and writers over the centuries and particularly in our own. And the fascination, in Yeats's case, was not only with the structure of verse but also with the creation of a means to express and explore another complexity—that of the many-faceted inheritance of modern Europe and of the Anglo-Irish tradition.

10

The Versecraft of Robert Graves

For many years Robert Graves has emphasized the importance of versecraft, and his own skill in prosody has been recognized by many critics. J. M. Cohen, for example, has written that "No contemporary poet is a greater master of cadence none more capable of achieving variety with a uniform verse pattern. Nor is there any with greater control of rhyme and half-rhyme, assonance and alliteration."[1] P. N. Furbank, on reviewing *New Poems 1962* in the *Listener*; called Graves's art "an art of proportion, the utmost spontaneity in the shape of the strophes being combined with the strictest mathematics in their laying together and poising upon one another."

John Press in a *Sunday Times* review said Graves was "the most accomplished craftsman now practising the art of poetry in these islands" (one assumes he meant Great Britain and Ireland and not the Balearics). There seems, indeed, to be a consensus among critics and reviewers that Robert Graves is a master craftsman, and yet there has been very little serious examination of his craft.

A thorough exploration of Graves's craftsmanship would occupy many years of study, because it would not only involve a close examination of his work sheets and of his many revisions of published poems but also demand from the critic an intimate and practical knowledge of Latin and Greek prosody as well as English, Welsh, and Irish, for Graves has learned his skills from many and diverse traditions. In this essay therefore I can do no more than offer one or two observations upon one aspect of

1. J. M. Cohen, *Robert Graves* (Edinburgh: Oliver & Boyd, 1960), 116–17.

Graves's craftsmanship which interests me particularly and which Graves himself seems always to have considered important. In his *Observations on Poetry* (1922–1925) which were collected together in *The Common Asphodel* (1949), he wrote under the heading "Texture":

> Classicists pay great attention to the texture of poetry; their aim is euphony and, within the strict metrical patterns approved by tradition, variety. "Texture" covers the interrelations of all vowels and consonants in a poem considered as mere sound. The skilled craftsman varies the vowel sounds as if they were musical notes so as to give an effect of melodic richness; uses liquid consonants, labials and open vowels for smoothness; aspirates and dentals for force; gutturals for strength; sibillants for flavour as a cook uses salt. His alliteration is not barbarously insistent, as in Anglo-Saxon poems or *Piers Plowman*, but concealed by the gradual interlacement of two or three alliterative sequences. He gauges the memory-length of the reader's inward ear and plants the second word of an alliterative pair at a point where the memory of the first has begun to blur but has not yet faded. He takes care not to interrupt the smooth flow of the line, if this can possibly be avoided, by close correspondence between terminal consonants and the initial consonants that follow them—e.g. *break ground, maid's sorrow, great toe*. Non-Classicists either disregard texture as another of the heavy chains clamped on the naked limbs of poetry, or use their understanding of it for deliberate exercises in cacaphony or dislocation: by judicious manipulation of vowels and consonants a line can be made to limp, crawl, scream, bellow and make other ugly or sickening noises.

Some years later, in the foreword to his *Collected Poems* of 1938, he said of his schoolboy writings:

> In those days my disgressions were chiefly towards difficult technical experiments in prosody and phrasing. In 1909, for example, I tried my hand at a set of translations from Catullus; and also adapted to English the complicated *englyn* metre, the chief feature of which is matching sequences of consonants. In 1910 I addressed some lines "To a Pot of White Heather Seen in the Window of a House in a Mean Street":
>
> Thou, a poor man's fairing—white heater,
Witherest from the ending

Of summer's bliss to the sting
Of winter's grey beginning

Here the devices of rhyming unstressed with stressed syllables (the second stanza had *nature, rapture, pure* and *treasure* as its end-rhymes) and of internal assonantal rhyme (heather, wither) were derived from the Welsh. I found the strictly matching consonantal sequences of Welsh bardic poetry too crabbed for English, but modified them to cross-alliteration—as in a poem, "The Dying Knight and the Fauns" written in 1911:

Woodland fauns with hairy haunches
Grin in wonder through the branches,
Woodland fauns who know not fear:
Wondering they wander near,
Munching mushrooms red as coral,
Bunches, too, of rue and sorrel,
With uncouth and bestial sounds,
Knowing naught of war and wounds.
But the crimson life-blood oozes
And makes roses of the daisies

I was preoccupied with the physical side of poetry—the harmonious variation of vowels and the proper balance, in a line or stanza, between syllables difficult and easy to articulate.

Over thirty years later in the preface to his *Poems 1970–1972*, he returned to the subject or prosody and wrote: "Recently in a broadcast I admitted my constant debt—with which I had, however, never been charged—to early Welsh prosody. In my boyhood at Harlech, North Wales, I was indoctrinated by "Gwynedd" (the bardic name of our celebrated neighbour Canon Edwards) in *cynganedd* and other ancient metrical devices. In 1913 I even published an English *englyn* without transgressing too many of its ninety-five statutory rules. Briefly, the subsequent use I made of cynganedd was to strengthen my verse with complex half-concealed chains of alliteration. But I also borrowed the ancient Irish use of internal rhyme."

Graves's statements about poetry are often enlivened with hyperbole. It is necessary to point out, therefore, that the twenty-four official measures of Welsh verse, first codified by Einion Offeiriad and edited in the fourteenth century by Dafydd Ddu Athro, are of three kinds, the *Englyn*, the *Cwydd*, and the *Awdl*. There are eight *Englynion*, and no *Englyn* has more than three or four rules. It must also be pointed out that while the ancient Irish did use internal (or Aicill) rhyme, so did the Welsh, and much more elaborately. There are, so far as I can detect, no precise imitations of any of the twenty-four Welsh measures in Graves's canon, though he has certainly made considerable use of *cynghanedd* and some of his poems approximate to the Welsh stanzas. *Cynghanedd* is a word meaning simply "harmony," and there are three main modes. *Cynghanedd Gytsain* refers to the organization of consonantal repetition and can be itself divided into three submodes. In *Cynghanedd Groes* the same consonants appear in each half of the line and in the same order. An example in English is:

May I peel my apple?

There are several kinds of *Cynghanedd Groes* according to whether the stresses are placed in the same position in each half of the line or not, and whether or not the word ending of each half line is stressed or unstressed. This form of *cynghanedd* is difficult to manage in English. The second form of *cynghanedd, Cynghanedd Sain* occurs when the line is constructed of three parts, the first two rhyming with each other and the third one being consonantally linked to the second. Again, there are different varieties according to the positioning of the stressed syllables. This form is not impossible in English. One example is:

The hand has planned the pose,
the line defined the dove

From this one can see that the rhyme may be partially concealed by splitting it between two words, as in "line d/-fined."

The third form of *cynghanedd* is the *Cynghanedd Lusg*, in which the concluding syllable of the first half of the line rhymes with the penultimate syllable of the whole line, as in

The old well in the cellar

To these chiming devices of *cynghanedd* must be added the rules of rhyme of the various measures, such as the rhyming of the *Toddaid* in which a word in the middle of the first line rhymes with the end word of the second, and the end word of the first line rhymes with a word in the middle of the second, and the Englyn Lleddfbroest in which the rhymes must all be dipthongs.

Graves, again from the preface to his *Poems 1907–1972*, says that "English poetry . . . combines the Anglo-Saxon metre of the tugged oar with the dancing metres of Ancient Greece and with the resolute marching metre of the Roman legionaries," and he admits that this is "complex enough without recourse to Welsh prosody." Nevertheless, it is Welsh prosody that enabled him to create the greater part of that individual harmony which distinguishes his verse. Whether this was an altogether consciously planned maneuver or the result of intuition and accidents of circumstance need not concern us. What should concern us, however, is the way in which Graves, by use of the *cynghanedd* and allied techniques, contrived to enrich and vary the conventional verse tunes of the Anglo-classical tradition to such a degree, and with such subtlety, that he created a new mode for English lyric verse.

It is easy to see that the Welsh elements in Graves's poetry are most carefully and meticulously organized. A brief examination of the work sheets of "A Bracelet" shows that, while the early drafts reveal a good many chiming words within the lines, the process of "secondary composition" (to use Graves's own expression) has led to a marked increase in the number, and a much more rigorous organization, of these internal rhymes. Thus in what appears to be the first draft, while we have two lines echoing each other on the syllable "is,"

ThIS bracelet invISible
for your bUSy wrISt,

and while we may also note the recurrence of the plosive *b*, the following three lines are not linked to each other but simply alliterate internally:

EighT and TwenTy moonleTs
Sent to SurpriSe you
Waxing and Waving

In the intermediate drafts the lines are sometimes strengthened by means of end rhymes and a dancing rhythm as in

Moonface, pray wear this
Bracelet invisible
Twenty eight lunulas
Sent you for jingling
On your busy arm.
Wear it for a charm.

The variety of chiming devices here does not give the poem that ritual formality necessary to a spell or charm. A late draft relineates the poem and presents it as a rhymed quatrain, and thus relates it to the tradition of the English epigram:

A bracelet invisible for your busy wrist,
Twisted from silver of a chill night,
From silver of the full moon, from her sheer halo:
Hence the scheming demons pale in their flight.

It is an indication of Graves's extraordinarily rigorous approach to his own work that this draft was not allowed to stand, for another poet would have considered the poem completed. It certainly seems completed. The syllable count is 12, 9, 12, 10, and the stress count is 4, 4, 5, 5. The meter is mixed, and as the organizing principle is that of counting stressed, but not unstressed, syllables, it might be described as "sprung rhythm." The chiming devices are many. In the first three lines the first half of the line repeats a consonant or vowel which then recurs in the second half of the line. In the first line the sound is *b*, in the second *i*, and in the third *l*. It must also be noted that the penultimate syllable of one line rhymes with a syllable in the middle of the next line (as in the *Toddaid*), thus "bUsy" is echoed by "sIlver," which is at the center-point of the second line, as well as by "twIsted" and "chIll" (and, earlier, "wrIst"), and the first syllable of "hALo" chimes with "pALe." Moreover, the last two consonants in each line echo two adjacent consonants in the preceding line; thus "NighT" echoes "braceleT iN," "SHeer haLo" echoes, approximately, "CHiLL" (or "SiLver"), and "FLight" echoes "FuLL." The last line has a rich internal rhyme at the center and proceeds by means of three sections of linked words. The chain effect can be demonstrated thus:

Hence the scheming demons pale in their flight

This last line is not constructed in the same fashion as the earlier lines, although it is firmly linked to them. Moreover, the long line makes the poem move too quickly and also does not fit well with the notion of a spell or charm, for these, in the Anglo-Celtic tradition, are almost invariably short lined. The next draft, therefore, relineates the poem, removes the emphatic rhyme that suggests the precise click of epigrammatic wit, and unifies the mood by removing the negative reference to demons. In what appears to be the next and penultimate version the system of chiming sounds is perfected. One word is added and one change in order to complete the sound pattern.

"From silver of the moon" becomes "From silver of the clear Moon" so that "clear" may rhyme with "sheer" in the next line, and the phrase "clear beauty" is changed to "male beauty" so that "male" may rhyme with "halo" in the preceding line. The final version is beautifully crafted. In the first four lines, the vowel of the last stressed syllable in the line chimes with that of the first stressed syllable in the next; in the last three lines, the last stressed syllable in the line rhymes with the penultimate stressed syllable of the next line. The fifth line is pivotal, both in sense and in structure, the first stressed syllable rhyming with the first stressed syllable of the preceding line and the penultimate stressed syllable with the penultimate stressed syllable of the line following. This pivotal fifth line contains three stresses, the remainder two, and the poem is given formal strength by means of epanaphora utilizing the word "From," which this line introduces.

A bracelet invisible
For your busy wrist,
Twisted for silver
Split afar,
From silver to the clear Moon,
From her sheer halo,
From the male beauty
Of a shooting star.

I have spent a good deal of space upon "A Bracelet" because we have the work sheets and can see from them, very clearly, that the process of "secondary composition" consisted both of a careful manipulation of sound in a manner characteristic of Welsh verse as well as a clarification and intensification of the poem's message. It may be suspected that "A Bracelet" is in some ways atypical, being a lyric in a mode in which complexity of chiming might be considered de rigueur. I feel therefore that I should indicate from other poems the range and subtlety of Graves's use of Welsh prosodic devices. I take my illustrations entirely from the poems published over the last twenty-five years, because it is generally accepted that it is in the poetry of this period that Graves perfected his style and because that style (apart from some excursions into light verse) remains consistent from collection to collection.

Firstly, here are examples of Graves's delicate use of the principle of *Cynghanedd Llusg*, in which the word concluding the first half of the line chimes with the line's penultimate syllable:

Circling the SUN at a respectful distANce
("Problems of Gender")

Love is a gAme for only two to plAy at
("Jus Primae Noctis")

Boys never fall in lOve with great-grand mOthers
("Age Gap")

These are not emphatic usages; a richer chiming involving full syllables would be more orthodox; nevertheless, the structure is clearly there. *Cynghanedd Sain* is used with similar delicacy, the first two thirds of the line chiming with each other and a consonant in the second third of the line recurring in the final section:

COmpassion for your SCHOlars—yeS
("Complaint and Reply")

And ENdless MomEnt of once More
("Song: Once More")

But beware agAIn: even a shy embrACE would be too expliCit
("Gold and Malachite")

Cynghanedd Groes, in which the same consonants appear in the same order in each half of the line, occurs only in a modified form, as in:

AloNe, you are No More thaN MaNy aNother
("Son Altesse")

Here the general effect is achieved by means of an approximation to the rule. In this line we should also notice the repetition and variation upon the long *o*, and the repetition of *th*. Another example of slightly modified Cynghanedd Groes is:

NeVeR agaiN RemiNd me oF it
("Bank Account")

As the voiced *f* and the *v* are the same phonetically, we have here the repetition of the sequence *n* then *v* in both halves of the line, (assuming that the line breaks after the word "again"). *R* appears in both halves of the line also, and the second half of the line uses a repeated *n*. The *d* and *t* in the line are also very similar in sound., Thus, there is, effectively, only one consonant in the line, the *g*, which is not repeated.

It is not Graves's practice to imitate the Welsh devices slavishly, but to utilize the principles behind the practice of creating harmony by means of clearly organized patters of rhyme, consonance, and alliteration. The following examples need no typographical tricks for their chiming effects to be revealed:

Warring with love of love in your young eyes
("The Gentleman")

Which, when you see, you smile upon and bless
("Druid Love")

Confess, Marpessa, who is your new lover?
("Confess, Marpessa")

Many of Graves's revisions of already published poems reveal a desire to improve the verbal music of the lines which is quite as intense as the desire to clarify their message. In his revisions of his poem "Alice," we see him altering line 6, "She being of true philosophic bent," to "She being of a speculative bent," and thus adding to the existing repetitions of *b*, *t*, and the sibilants a repetition of the *e* sound in the second half of the line and a third plosive at the line's center. The number of *n*'s in line

11, "That what I'd see would need to correspond" is increased in the revised version, "That what I see now needs must correspond," thus producing a more tightly knit sound pattern. Similarly, the number of chiming *t*'s in line 18, "Moreover, uncontent with what she had done" is increased in the later version, "Proved right, yet not content with what she had done," and the phrase "full holiday" in line 43 is made alliterative by the change to "whole holiday." Some of these revisions may not seem as important as others which appear to have been made for different reasons. They are, nevertheless, significant, and an examination of other instances of Graves's revisions of published texts reveals that they are typical. One might even state, quite emphatically, that Graves's revisions of his published poems invariably involve a deliberate "Celticization" of the harmonies. Indeed, the point of all this is not merely to show that Graves is a master manipulator of assonance, consonance, rhyme, and near-rhyme, but also to suggest that this mastery is based firmly upon a profound understanding of the nature and utility of the Welsh tradition of versecraft, and that it is this Welsh element in his work which gives his cadences their peculiar authority and subtlety. These prosodic devices are not simply decorative elements they are integral to the structure of the poetry, and the greater part of Graves's poetry of the last twenty-five years can only be properly understood, as craft, if it is examined with these techniques in mind.

Another characteristic of Graves's later work is the preponderance of poetry that is apparently ametrical. While some of the songs and occasional verses are constructed in orthodox Anglo-classical metrics, the majority of them are written in "sprung rhythm." The problem with "sprung rhythm" is that by itself, without rhyming devices, it tends to approximate so closely to the rhythms of conversational speech that all intensity is lost. Hopkins, who invented the term, forced intensity upon his poetry in "sprung rhythm" by means of compound words, wrenched syntax, and idiosyncratic diction, as well as some of the devices of *cynghanedd*. Graves has almost always written in a bare direct manner, with close attention to syntactical proprieties and with a lexicographer's distaste for the distortion of commonly received meanings. Consequently, he has had to find a way to provide an apparently unmetrical piece of conversational speech with a sound pattern strong enough to "hypnotize" (his own word) the reader without making the speech itself appear forced or tricksy. He has achieved this by means of sound patterns that alert the inner, subliminal ear of the poetic receptor without alarming the outer ear of commonsense.

A good example of the method is the poem "In Disguise." It is somewhat bland in diction; Graves frequently eschews the use of multiple vivid images and prefers to maneuver the reader gradually into a sense of the particularity of the moment by way of unostentatious phrases that are acceptable as common usage. Some phrases are even a little shopworn, the common coin of exchange, such as "dirty subterfuges," and "a veteran on the pensioned list." In this particular poem the bland and worn diction does, of course, act as a means to an end; were the poem initially more impressive the final lines would lose their dramatic effect. The strategy of the poem is not however limited to its careful diction, nor even to the provision of a well-balanced stress pattern—the two quatrains being stressed 5,4,5,4, and 4,5,5,4, if the poem is read with the cadence of ordinary speech. Indeed, it is the unobtrusive sound effects that provide a pattern that authenticates the piece as poetry.

In Disguise

Almost I welcome the dirty subterfuges
Of this sunreal world closing us in,
That present you as a lady of high fashion
And me as a veteran on the pensioned list.

Our conversation is infinitely proper,
With a peck on either cheek as we meet or part—
Yet the seven archons of the heavenly stair
Tremble at the disclosure of our seals.

Once we begin to look for the poem's sound patterns we can see that in every line but the first and last there is a chiming sound making use of the consonant *n*. The sequence begins with "uNreal/iN" in the second line, and continues with "preseNt/fashioN/veteraN/peNsioNed/, coNversatioN/iNfiNitely,pEck oN" (close to 'PEnsioN'in sound), "seveN/archoNs/heaveNly." Our appetite for exploration whetted, we then may notice that the first half of the first line has a chime in *l* and *m* (aLMost/weLcoMe) and the second half chimes on *t* and *er* (or *ir*) (dIRty/subtER-); similarly the last line begins with a chime in *l* and a near chime between *t* and *d* (TrembLe/DiscL-), and that the second half of the line chimes also in *l* and with a sibilant (-loSure/SealS). Moreover, the sixth line has a structure all its own, and an obvious one; it draws attention to itself, as it should, for this is a crucial and pivotal line for the poem. It proceeds by way of a sequence of chimes, "WiTH a peCK" chimes with "eiTHer cheeK," and "Either chEEk" (if "either" is prounounced "EEther," not "IGHther") chimes with "wE mEEt," while "meeT" is in consonance with "parT." Such a heavily chiming line must, if the poem is to move towards climax, be followed by a similarly effective piece of internal rhyming, and so we find that the next line rhymes "sEVEN" with "hEAVENly," and the consonantly chiming "archoNs" lies between them. Thus, as we read this poem, we receive, though probably subliminally, a series of sound patterns that lead us to believe we are hearing something of importance, and that does indeed hypnotize us, persuade us without our being aware of the means by which we are being persuaded.

It is this "art concealing art" of which Robert Graves is the poetic master. Sometimes, it must be admitted, he succeeds so well in his concealment that only other poets as concerned with the craft as he are likely to recognize what is happening, and some of the more cloth-eared critics have dismissed many of his later love poems as trivial, which is rather like dismissing Monet's paintings of water lilies as trivial.

I use this parallel deliberately, for it is not in the actual content of the poem that we must always seek for greatness; it is in its implications, both particular and general. There is implied by Robert Graves's practice, a view of the profession of poetry, of the scope and range of the medium, and of the morality of craftsmanship that is of extreme importance. In his preface to *Poems 1970–1972*, from which I have quoted already, he says, "Prosody is now generally underrated by English and American writers, who fail to recognize it as a necessary means of hypnotizing the reader into the same dream-like mood—the top level of sleep—which the true poet himself must enter." In this "dream-like mood," in this "poetic trance" (to use Graves's own expression), both poet and reader are able to sense a pattern in experience that is at once more multifaceted and more profound than that which they perceive when fully awake. It is not only the state of mind in which all true poems (and all works of art) are created but also that in which many scientific discoveries are made. It is, indeed, the place where the boundary between conscious and unconscious knowledge, between reason and intuition is crossed; it is, perhaps, the place where ego and anima meet, the wedding chapel for that union of complements which creates the total self.

There is a poem by John Peale Bishop which puts the nature of Graves's strategy into clear perspective. The poem "Speaking of Poetry" opens:

> The ceremony must be found
> that will wed Desdemona to the huge Moor

The ceremony 'found' by Robert Graves is all the more effective because it is so often secret; the union happens before the participants are aware of its immanence. John Peale Bishop's poem ends:

> The ceremony must be found
>
> Traditional with all its symbols
> ancient as the metaphors in dreams;
> strange, with never before heard music, continuous
> until the torches deaden at the bedroom door.

It is from this viewpoint that Robert Graves's craftsmanship, his fusing together of Welsh and Anglo-classical prosody, must be seen. He provides us with the ceremonies we need to achieve wholeness and proves to all who have ears to hear that the craft of verse is more than cleverness, but it is a skill and a mystery which must be practiced with incessant labor and vigilance if poetry and vision are not to vanish from the face of the earth.

11

The Craftsmanship of Louis MacNeice

Though Louis MacNeice is most usually regarded as an English poet he was, in fact, an Ulsterman born in Belfast. His paternal grandfather was a Sligo man, and his father's Irish blood was only qualified by his being a quarter Welsh. His mother and her family were from Connemara. Louis MacNeice, however, was educated in England, and, though he returned to Ireland frequently, he spent most of his life out of the country of his birth. William T. McKinnon in his sensible book on MacNeice says of his work: "An almost obsessive theme in the poetry of Louis MacNeice is the search for identity and home" and tells us that MacNeice frequently refers to ancestral influence.

To the conflicts presented by his Irish background and the English public school education, MacNeice added a further complication. Like Wilde, he was trained as a classical scholar and, from his prep school days onward, was obliged to spend a good deal of time in the scansion of classical meters. In his unfinished autobiography published under the title of *The Strings Are False* in 1965, he says that his classical teacher at Sherborne "was the first who thrilled me by reading poetry" and tells how, in teaching the pupils to scan Latin hexameters, "he would stride up and down the room slowly, yards to each stride, intoning "Spon-dee! Spon upon the left foot and Dee upon the right." In his senior year at Marlborough his classical teacher "concentrated with gusto on grammar and syntax." It is not, therefore, particularly surprising to discover that at Oxford "Style remained more important than subject" to him. His interest in style and in prosody persisted. In 1941 he told L. A. G. Strong in a BBC discussion, "Well, I have read a good deal about the theory of metre and I do know how to analyse the various traditional metrical forms, and actually I do know how to practise them if I want to." Nevertheless, he felt that "the point of having rules is that you can break them. The artist needs a limit within which to work and he needs a norm from which to deviate." MacNeice deviated from the "norm" with real brilliance. McKinnon describes his variations as resulting from an "interplay of intuited rhythm and regular metrical pattern" and gives some interesting examples of the way in which MacNeice brought new vitality to an established verse medium or form by utilizing skillful substitution and by deploying elaborate patterns of near-rhyme, assonance, and consonance. That MacNeice was a master practitioner of orthodox metrics hardly needs to be proved. We can point to the regular ballades of 1940, the octosyllabic couplets of "Childs Unhappiness," the terza rima of "Autumn Sequel," and numerous other poems whose deviations from the norm would be totally acceptable to disciples of Saintsbury. What does perhaps need to be examined anew is the way in which he developed methods of verse construction which have little to do with the schemae of classical prosody and yet which, when applied to classical structures, provide the verse with a new bite and brilliance.

It is necessary here to digress a little. McKinnon, and most other writers concerned, if only briefly, with English prosody tend to assume that rhythmical verse must necessarily be based upon metrical structures familiar to students of the classics, and that any variations they exhibit are likely to be (to use McKinnon's word) "intuitive." This may be true in the majority of cases. When one is tackling the work of a Celt, however, one must remember that the Welsh and the Irish utilized devices and structures that only a minority of the English even now understand. It is true that one can detect in the English poetry of the sixteenth and seventeenth centuries a good many forms which appear to derive from the simpler of the twenty-four official Welsh meters. Herrick has examples of a number of these. It is also true that the octosyllabic rhyming couplet was familiar to Welsh poets long before it became a feature of French poetry, whence (it is usually supposed) it came into use in England. If one were to attempt to list the ways in which Welsh and Irish practice differ from English (which means, I suppose, Anglo-French, Anglo-Italian, and neoclassical) practice, at least after the beginning of the fifteenth century, one would have to make a number of basic points. Firstly, although there are many Welsh and Irish meters which use lines with an even number of syllables (the Welsh being particularly addicted to four-syllable and eight-syllable lines), there are quite as many which employ lines of three, five, seven, and nine syllables. Lines of this length rarely occur regularly in English verse, perhaps because of the dominance of the iambic and trochaic tradition. Secondly, in both Welsh and Irish verse, more attention is paid to patterns of assonance, consonance, and alliteration than in English verse. Indeed there are established patterns upon which the verse is based rather than upon stress patterns. Moreover, in both Welsh and Irish verse it is not infrequently laid down that certain words which are crucial to the structure should possess a defined number of syllables. Thus, in the Irish *Rannaigecht Gairit*, a quatrain rhyming *abab*, the end words of the first and third lines are monosyllables and the end words of the second and fourth lines are disyllables, the end word of the third line also rhyming with a word in the middle of the fourth line. The first line has three syllables and the remainder have seven. Moreover, in some Irish and Welsh forms, it is clearly specified that certain rhymes should be "near-rhymes" and not masculine ones. Indeed, the Welsh *Cywydd deuair hirion* and the Irish *Deibide* are both composed in seven-syllable couplets which rhyme a stressed with an unstressed syllable, and the *Englyn proset dalgron* is composed in stanzas of four seven-syllable lines all linked by an assonantal form of near-rhyme; no masculine rhyme is permitted.

Louis MacNeice, though he spent a great deal of his life in England was an Irishman. He described himself in *Letters from Iceland* as "descended from an Irish king—the name MacNeice being derived from Conchubar MacNessa, the villain of the Deirdre saga. (In later years I was told that the derivation was much more probably from Naoise, the hero of the same saga, and since then I have, in defiance of natural history, claimed descent from both of them and in each case by Deirdre.)" MacNeice was very conscious of his Irishry, especially as a boy and young man, and while he did not know Gaelic, it is unlikely that one so sensitive to speech-tunes and so interested in metrics, would not have picked up something of Irish verse in his many visits to the West. Moreover, he was sufficiently interested in Irish poetry to write a book on W. B. Yeats, and in his book, on modern poetry, he suggested that one way to avoid giving the impression of artificiality in formally structured verse was to use "internal rhymes, off-rhymes, bad rhymes, 'para-rhymes'"; he also suggested that one might rhyme stressed with unstressed syllables. In this he may not have been doing more than commend methods he had arrived at "intuitively"; it is, however, not unlikely that his intuition had been assisted by his memories of Irish speech and by his reading of Irish and Welsh literature.

There is no doubt that a number of his poems had their beginnings in technical experimentation. He once told me that he sometimes selected a form and then worked within it until lines began to be "given," finding that the form and meter occupied his conscious mind and allowed intuition full play, even that a meter could "hypnotize" him and permit inspiration to occur. Certainly when one looks at some of his poems it is clear that, while some variations may be chance, many are deliberate. The poem "Aubade" of 1934 shows him approximating the *Deibide* already mentioned, though the line has been lengthened from seven to eleven syllables (to take the average, for the syllable count is 11, 10, 11, 11, 12, 12). In the couplet the lines are linked by assonance ("apple"/"happy"), in the second by true *Deibide* rhyme ("blue"/"to"), and in the third by assonance ("dawn"/"war"). Moreover in the first two couplets, which are dominated by lyrical recollection, we find both alliteration and a touch of that echoing of the final syllables of one line in the first syllables of the next which is part of the formula for *Englyn penfyr* ("apple"/"Or, pl" . . .). Moreover, in the middle of all the first four lines we find an *f* sound which is made prominent by its being accompanied by a number of *f*'s and *v*'s (*v* being, after all, a voiced *f*) surrounding it. The last two lines have a hard *g* as the central consonant. These features may, just possibly, have been created "intuitively," but they certainly form a quite precise pattern.

Aubade

Having bitten on life like a sharp apple
Or, playing it like a fish, been happy,

Having felt with fingers that the sky is blue,
What have we after that to look forward to?

Not the twilight of the gods but a precise dawn
Of sallow and grey bricks, and newsboys crying war.

November 1934

A search through MacNeice's verse reveals that, at one point or another, he has used almost all the rhyming and near-rhyming devices of Welsh and Irish poetry. *Aicill* (or internal) rhyme is frequent, and lines are frequently linked by consonance as in many traditional Irish and Welsh meters. Thus the first verse of "Order to View" (March 1940) reads:

It was a big house, bleak;
Grass on the drive;
We had been there before
But memory, weak in front of
A blistered door, could find
Nothing alive now;
The shrubbery dripped, a crypt
Of leafmould dreams; a tarnished
Arrow over an empty stable
Shifted a little in the tenuous wind.

The end words of the first three lines have *aicill* rhyme with lines four, five, and six. The last consonant of line seven reappears in the penultimate word of line nine, and the last word of line eight is in consonance with the penultimate word of line ten.

The second stanza follows a different scheme, being structured around the repetition of a small number of consonants and vowel sounds. The words thus connected are: unable, wall, loose, loops, bubble, Faltered, dull, bell-pull, pull, ill, world (all using *l*), rise, trees, loose, loops, rose, use, place, supposed, closed (all using sibilants), and wishes, were, wall, one, wish, what, one, was, world (the *w* sound). There are other links: "loose" rhymes, *aicill* fashion, with "loops"; "pull" with "whole"; and "supposed" with "closed"; and the word "pull" appears twice in one line.

And wishes were unable
To rise; on the garden wall
The pear trees had come loose
From rotten loops; one wish,
A rainbow bubble, rose,
Faltered, broke in the dull
Air—What was the use?
The bell-pull would not pull
And the whole place, one might
Have supposed, was deadly ill:
The world was closed.

The third stanza is similarly dominated by patterns of repeating consonants and vowels.

Neither of the two poems we have glanced at are metrically regular, and it may therefore be suspected that MacNeice rarely utilized the same pattern in successive stanzas. The lie to this can be given by glancing at the extraordinarily deft and precise construction of "The Sunlight on the Garden." In each stanza the pattern is the same, with only tiny variants. Line One is of seven syllables and is in catalectic iambic tetrameter; line two varies in length from five to seven syllables but is made up of a choriamb and one to three additional syllables, one of which is always stressed and concludes the line; line three is, again, a seven-syllable catalectic iambic tetrameter; line four is of six syllables and is iambic trimeter with trochaic substitution in the first foot; line five is regular iambic diameter; and line six is of seven syllables (if we read "we are" as approximating to "we're" as the cadence demands and as MacNeice himself read it) and is catalectic iambic tetrameter, with trochaic substitution in the second foot of the last line as in the first line of the whole poem.

This regularity of form is also revealed in the verbal repetitions. The poem begins and ends with what is, to all intent, the same line. Similarly the middle two stanzas each contain the words "The earth compels." In all stanzas the end word of the first line rhymes disyllabically with the first word of the second, and the last word of the third line and the first of the fourth are similarly connected. The end rhyme scheme in each stanza is *abcbba*. The *a* rhyme is disyllabic and the *b* is monosyllabic. The poem utilizes internal consonance and assonance to good effect, and a small group of words are repeated several times during the poem, sometimes within the lines (Epanorthosis) and sometimes at the beginning of them (Epanaphora). These patterns are so organized as to give the poem musical coherence and progression. Thus in the first stanza four of the six lines begin with the sound *w*. In each of the next two stanzas one line begins with the word "We"; in the final stanza the w sound appears only once and unobstrusively in the word "anew." This pattern is reversed in the handling of the word "and." In stanza one, as in all the stanzas, it appears in the middle of one line. It first appears as the opening word of a line in the second stanza; it also begins one line of the third stanza. The final stanza uses it twice as the beginning of a line.

Other patterns emerge as soon as one begins to look for them. The first two lines of each stanza are linked by similar vowel and consonants being used in the first foot of the line, these being *n* in stanza one, *f* (voiced as *v*) in stanza two, *y* in stanza three, and *d* and *n* in stanza four. A consonant in the first foot of the last line of stanzas one, three, and four reappears in the last foot of the line; in stanza two a vowel sound is repeated. This pattern of repeated sounds is given climatic emphasis in the last stanza by consonantal links between the first foot of the third and the fifth line, (But "glad"/"And grate-") and the first foot of the fourth and sixth ("Thund-"/"For sun-"). There are other, less regularly patterned, instances of alliteration, consonance, and assonance in other parts of the poem.

When "The Sunlight on the Garden" is read from this structural point of view it reveals a subtlety, strength, and cunning which places it as one of the most impressive lyrical constructions of the century.

The Sunlight on the Garden

The sunlight on the garden
Hardens and grows cold,
We cannot cage the minute
Within its nets of gold,
When all is told
We cannot beg for pardon.

Our freedom as free lances
Advances towards its end;
The earth compels, upon it
Sonnets and birds descend;
And soon, my friend,
We shall have no time for dances.

The sky was good for flying
Defying the church bells
And every evil iron
Siren and what it tells:
The earth compels,
We are dying, Egypt, dying

And not expecting pardon,
Hardened in heart anew,
But glad to have sat under
Thunder and rain with you,
And grateful too
For sunlight on the garden.
1937

Most of MacNeice's regularly formed lyrics reveal the same group of technical devices. The "Finale" of the sequence from "Out of the Picture" is another instance of the expert handling of Celtic devices. The last word of the first line is linked by consonance to the first foot of the second, and all the lines have internal consonance. The last stanza (in which the devices are used most obviously) may serve as an example:

A kiss, a cuddle,
A crossed cheque,
The trimmed wick burns clear,
Walk among statues in the dark,
The odds are you will break your neck—
Here ends our hoarded oil.

MacNeice is fond of epanorthosis. In "London Rain" he uses it at the end of lines four and six of each stanza, making it appear to be rime riche, though in fact only in one stanza (stanza three) does the second appearance of the word carry a meaning different from the first and thus present the true rime riche phenomenon. In this poem he also uses locution patterns and parallelism, repeating a syntactical construction in adjacent lines, as in

The randy mares of fancy
The stallions of the soul

and

The world is what was given
The world is what we make

Although the rhymes scheme of each stanza could be described as *abcbdb*, two of the *a, c*, and *d* lines are usually linked either by consonance or assonance, and the third is only similar to the others in being a trochaic disyllable. Thus in stanza one we have the *a, c*, and *d* words, "pimples"/"London"/"jungle." In stanzas two and three, they are "violent"/"fancy"/"fences" and "chimneys"/"channel"/"No-God," the last being (exceptionally) a spondee. The pattern is varied in only two of the remaining eight stanzas. Again there is much internal consonance and assonance throughout. The first stanza may serve as an illustration.

The rain of London pimples
The ebony street with white
And the neon-lamps of London
Stain the canals of night
And the park becomes a jungle
In the alchemy of night.

All these poems are orthodox and regular metrically. Sometimes, however, MacNeice abandons meter altogether and structures his work entirely upon the kind of patterning I have been describing. When he does this he relies heavily upon locution patterns and parallelism, epanaphora and epanorthosis. A good example is, of course, "Prayer Before Birth." The fifth verse paragraph runs:

I am not yet born; rehearse me
In the parts I must play and the cues I must take when
  old men lecture me, bureaucrats hector me, mountains
    frown at me, lovers laugh at me, the white
      waves call me to folly and the desert calls
        me to doom and the beggar refuses
          my gift and my children curse me.

It does not require much acuteness of observation to see the internal rhyming, the consonance, the assonance, and the parallelism. The whole poem is, of course, built up on incantatory repetition. Other obvious instances of this are "Visitations I" and "VI," "Bagpipe Music" (which, however, is obtrusively and deftly metrical), "Jericho," "Invocation," and "Chateau Jackson," which is based upon "The House that Jack Built" but improves the original with many internal rhymes and consonantal patterns. The first part of the poem runs:

CHATEAU JACKSON

Where is the Jack that built the house
That housed the folk that tilled the field
That filled the bags that brimmed the mill
That ground the flour that browned the bread
That fed the serfs that scrubbed the floors
That wore the mats that kissed the feet
That bore the bums that raised the heads

That raised the eyes that eyed the glass
That sold the pass that linked the lands
That sink the sands that told the time
That stopped the clock that guards the shelf
That shrines the frame that lacks the face
That mocked the man that sired the Jack
That chanced the arm that bought the farm
That caught the wind that skinned the flocks
That raised the rocks that sunk the ship
That rode the tide that washed the bank
That grew the flowers that brewed the red
That stained the page that drowned the loan
That built the house that Jack built?

The sheer dexterity and brilliance of this poem, and its air of spontaneity, should not blind us to the tight patterns of its structure, any more than the ease and masterly poise of "Autumn Journal" should prevent us from noticing the extraordinary richness of its music and the way in which almost every known device of versecraft if brought in to support and control the structure. In the twenty-fourth canto, for example, we find a strong and effective use of epanaphora and consonance:

Sleep, my fancies and my wishes,
    Sleep a little and wake strong,
The same but different and take my blessing—
    A cradle-song,
And sleep, my various and conflicting
    Selves I have so long endured,
Sleep in Asclepius' temple
    And wake cured.

In other parts of the poem, we find the incidental use of internal rhyme and are dazzled by the cunning of such lines as "Still alive even if forbidden, hidden"—in which every word in the line chimes with another one, and "Come over, they said, into Macedonia and help us." This line is particularly interesting, for it is a cunningly rearranged quotation from the Bible, Acts 16 verse 9 reads:

And a vision appeared to Paul in the night; There stood a man of Macedonia, and prayed him, saying, Come over into Macedonia, and help us.

MacNeice's tiny amendment has ensured that the main consonants and vowels of the first half of the line are repeated in the second half of the same line in the same order ("come"/"Mac"—"over"/"onia"—"said"/ "help"). This particular device, which in Welsh would be regarded as a form of *cynghanedd*, is not infrequent in MacNeice's longer and more discursive poems, though it is never permitted to obtrude except when it is used to point up a joke or contribute to helter-skelter levity. It is, indeed, often unnoticeable, art concealing art, as perhaps in the lines

> We wrote compositions in Greek which they said was a lesson
> In logic and good for the brain

in which a hard *c* is followed by a hard *g* in each line, and the last foot of the first line is linked to the first of the second by consonance in *l*.

It may be, as McKinnon suggests, that MacNeice contrived these effects intuitively rather than with full awareness of what he was doing, but it seems unlikely. There are many effects which might have been the result of simply seeking a musical language, but there are many others which are so schematically organized as to make accident improbable. Clearly, either MacNeice managed to arrive at the same conclusions about verse structure as the early Welsh and Irish poets, or he deliberately studied and learned from them. It is true, of course, that the Welsh and Irish poets were not alone in employing the devices I have uncovered; many of them can also be found in the classical literature of which MacNeice was a scholar. Nevertheless, I am persuaded that MacNeice, conscious and proud of his Irish ancestry from an early age and a man clearly and admittedly fascinated by technique, could not but have dipped into Celtic prosody. He found there principles of structure which he then used both together with, and apart from, the classical meters he knew so well.

MacNeice brought to English verse a dexterous verbal music which has received much less attention than the more obvious, and sometimes ostentatious, "mouth music" of his friend Dylan Thomas who, though not a Welsh speaker, also clearly learned from traditional Welsh forms. MacNeice, in his versecraft, brought together the English and the Celtic traditions, as did Yeats in some of his later poems. He was, however, stylistically a more various poet than Yeats; he was, indeed, in his enthusiasm for technique, closer to the multiskilled Pound who also brought into English verse devices and effects learned from other tongues and centuries. Now, a quarter of a century after his death, it is high time for

Louis MacNeice to be recognized as one of the master craftsmen in our poetry, and for his poems to be established as essential reading for any who care to study or to practice the intricacies of English and Anglo-Celtic verse.

12

The Poetry of Thomas Kinsella

Thomas Kinsella was born in Dublin in 1928. He remained a Dubliner until 1965 when he left the Irish Civil Service and took up a position in the University of Southern Illinois, later moving to Temple University. He now divides his time almost equally between Ireland and the United States. From the very first his central themes have been those of divided man plagued by the contrary drives of sense and soul, troubled by dichotomy, and his style has reflected this tension and this conflict throughout.

Kinsella's earliest poems were published in pamphlet form by the Dolmen Press, and the first two of these have never been reprinted. *The Starlit Eye* (1952) consists of a single poem of fifty-one lines. It is a meditative poem in which the speaker contemplates the sea at night while lying on the beach of Dublin Bay with a girl. Even in this early and suppressed poem, characteristics of Kinsella's mature style are foreshadowed. The divided nature of the human creature is presented by means of a diction which neatly combines the self-regarding niceties of intellection with the broadly affective and extroverted cadences of colloquial ease. Thus he perceives that

> That spare and rigid frame of stars
> And the minute particulars
> Of this girl's patient, cool intent
> Are not at one, and scarcely meant
> To occupy me both together.

The sophisticated tone of the first line of this stanza contrasts deliberately with the flat, almost bathetic, tone of the last line. This consideration of the divided nature of the experiences leads, predictably, by way of an almost Donnian argument, to the lover yielding to the girl. The silence of the scene replies to the invitation to love,

> insinuating: why imply
> That there is a dichotomy?
> Earthly strand and abstract ocean
> Mingle both in soft commotion

Consequently, in the agreement to love, the world becomes unity once more:

> Suddenly she beside me seems
> The meeting place of various streams
> converging in a placid mirror
> That reflects my simple error.

Orion, the hunter, has watched the whole proceeding and provides a final comment:

> Night grows around our satisfaction
> Till we tire. In quiet reaction,
> Standing apart on the sands, in soft
> Mood we talk and look aloft
> At glittering gravel in the sky
> To see Orion striding by
> Suspended handsome, broad and high.

This early and admittedly immature poem established several of Kinsella's main concerns. The theme of a world or of a human creature, divided against itself and seeking unity by way of some overmastering experience or belief, is pervasive in Kinsella's work. As time goes on, the divisions become more severe, and the unification more difficult and perhaps more temporary. Moreover, just as the lovemaking in "The Starlit Eye" is seen as valuable primarily for its clarification of the speaker, so the later poems, whether adopting the first person stance or not, tend towards this implication of the unconquerably self-regarding solitude of the individual creature.

Kinsella's second pamphlet, *Three Legendary Sonnets*, appeared in December, 1952, and is notable more for its attempt to intensify the vision of life's tensions than for its poetic success. Here are references to "dreams disordered," to the shrieking of nerves, to "Orestes, image-throttled," together with statements of conflict resolved in some miraculous event. Kinsella sees, in these poems, "that from burned bodies staked at creation's verges/The unplanned Phoenix constantly emerges."

The Phoenix of unification or resolution is always unplanned. In Kinsella's third pamphlet, *Per Imaginem* (1953), which was published in a private edition of twenty-five copies for presentation at a friend's wedding, love is considered "a difficult, scrupulous art," and its "course of argument" must lead to a point when "word and image are gone." At this point, "Out of a certain silence it may bring/The softer dove or a skylit, glittering wing." The whole poem, dwelling gracefully upon romantic images, is a series of variations and developments of this theme. There is something Spenserian about its "lapping airs and graces," and yet there is no actual echo of Spenser. "Per Imaginem" is the first of a number of poems in which Kinsella, while preserving his individuality, works within the milieu of an older tradition and allows its decorum to qualify his sensibility. This is not, perhaps, surprising in a poet who has devoted much time to the translation of medieval Irish stories and poems, but it is indicative of the way in which Kinsella approaches the past. Many of his later poems adopt the stanzas of earlier traditions and play this element of pastiche against the pressures of the present. The human creature is divided also by his perception of time, by his understanding being always and only the understanding of a particular time and place.

Kinsella's fourth pamphlet, *Death of a Queen*, appeared in April 1956 and was followed in June of the same year by the appearance of his first book, *Poems*, which was issued in a limited edition of 250 copies. *Poems* includes, of the earlier pamphlet material, only "Per Imaginem," which is given pride of place at the beginning of the collection. It does, indeed, act as a summary of the book's main themes, for *Poems* is largely concerned with love.

It is in *Poems* that the theme of division and unity begins to take on the complexities which later attend all its reappearances in Kinsella's work. "First Light," for example, presents a vision of the visitation of some goddess by night, her "flocks flickering in darkness" as "omens hatched in the marshes." At this visitation "all manner of birds/ Exploded across the estuary" and the whole world of nature was troubled. The poet, however, finally discovers that "For reply, I find I am left/With an unanswerable dawn upon my hands."

Thus the response to vision is as difficult to make as the conflict preceding the vision was difficult to comprehend. Love, or the visit of the Muse, may bring resolution of conflict, but it also breeds further disturbance. In "Soft, To Your Places" the girl tells the animals that their "legendary duty" is to be "Lucky for my love and me," and decides "that all's/ A fiction that is heard of love's difficulty." "Beauty," she says confidently, is "an easy thing." Her less confident lover, however, sees that beauty is threatened by time, and therefore "the heart's calling is but to go blinded and diffident." It is this perception of the heart's limitations, however, that causes the lover to love. He states finally that he kisses because of, not in spite of, the heart's mortality.

This is not a notable philosophical proposition, but it is the first of Kinsella's poems in which the acceptance of man's mortality and imperfect understanding is seen as a necessary attribute, and part cause of human endeavor. In "Dusk Music" the lover discusses again this limitation upon human affairs. He confesses that

> under this hygienic ceiling
> Where my love lies down for healing
> Tiny terrors grow,
> Reflected in a look, revealing
> That her care is spent concealing
> What, perhaps, I know:
>
> The ever-present crack in time
> Forever sundering the lime-
> Paths and the fragrant fountains,
> Photographed last summer, from
> The unknown memory we climb
> To find in this year's mountains.
>
> 'Ended and done with' never ceases.
> Constantly the heart releases
> Wild geese to the past

In "Ulysses" the anguish of mortality is expressed by way of the tormented ghosts of the dead heroes recalling their passions, and in both "An Ancient Ballet" and "Who Is My Proper Dark," the Muse figure is again related to the speaker's needs and limitations.

In the first of these, "An Ancient Ballet," the moon shines in upon the speaker, transfiguring his room:

> She draws our gazes thronging
> Into the figured void
> Her light feet deck, where we forget
> We know her power is our longing
>
> And I think that her stare discovers
> Only what we pretend,
> That the moon is lovely, and will descend
> Through the night's honest endeavours.

The room, as a consequence of this visitation, "Disengaged . . . its serious dancers from/ Their stations and their time." This dancing "laid waste" the speaker's pillow with his "tears" and "joy."

> O that mastering huge sky-
> Stare, downstreaming, witnessed!
>
> All about her lit as though
> Blood rang, Marvels toiled.
> Close at heart there sailed
> A stately vast plateau . . .

Rapt by this vision, the speaker "died / The light death," and descended into

> the salt still water
> Where quietly, for miles,
> Time lowers its twinkling shells
> To a freighted bed, to a travelled floor.
>
> Of time, of longing. Their recorder sleeps
> Sleeps and they retire
> In the deep reaches of the night
> The ticking stars keep order.

The consequence of the moon-goddess's visitation is thus the temporary solution of the problems of mortality and desire. Nevertheless, it must be recognized that the speaker thinks the moon's stare "discovers/ Only what we pretend." The visitation is, perhaps, a manifestation of the speaker's longing for such a visitation to occur.

"Who Is My Proper Art" is less lyrical, a much more forceful vision. The Muse figure, moreover, is regarded with fear as well as adoration. The poem opens: "Much as calamities do, she took/ Her station near the heart . . ." The vision develops in terms of the two white horses which draw her chariot. These horses are Pegasus-like:

> They galloped the years and grew wing-
>   Tipped, brighter, supple—soaring,
> Much as calamities do, straight
> Into the shape of the heart-beat,
>   Wide-nostrilled, terrifying,
> And pastured in our sight. That latest
> Look she drew from the world's sweetest
>   Well, that scene lying
> Imagery for her, I will make
> Fix its true state for her sake
>   Into my clearer, blinder
> Eyes. Who is my proper art,
> Who rested here her soaring heart,
>   The fashioner, the finder.

The language here is wrenched and tricksy, so that the reader is aware of multiple possibilities in each statement. The word "lying" is given ambiguity by being contrasted with "true" in the following line. The last sentence is neither statement nor question, but both. The "Who" is never named. It is only "She." Earlier in the poem there is a riddling reference to "three Springs ago" and to the horses being, at that time, unbroken to double harness. This touch of the specific adds conviction to the poem's tone without lessening its total dependence upon plurivalent symbolism. The sentences are often complex and eventful in this poem, and frequently appear to change direction. Thus the speaker states:

>   I kissed
>   The effort in her wide
> Eyes and crowned the breasts where I
> Find order and sanguinity
>   Beyond hope's finest-drawn

Proposals, jittering as those
Her white horses made when seiz-
    Ing onto their first dawn
With foals' hooves.

Here the stanza changes directions at the word "jittering"; what appears, syntactically, to be a subordinate statement attached to the word "proposals" becomes, because of the physical power of its imagery, a new departure. Moreover, the sentence which begins by carrying the argument forward, ends by referring us back to the image of the horses which was introduced earlier. Thus the poem developes a muscular restlessness, a dynamic complexity that supports the effortful rhetoric of its imagery by an athletic syntax.

It is the final poem in the book which sums up much of the conflict perceived here. Called "A Shout After Hard Work," it is a vigorous angry statement of the "bloody labour" involved in making poems, and it ends with the perhaps over-trenchant couplet: "I hack these words across the belly of the earth:/ IMMACULATE PERCEPTIONS NO IMMACULATE BIRTH." It is the conflict between the desire for "immaculate perception" and the recognition of the far from immaculate nature of the human creature which provides much of the dramatic excitement in Kinsella's work. This conflict is presented by means of a mixed diction in which echoes of nineteenth-century romanticism or Renaissance decorum are juxtaposed against thrusting colloquialism and laconic understatement. The dialogue of heart and mind which troubled Yeats, and, earlier, Donne and the metaphysicals, is also expressed by juxtaposing images which must be accepted as affective truth against adjectives whose sophisticated nicety demands that they be scrutinized with almost clinical detachment. One might say that the theme of human love which dominates Kinsella's poetry up to 1956 provides an overture, or prologue, to the more complex work to follow. One might also suggest that the persona of the self-regarding, heart-searching lover is a rough sketch for the persona which gradually emerges in the later books.

Another September, the first book of Kinsella's to be published in an unlimited edition, appeared in 1958 and was a choice of the Poetry Book Society. It included "Death of a Queen," nine of the thirteen poems appearing in *Poems*, and nineteen new poems. "Per Imaginem," curiously, was not included. The book opens with "Death of a Queen." This poem introduces the theme of despair, which remains one of Kinsella's central subjects. The Queen, faced suddenly with the recognition of her own mortality, "could not/ Breathe without wondering/ What it would be like to end." Her despair increases throughout the poem. Reality undermines her. Counsellors and Music result only in angering her. Memories make her mourn. In the very depths of despair, however, she faces death. Proud, she walks "with the step of a goddess" and with "hypocritical" courage (because her regal bearing is a pose) forms Death into the shape of a lover. In his eyes she sees two figures, "a knight and a queen," images of herself and her desire. "Her death and her lover" are now "utterly mated." This somewhat allegorical poem could appear the merest medievalism, were it not for the last stanza, which in some ways could stand as a prologue to the whole collection:

> Yet it is not so much
> For disintegration of a lover or a kingdom
> Or burning of oak—and bronze leaved
> Capitals that a queen grieves
> But that life, late or soon,
> Suddenly becomes, on the face, a jaded rouge.

The heroic tone and vocubulary of "Death of a Queen," its carefully sophisticated diction, its slow and decorous thematic development—these are all typical of one aspect of Kinsella's work. He frequently adopts a "high serious" style as his main mode of communication, and then he proceeds to highlight or undermine it with vulgar elements and to give it intellectual toughness by means of sophisticated abstraction or exquisitely pedantic syntax.

Thus in "Test Case," the second poem in the book, we have a portrait of the Hero considered almost as a laboratory specimen. The opening, because of its mixed diction, is ironic in tone:

> Readier than flags rippling in the sun
> To turn tragic in elegiac weathers,
> More striking, forked and longer than lightening,
> Is the heroic agenda, full of frightening
> Things to kill or love, or level down—
> A man's life, magnified with monumental bothers.

Here the epic tone is maintained by references to "flags" and to "lightning" and by the use of such words as "tragic," "heroic," "Magnified," and "monumental." Ironic distancing is achieved by the self-conscious urbanity of "elegiac" and "agenda," and it is given an added wryness by the sudden drop into the commonplace on such words as "frightening," "things," and the final bathetic "bothers." Thus the voice of the poem could be described as a trio; one might suggest, perhaps frivolously and with wanton exaggeration, that the trio consists of the Bard (B.1), the Bookman (B.2) and the Bourgeois (B.3). The second stanza might be split up between the voices thus:

B.1 Naked save for the skin of a [B.2] preferably
B.1 Ferocious beast, [B.3] pulling down roofs
B.2 Seriously to demonstrate some fact,
B.3 His queer [B.2] quality is noticed—direct
  Approach, statuesque faith—clearly he
  Is unforgettable. [B.1] Events will circle him with graves.

From this mingled speech one voice emerges clearly to take over the next stanza. It is the voice of the Bookman, the observer, the commentator:

Curious to discover how far in given
Conditions a human attribute
May be goaded, what ultimate in grief
Can be tolerated for a belief,
What is utter love, how forgiving
Is degradation, what justice would rather die than commit.

The last line has a touch of the Bourgeois, the commonplace prolixity of casual speech about it, but only a touch. The next stanza is again in several voices, though here the Bard dominates, and in the last syllable it is the Bard who concludes the poem, though the intellectual accuracy of the final grandiose image makes one also hear the tone of the Bookman:

His native village, vaguely honoured
And confused by stories newly arriving,
Would have a little of minor value to add
—Anecdotes to charm students of his mad
Bleeding retreat to a stoic beloved,
The famous towering Death already avalanching.

"Test Case" is appropriately named in more than one respect, for, more clearly than many of the poems in *Another September*, it lays bare the diction strategy which is at the heart of Kinsella's method. Moreover, its diction reflects the poem's own ambivalence about its subject matter, and in setting the High Poetic against the Commonplace, the Aristocratic against the Vulgar, or—to use a Yeatsian image—the Noble against the Beggarman, it presents the conflict inherent in the poet's awareness of his role in our time. Kinsella has, however, added the qualifying, meditating voice of the observer, the cool recorder, the wielder of adverbs, the shrewd ironist, the clinician, so that there is also a tension between the poem's claims upon emotional involvement and its claim upon the scrutinizing intelligence.

Once this diction is perceived it becomes easy to read Kinsella with the proper kind of attention. Sometimes the Bard takes over almost completely and betrays a fondness for images of violence and distortion as well as hectic and highly colored adjectives. Thus in "The Travelling Companion," we have "blind turmoil," "snarling," "knotted," and "brightening muscles"; and in "Night Songs" there are "crippled leopard," "yellow light," and "golden skin." Sometimes the Bookman controls the poem, only allowing the Bard to insist upon the occasional grandiose adjective or heroic image, without allowing him to take over the cadences of the lines. The Bourgeois is allowed, on occasion, to begin or to conclude a poem, but never speaks unattended.

I have, of course, grossly simplified the nature of the mixed diction in Kinsella's work, and my account must make it appear as if the poems lack subtlety. This is far from the case. There are infinite gradations of tone between the three *B*'s I have mentioned, and, if one were to elaborate my formula in order to make it applicable to all poems, one would be obliged to create other personae. The ménage à trois, one might say, produces offspring of a richly varied inheritance, always identifiable as part of the household, but only generally so. Take, for example, the opening lines of "The Monk":

He tramped in the sliding light
Of a late February day
Between hedges stiff with the wind.
His boots trod stone and clay.
His blown habit crouched
In the wet daylight's decay.
A clotted spade over his shoulder
Slanted into the sky.

Here the syntax is simple, and the effect is that of a very straightforward speech being enriched by qualification from a speaker concerned with sensual accuracy, a sort of sensual Bookman standing behind the shoulder of our Bourgeois anecdotalist. Thus "sliding," "stiff," "blown," "wet," "clotted," and "slanted" are all intensely particular and physical, as well as being intellectually surprising. How can a hedge be "stiff with the wind"? How can any sort of light be "wet"? How can any light be thought of as "sliding"? The emphatic nature of these words reminds us of the grandiose Bard, but their intellectual accuracy, their shrewdness of observation, reminds us of the Bookman. The other voice seems simply a norm. It is not vulgar; it is not prolix or overcasual. If we abstract from the poem what is most obviously in this speaker's voice, we get a series of bold statements thus: He tramped in the light of a late February day between hedges. (He) trod stone and clay, his habit blown (out by the wind), a spade over his shoulder. This exercise reveals that some of the intensifying is done by compression; "blown habit,"—partly because of the speed with which the total image is conveyed and partly because the secondary associations of the word "habit" emerge more easily when the word is not limited in its connotations by the easy contextual qualifications or ordinary conversation—is a much more intense image than that given in the prose version above.

My contention is that, in *Another September*, Kinsella uses mixed diction. He organizes devices of ellipsis, compression, and apposition in order to provide and maintain the diction tension and, consequently, the enriching ambivalence of his poetry.

This ambivalence is not, however, a superficial device but an essential part of the book's vision. *Another September* was originally called *Baggot Street Deserta* after the poem of that name which it contains, and this poem reveals much of what we might call the mastering persona in Kinsella's work. It opens with a summary crypto-sentence which, lacking a verb and therefore a direction, presents a state of being, an attitude, with casual brusqueness:

Lulled, at silence, the spent attack.
The will to work is laid aside.
The breaking cry, the strain of the rack,
Yield, are at peace. The window is wide
On a crawling arch of stars, and the night
Reacts faintly to the mathematic
Passion of a cello suite
Plotting the quiet of my attic.

The meditation which follows is one haunted by ambiguity and unresolved conflicts. The speaker refers to his "half-buried longing," his "half-serious anger," and his "rueful laugh." He announces that "We fly into our risk, the spurious," and thereafter attempts to relate fantasy to reality and to perceive and grasp some kind of unity. The speaker sees himself as both inflicting and enduring:

> Tedium, intracordal hurt,
> The sting of memory's quick, the drear
> Uprooting, burying, prising apart
> Of loves a strident adolescent
> Spent in doubt and vanity.

He then adds: "All fuel a single stream, impassioned/ Now with obsessed honesty,/ A tugging scruple." It is this "obsessed honesty," this "tugging scruple," which accounts for the toughness of Kinsella's poems and also, perhaps, for his main theme of man divided. This theme appears in almost all the poems in *Another September* and is equally central to Kinsella's pamphlet of 1960, *Moralities*.

Moralities, even by its title, suggests Kinsella's obsession with morality and his nostalgia for the certainties of the past, the simplicities, even, of medieval faith. Yet, as always in Kinsella, the nostalgia is qualified by skepticism; the impulse of the heart is countered by the "tugging scruple." Thus it is only when heart and conscience, desire and scruple, are at one that Kinsella can celebrate the stature of man without hesitation or challenge. The morality of these short poems is, one might say, traditional. The beer drinkers are dismissed as "a puff of smoke"; reason and drunkenness are opposed melodramatically as satyr and nymph; the rump of the devil is inscribed: "Do good./Some care and a simple faith will get you on." Violence obtrudes in diction and theme. Death and the fear of death are everywhere. Thus *Moralities* adopts a severe, a rigorous stance, and emphasizes yet again the divided nature of fallen man.

Kinsella's next book was *Poems and Translations*, published by the Atheneum Press in New York in 1961. This, in effect, was a volume of selected poems and need not detain us here. The next collection, *Downstream*, published in 1962 by the Dolmen Press, reveals new developments.

The book is prefaced by an untitled forty-two line prologue in rhyming couplets which, in its procedures, is not dissimilar to "Baggot

Street Deserta." Here the speaker comments upon his bourgeois way of life, the smug ordinariness of his suburban existence, and describes the way in which it is occasionally disturbed by the demands of poetry. The third verse paragraph begins with what is surely an allusion to Yeats's "The Circus Animals' Desertion" and continues with the presentation of figures strongly reminiscent of those in medieval allegory or, perhaps, in the Dance of Death:

> And so my bored menagerie
> Once more emerges: Energy,
> Blinking, only half awake,
> Gives its tiny frame a shake;
> Fouling itself, a giantess,
> The bloodshot bulk of Laziness
> Obscures the vision; Discipline
> Limps after them with jutting chin,
> Bleeding badly from the calf:
> Old Jaws-of-Death gives laugh for laugh
> With Error as they amble past,
> And there as usual, lying past,
> Helped along by blind Routine,
> Futility flogs a tambourine . . .

The first section of *Downstream* is devoted to portraiture. "The Laundress" is a simple description of a pregnant woman at the house door in Flanders. Its only gloomy note is that provided by the phrase "harrowed Flanders." The poem as a whole asserts the possibility of calm, human fruition in a war-torn world. The last verse hints at metaphysical ambiguities with its reference to the "winds of Heaven" and their winnowing, but it does no more than hint. "Wedding Morning," however, after describing the walk from the church after the ceremony, concludes more ominously: "Down the bright gravel stroll the families/ With Blood, the trader, profiting in their peace." "A Portrait of the Engineer" presents the speaker's "hatred" for "the flesh his engines ate." "Charlie," describing an ape at the zoo, implies derision of pontificating authority and self-satisfaction. "Scylla and Charybdis" opposes the fruitmonger's dream of the orange-rich South to the fishmonger's yearning for bracken and hill streams, ending with a presentation of the speaker as one having a third, unstated viewpoint. "Carol" balances imagery of harvest against that of waste and withering. "Dick King" is in two parts: The first is contemplative, slow-moving, colloquial; the second is in ballad form. Together they give an antiphonal view of the poem's subject. From these poems one can see that Kinsella's sense of divided man has now become more explicitly part of his subject matter. The individual is divided against himself; the world is ruled by dichotomies.

These dichotomies are presented at greater length in the third section of the book (the second being devoted to *Moralities*). The most important poems here are "Old Harry," "A Country Walk," and "Downstream." "Old Harry" conceals its subject matter in a turmoil of symbolism and sensual imagery. It is not about the Devil, but about the decision to drop the atomic bomb and the personality of the man who took that decision. Nevertheless, in the first section, where "Death states the theme," we are given a much broader subject:

> "Master Love," my grim instructor assured me,
> "Moved already in the criminal darkness
> Before our dust was chosen or choice began,
>
> Devising, for spirits that would not crumple
> At a touch, a flesh of thirst and pain, a blood
> Sped onward by self-torment and by desire."

God, in other words, and simplifying somewhat, "chastizeth those whom he loveth." The innocent spirit "In accurate pursuit of the ideal," we are told, is given the fate that his "flesh" shall proceed to its "harmonious end." The guilty, however, have another fate: "The spirit that invites/ The criminal darkness to the human womb/ Repays with flesh and blood." This viewpoint is likely to lead to a belief that the suffering of the flesh is always the result of guilt, although this is not strictly a logical deduction from the premise. As the poem proceeds we are given a portrait of a war leader who is himself slowly decaying.

In the third section we find biblical references: "Then the notorious cities of the plain,/ Groves of the temporal, lost their flesh and blood,/ Tiles, leaves, wild cries, stripped away by gales of light." The atomic transformation of the cities is described with Shelleyan richness:

> Anthropophagi moaned in the buckling cloud,
> Amazons and chimaerae, leaving the world.
> Where once the cities of wickedness had stood

An eye socket with nerves and ducts smouldering,
A mouth with torn vulva and with no tongue,
Moistened like two wells the plain's enameled face.

The wood, through which old Harry, contemplating and remembering, now walks is confused, terrified, "a nest of twittering naked animals." Old Harry is only momentarily disturbed by a chill breath of wind. He turns for home, and the poem ends with a reflection upon mortality:

Soon, with God's goodness, the nettle turns to dust,
Bees seek their clustered sleep, the loam packs tighter
And cracked boughs deliver up their final bronze.

Do not let this allay your soft suspicion,
Rightly terrified sentinels of the wood
In certain cases death is a criticism.

The moral concern of the poem is revealed by the many references to abstract virtues—to wisdom, reason, and good. Nevertheless, the poem remains ambiguous. Are we to believe that Hiroshima and Nagasaki were the equivalents of Sodom and Gomorrah? Are we therefore to see Old Harry as a God figure, or as that Satan who, in obedience to God, plagued Job? The description of Old Harry as "shaggy, gasping," and of his eyes hidden behind spectacles as "two sightless coins" does not endear him to us. Yet he is described also as "Jaw jutting with power for good." Is this sarcasm or not?

The difficulties present in the second section of this poem are solved only if we return to the first section and realize that Death's statement of the theme enunciates a principle which "The Twilight of Old Harry" illustrates: Our spiritual health and sickness are embodied in the health and sickness of the flesh, and our moral confusions produce confusions of the body and of the universe. The physical twilight of Old Harry is also a moral twilight. Nevertheless, even while intellectually the poem presents a coherent system of ideas, the imagery of confusion is so powerful as to leave the reader more aware of disorder than of order.

"A Country Walk" is also concerned with the appearance of disorder. The speaker wanders through the countryside, observing and recalling passion, tumult, confusion, pettiness, and debris. He observes the flux: "grimly the flood divided where it swept/ An endless debris through the failing dusk/ Under the thudding span beneath my feet." The final statement is the speaker's artistic response to this awareness and to his memory of his encounters with life. He ends his poem: "The waters hurtle through the flooded night."

"Downstream" takes up this flood image and extends it. The first version, published in the book of that title, was followed in 1964 by the publication of a revised version in the *Massachusetts Review*. The first version is 166 lines long and the second 83. The poetic strategy of both versions is the same. The narrator and an unnamed friend set out, in the sunset, on a sail downstream. In the process the narrator reflects upon the scene before him and upon the war-torn past. He also recollects the corpse of one particular man who died in the bushes on the river bank. In the first version this last matter is of less importance thant the references to Durrow, and to the medieval and even more remote past of Ireland and Europe. The second version, however, leaves out the medieval references almost completely and places the image of the dead man at the very center of the poem's concerns. The second version is, thus, much more cohesive and dramatic than the first. Moreover, the extremely lush, Tennysonian vocabulary of "Downstream I" has been much simplified for "Downstream II," largely by omitting much beautiful but directionless description.

These discarded passages are not without interest, and imply a good deal about Kinsella's poetic attitudes. "Downstream I" opens with a line in which the almost decadent romanticism of the imagery is only partly qualified by the intrusion of abstraction: "The West a fiery complex, the East a pearl,/ We gave our frail skiff to the hungry stream,/ Ruffling the waters." The adjectival richness and romantic orthodoxy here have been noted by other commentators upon Kinsella. Certainly he seems in "Downstream I" unable to avoid attaching an adjective to every noun; the adjectives are often witty, semi-paradoxical, and extremely sensual, but as a result we find ourselves interested only in a sequence of superb effects rather than in the development of a theme. We note, and are delighted by such phrases as "the mirrored heavens' liquid casque," "the tinkling blades," "a spinal cry/ Of distant plover," "A swan in muffled stress," "ploughing wings," and "silken kings/ Luminous with crisis," and yet we are also disturbed by the implications of this aesthetic. It is as if Kinsella had adopted a Keatsian conviction that every rift should be loaded with ore. The result is what might be termed Kinsella's "Endymion," a richly fraught poem whose detail obscures its structure and whose sensationalism of language implies a hedonism at variance with the philosophical stance of the whole poem.

This last statement, however, demands more examination. Is this hedonism really at variance with the poem's "message"? In part, the language *is* the poem's message. It portrays a yearning for romantic nebulosities, for vast dream-ridden generalizations, for the blurred comfort of rapt entrancements, which is set against the harsh remembrance and contemplation of man's crudity and the nastiness of death. Unfortunately, however, the language of those passages devoted to the harsher realities is as epithet-cluttered and as romantic as those devoted to ideal mystery:

Then the cold of hell,

A limb-lightness, a terror in the glands,
Pierced again as when that story first
Froze my blood: the soil of other lands

Drank lives that summer with a body thirst
While nerveless by the European pit
—Ourselves through seven hundred years accurst—

We gazed on barren earth obscurely lit
By tall chimneys flickering in their pall,
The haunt of swinish men—each day a spit

That, turning, sweated war, each night a fall
Back to the evil dream where rodents ply,
Man-rumped, sow-headed, busy with whip and maul

Among nude herds of the damned.

This intensity, therefore, is of the same kind as that devoted to "the heavens' bright continuum," "the birth of soul," and "ancient Durrow." In fact, "Downstream I" emerges as a consistently gothic poem—its intensities are those of Horace Walpole, Monk Lewis, and Charles Robert Maturin. Its medievalism is that of the romantics, and its presentation of Hell is as firmly in the romantic-gothic tradition as *The City of Dreadful Night*, which is similarly prolix and similarly grandiose in generalization and in the evocation of vague beauty and indefinite horror.

When we turn from "Downstream I" to "Downstream II," however, the picture alters. Though "Downstream II" is rather a cut-down version than a rewriting of its predecessor and includes many of the gothic passages (including the one above), the poem's concentration upon one central image gives it greater coherence and enables the philosophical comments to achieve greater prominence and clarity.

Thus the imagination of the "formal drift of the dead/ Stretched calm as effigies on velvet dust," which follows immediately the hell passage I have already quoted, is itself followed immediately by the sick recognition that one must face not general but particular mortality. The story of the dead man on the river bank who "left his shell/ Collapsed, half-eaten like a rotted thrush's/ To frighten stumbling children" which led to the contemplation of the "cold of hell," returns to thrust

> Pungent horror and an actual mess
> Into my very face, and taste I must!
>
> Then hungry joy and sickening distress
> Met in union by the brimming flood
> And Night devoured a hopeless loneliness

This loneliness remains as the boat sails on "into a pit of night" to be confronted with a "soul of white with darkness for a nest" (the "Swan" of "Downstream I") and to be comforted by a vision of "The slow, downstreaming dead" of Heaven. The poem ends shortly after this vision with the boat coming up against

> A barrier of rock that turned and bared
> A varied barrenness as toward its base
> We glided—blotting heaven as it towered—
>
> Searching the darkness for a landing place.

Thus "Downstream II," taking the stream as an image of life's flow, faces mortality and balances a vision of earthy hell against supernatural heaven, leaving us with the picture of man seeking a "landing place." The gothic elements are still present but disciplined into a pattern. The romanticism remains but is qualified by a more rigorous and disciplined structure. "Downstream II," in fact, stands out as one of Kinsella's most important single poems, and it establishes many of the themes that are central to his work of the time.

The fourth section of the collection *Downstream* contains only five poems. Four of these are directly concerned with mortality and express their concern with that mixture of pedantry, colloquial ease, and (occasionally antique) romanticism with which we are now familiar. "Chrysalides" describes youth and its "last free summer" in a pleasing and vivid manner, but it concludes with a statement of youth's insensitivity to "the unique succession of our youthful midnights" as well as to "lasting horror: a wedding flight of ants/ Spawning to its death, a mute perspiration/ Glistening like drops of copper, agonised, in out path." "String-Puppets" describes, with graphic and obsessive intensity, a dying man, heroic in his contorted solitude, the figure of Death outside upon the lawn. This is, again, a gothic vision, and one M. R. James would have enjoyed. "Brothers" describes a man and a dog upon the heights of an island. The eager, storm-whipped body of the dog suddenly forces the speaker to see the animal as if he were made of glass:

> A model of sinews, fragile tissue and channelled blood,
> Of living translucencies crimson in the driving gale,
> To horrify and instruct. In the spasm of Sentience
> Beast and man are made one.

The phrase "spasm of Sentience" is Websterian in its bitterness, and in its mockery of the flesh's importance and the significance of its tyrannical appetites. And yet it is in this "spasm" that beast and man are at one. Thus the natural and the human world achieve common understanding in appetite and are (it is implied) separated by reason. Should we then praise or condemn that "spasm of Sentience"? Typically, the moral concern leads to no moral decision. The confrontation is established, but it is not resolved. "The Force of Eloquence" is little more than a powerful perception of an allegorical portrait of rhetoric enslaving humanity. It does, however, imply that, to the poet, his mastery of language is both a gift and a threat. Again the divided nature of all things is established. "Mirror in February," one of Kinsella's most moving poems, records the speaker's contemplation of himself while shaving, and his wry conclusion, after his recognition of his age, that he is "Not young and not renewable, but man."

These dark poems conclude *Downstream* and lead directly on to *Wormwood*, the last book completed by Kinsella before his departure for North America; it was published in 1966 by the Dolmen Press in a limited and signed edition of 350 copies.

The epilogue to *Wormwood* establishes the significance of the title. It reads:

> and a great star fell from heaven, burning as it were a torch; and it fell on the third part of the rivers and upon the fountains of waters; and the name of the star is called Wormwood; and the third part of the waters became Wormwood; and many men died of the waters, because they were made bitter.
>
> Apocalypse: chap. 8, vv. 10 and 11.

The prologue states clearly Kinsella's main themes and his obsession with suffering and division:

> Beloved,
> A little of what we have found
>
> It is certain that maturity and peace are to be sought through ordeal after ordeal, and it seems that the search continues until we fail. We reach out after each new beginning, penetrating our context to know ourselves, and our knowledge increases until we recognize again (more profoundly each time) our pain, indignity and triviality. This bitter cup is offered, heaped with curses, and we must drink or die. And even though we drink we may also die, if every drop of bitterness—that rots the flesh—is not transmuted. (Certainly the individual plight is only hideous. Believing so, we make it so: pigs in a slaughter-yard that turn and savage each other in a common desperation and disorder.) Death, either way, is guilt and failure. But if we drink the bitterness and can transmute it and continue, we resume in candour and doubt the only individual joy—the restored necessity to learn. Sensing a wider scope, a more penetrating harmony, we begin again in a higher innocence to grow toward the next ordeal.
>
> Love also, it seems, will continue until we fail: in the sensing of the wider scope, in the growth toward it, in the swallowing and absorption of bitterness, in the resumed innocence.

This is, perhaps, the definitive comment upon *Wormwood* and its eight powerful poems. The title poem presents a dream of a "black tree with double trunk." These two trunks "in their infinitesimal dance of growth/ Have turned completely about one another, their join/ A slowly twisted scar." The speaker recognizes this scar, even as he dreams of a "heavy blade in flight" that causes iron to sink "in the gasping core." The dream, he tells us, has occurred previously and will occur again. This dream is, obviously, symbolic of two lives united in marriage, or some other bond, and united not only by shared growth but also by shared suffering. The blade is ominous; death and division are ahead. The poem avoids comment: it merely presents a human predicament, a central fact of life, in symbolic terms. The second poem, "The Mask of Love," defines the woe that is in a marriage, or in any close sexual relationship. It speaks of "peaks of stress" and of the lovers "face to face, wearied with horror/ Screaming in ecstasy/ Across the narrow abyss." The bodies "lack peace"; the nocturnal dance is "Suicidal." She despairs; he, also grieving and despairing, mocks. The mask of love disappears as "Dumb vapours" roll down upon the scene. Hectic, possibly melodramatic and shrill, this poem again universalizes a particular personal agony by the use of vast symbols and romantic gigantism. The symbols themselves become larger, more obscure, in "Forsaken," which portrays the loss of religious confidence, the wavering of strength. The speaker cries: "*Choose, O Christ,/ One with better strength*" and, finally, laying his cheek upon the "heart/ of steel and cloth and stone" (the Sacred Heart) receives no response, and "all becomes stone."

Reality is unendurable. "First Light" describes the dawn as a "pale deadly light," and the kitchen of the house as "Blank with marriage—where shrill/ Unreason and Jew-face Law have kept/ Another vigil." The poem ends with a child awakening from a dream which daylight makes unendurable, and his whimper "lengthens to an ugly wail."

This theme of sour, unendurable reality is further presented in "The Secret Garden," the sentimentality of whose allusive title is intended ironically, for this secret garden is bitter. The child, one of an "angel race," is experiencing there "The first chill of curse." "The Serving Maid," however, establishes the bitter cheer of servitude, the humility of service, and the way in which the spirit, facing mortal decay, may derive strength from self-mockery as well as from an obsession with tidiness and a rejection of all forms of self-regard. The ego, it seems, must be opposed. Nevertheless, if, by denying the ego we also deny ourselves love, we lose all capacity for growth and remain static, spiritually or psychologically dead. Humble devotion to service may be as destructive as pride. "Remembering Old Wars" describes two lovers clamped together in decay by night, rising daily to face "the hells of circumstance," and each dawn renewing each other's vitality "with a savage smile." The battle of the egos reaffirms those egos and renews the will to live, even though life itself be a gradual and nauseous decay.

The last poem in *Wormwood* is called "On a Gift in the Shape of a Heart" and is, in effect, a statement both of Kinsella's poetic and of his vision of life's progress through suffering upon suffering, through self-torment upon self-torment. It is, in its way, the ascetic answer to romantic nostalgia; it is a poem of the solitary soul, not so much divided against itself as endeavoring to strip off all the delusions of division in which it is clad:

> Open this and you will see
> A waste, a nearly naked tree
> That will not rest till it is bare.
> It shivers, shivers in the air
> Scraping at its yellow leaves
> And suffers—when the tempest heaves—
> In fierce relief, the Heaven-sent
> Convulsions of self-punishment.
>
> *What cannot rest till it is bare,*
> *Though branches crack and fibres tear.*

This poem is a significant one. It employs fewer adjectives and more active verbs than much of Kinsella's work. In one way it might be regarded as Kinsella's equivalent of Yeats's farewell to his "coat/ Covered with embroideries" and of his decision to abandon the Circus Animals and lie down "in the foul rag-and-bone shop of the heart." It could be both a conclusion to Kinsella's first, Irish, period and the beginning of a new phase in his work. The theme of divided man seems to be giving away to the theme of unaccommodated man; the dichotomies and divisions are removed, not by the unifying experience of some all-mastering fusion of intellect and passion, but by the recognition of fundamental solidity in the identification of the irreducible core of being. Self-punishment, suffering, guilt—these are the means of removing the inessential.

Kinsella is, as I have said, a moralist but not a humanist. His moral concern stems not from a concern for human order but from a belief in struggling toward a conviction of the necessity of Divine Grace. His moralities lead to no other convictions; he may hypothesize, but he does not judge. He questions even the apparent clarity of positive good. His faith, his humility, his self-torment and self-ridicule permit him no certainty. He records suffering without animus and celebrates the necessary abandonment of the ego by despair. His personae are often similar to those in Graham Greene's novels, whose faith permits few certainties, and whose self-destructiveness is itself a positive recognition of the need of Grace and its incalculability.

The sequence *Wormwood* was included together with the long poem

"Nightwalker" (first published separately by the Dolmen Press in 1967) and a group of poems from *Downstream* in Kinsella's second comprehensive American collection, *Nightwalker and Other Poems*, in 1968. The title poem is introduced by twelve lines which suggest the emergence into preeminence of that "rage for order," which had always been one of the poet's subordinate concerns.

> Mindful of the
>   shambles of the day
> But mindful, under the
>   blood's drowsy humming,
> Of will that gropes for
>   structure—nonetheless
> Not unmindful of
>   the madness without,
> The madness within (the
>   book of reason slammed
> Open, slammed shut)
>   we presume to say:

These lines, in their balance of "shambles" and "order" and of "the madness without, The madness within," could serve as prologue to almost all of Kinsella's poetry for the next five years. The shorter poems in the book record with a combination of bleak candor and elaborate epithet a fusion of the ascetic and the sensual, the "shambles of the day," presenting us with ever more intense perceptions of the burden of human passion and suffering, the shocked paralysis of the will faced by the prospect of mortality, and the essentially ephemeral nature of all human experience. The two long poems, "Nightwalker" and "Phoenix Park" are lengthy meditations set in a framework of the wandering walker and the shifting mind. "Nightwalker" announces, bleakly, "I only know things seem and are not good" and comments obliquely and savagely upon present-day Ireland and upon fragments of Irish history, perceiving "Bottled fury in new hotels" and idiocies of the newspapers and turning to Joyce and his Martello tower for the comfort which is not there. The sea mew calls "Eire . . . is there none/ To hear? Is all lost?" and the speaker comments that "A dying language echoes/ Across a century's silence." The poem is allusive and oblique; at one point this obliquity becomes an obstacle, for the passage about the Fox, the Groom, the Weasel, and the Player King can only be understood as more than mere fantasy if the creatures are identified as standing for particular personages of the Irish literary and artistic scene. The poem is, indeed, private in some respects, and the forceful language therefore ends by creating the impression of something "full of sound and fury, meaning nothing."

"Phoenix Park," on the other hand, is much more direct. The walker tells us his route clearly, and the relationship between the speaker and the "you" of the poem is both lucidly and subtly protrayed. It is in the "Dream" section that the central theme of hunger for order is expressed most effectively.

> Laws of order I find I have discovered
> Mainly at your hands . . . of failure and increase,
> The stagger and recovery of spirit:
> That life is hunger, hunger is for order,
> And hunger satisfied brings on new hunger
>
> Till there's nothing to come—let the crystal crack
> On some insoluble matter, then its heart
> Shudders and accepts the flaw, adjusts on it
> Taking new strength—given the positive dream.
> Given, with your permission, undying love . . .
>
> That while the dream lasts there's a total hunger
> that gropes out disappearing just past touch,
> A blind human face burrowing in the void,
> Eating new tissue down into existence
> Until every phantasm—all that can come—
>
> Has roamed in flesh and vanished, or passed inward
> Among the echoing figures to its place,
> And this live world is emptied of its hunger
> While the crystal world, undying, crowds with light,
> Filling the cup . . . That there is one last phantasm
>
> Who'll come painfully in old lewd nakedness
> —Loose needles of bone coming out through his fat—
> Groping with an opposite, equal hunger,
> Thrusting a blind skull from its tatters of skin
> As from a cowl, to smile in understanding
>
> And total longing; aching to plant one kiss
> in the live crystal as it aches with fullness,
> And accommodate his body with that kiss;

But that forever he will pause, the final
Kiss ungiveable. Giving without tearing.

Is not possible; to give totality
Is to be torn totally, a nothingness
Reaching out in stasis a pure nothingness.
—Therefore everlasting life, the unmoving
Stare of full desire. Given undying love . . .

This vision of mortal life has a Dantesque grandeur and an intellectual authority, which makes Kinsella one of the very few living poets who can be said to be tackling the highest poetic task—that of creating a vision which makes sense of our universe.

It is the strength of this vision which supports the poems in Kinsella's next book, *Notes from the Land of the Dead*, published by Cuala Press in 1972. Indeed this collection contains a much more positive vision than any other. While the suffering is still very much in evidence, it is now, from time to time, given a kind of justification. The girl whose heart is cut out of her in a human sacrifice assents to that sacrifice and abandons herself to a recognition of spiritual triumph in the giving of herself. Although "Hen Woman" presents us with a blow-by-blow account of the laying of an egg which breaks upon a grating and clearly identifies this egg as "the egg of being," the tone is not one of black grotesquerie as one might expect.

Through what seemed a whole year it fell
—as it still falls, for me,
solid and light, the red gold beating
in its silvery womb,
alive as the yolk and white
of my eye; as it will continue
to fall, probably, until I die,
through the vast indifferent spaces
with which I am empty.

It smashed against the grating
and slipped down quickly out of sight.
It was over in a comical flash.
The soft mucous shell clung a little longer,
then drained down.

She stood staring, in blank anger.
Then her eyes came to life, and she laughed
and let the bird flap away.
"It's all the one.
There's plenty more where that came from!"

Hen to pan.
It was a simple world.

Here the lyrical and the preposterous are neatly brought into unity, and the concluding statement is wry rather than savage, amused rather than accusatory. Moreover, in this poem as in the other poems in this collection, the diction has largely lost its internal stress and strain; the voice is one voice and not several. Moreover, the sensuality is more candid, the sexuality more explicit, and there is little of that ridding obliquity which afflicts the earlier "Nightwalker" and "Old Harry." Indeed in "Notes from the Dead" and in the following long poem, "Finisterre," published by the Dolmen Press in a limited edition in the same year, Kinsella appears to have reached his full stature as a poet, a situation perhaps implicitly recognized by the appearance in 1973 of his *Selected Poems 1956–1968* from the Dolmen Press.

I have not commented upon all Kinsella's poems. I have deliberately avoided discussion of his verse pamphlet on the Ulster troubles called *Butcher's Dozen* which seems to me to be little more than well-made verse presenting commonplace and predictable sentiments. I have also left out of consideration his many translations from Irish. I have tried only to explore the development, thematic and stylistic, of the main current of his work from its beginnings to the appearance of the *Selected Poems*. It is too early to be certain of Kinsella's place in twentieth-century poetry, for his work is still developing. Nevertheless, it appears to me that there is little doubt that he will be considered a major poet of our time not only for the tense energy and athletic wit of his style but also for the brooding strength and authority of the vision his poetry has developed. He has, over the years, brought unity out of division without ever denying the presence of division and without evading the challenges presented by the conflicts within the human creature. He has taken human suffering, human affliction, as one of his themes, and it is interesting to relate his essentially romantic treatment of the coexistence of sensual pleasure and spiritual pain to that of Wilde and the other decadent romantics of a little under a hundred years earlier. Both Wilde and Kinsella indulge in lush descriptiveness, in the hunger for ideal beauty, in the presentation of pain, and in the portrayal of a dangerous Muse. Moreover, both poets utilize a vocabulary that owes much to the romantic excesses of Keats, Shelley, and Swinburne. That Kinsella has managed to contain and master nineteenth-century romantic decadence within a poetry that also contains a toughness of language and a manipulation of staccato phrasing, which is very much that of the second half of the twentieth century, points to his quality as a craftsman as well as to the way in which his poetry is rooted in the past. Indeed, we can see in Kinsella's language and themes something approaching the syncretism of Yeats; his work is broadly and firmly based upon the literature and the vision of the past, and yet it is also a reflection of those divisions and conflicts, in society and in the individual, which are characteristic of present-day Ireland and indeed, the whole of the English-speaking world.

13

Aidan Higgins and the Total Book

Aidan Higgins was born in 1927 in county Kildare and educated at Clongowes Wood College, after which he became a member of a marionette troupe and with his wife toured Europe and Africa. Since then he has lived for different periods in Dublin, London, Berlin, and Spain. His book of short stories *Felo de Se* (called *Killachter Meadow* in the United States) was published in 1960, and his first two novels, *Langrishe Go Down* and *Balcony of Europe*, in 1966 and 1972 respectively.

This bald summary of Higgins's varied experience may serve to explain, in part, why his two novels deal so successfully with the mingling of cultures in present-day Europe, and why he is able to set his stories against a background, not merely of Irish, but of European history. It does not, of course, account for the manner of the stories, their subtlety of allusion, their rhythmic power, and their elaborate structure. These may perhaps usefully be viewed from the standpoint of Roland Barthes who has suggested that

> literature and language are in the process of finding each other again. The factors of this rapproachement are diverse and complex; I shall cite the most obvious. On one hand, certain writers such as Mallarmé, such as Proust and Joyce, have undertaken a radical exploration of writing, making of their work a search for the total Book. On the other hand, linguistics itself, principally following the impetus of Roman Jakobson, has developed to include within its scope the poetic, or the order of effects linked to the message and not to its referent. Therefore, in my view, we have today a new perspective of consideration which, I would like to emphasize, is common to lit-

> erature and linguistics, to the creator and the critic, whose tasks until now completely self-contained, are beginning to inter-relate, perhaps even to merge. This is at least true for certain writers whose work is becoming more and more a critique of language.

One reviewer of *Felo de Se* detected "muted echoes of James Joyce." He was, I think, both right and wrong—wrong in that the whole thrust of these early stories is towards a most un-Joycean end—and right in that Higgins, like Joyce, was providing himself with the first of a series of books which relate intimately to one another, each of which reveals a deepening of intention and a development of stylistic methods. Joyce's progress was like Higgins's only in as much as both reveal a movement towards an overview which offers us human life as a unity combining present with past, conscious with unconscious, and man with myth. Joyce brought his work to a conclusion (or so we must believe) with *Finnegans Wake*. Higgins is still moving towards that final vision.

That Higgins is one of those who are searching for "the Total Book" can hardly be doubted by anyone who has read his three works of fiction. The shape that "total Book" will take is something we cannot as yet guess at with any safety, but the "rejected epigraphs" to the third work, *Balcony of Europe*, do give us a hint. There we read a passage from Edmund Husserl, who, we must remember, was once the teacher of Otto Beck, the central priapean figure of *Langrishe Go Down*. The passage from Husserl runs:

> This world now present to me, and every waking "now" obviously so, has its temporal horizon, infinite in both directions, its known and unknown, its intimately alive and its unalive past and future. Moving freely within the movement of experience which brings what is present into my intuitional grasp, I can follow up these connections of the reality which immediately surrounds me, I can shift my standpoint in space and time, look this way and that, turn temporarily forward and backwards; I can provide for myself constantly new and more or less clear and meaningful perceptions and representations, and images more or less clear in which I make intuitable to myself whatever can possibly exist really or supposedly in the steadfast order of space and time.
>
> In this way, then consciously awake, I find myself at all times, and without ever being able to change this, set in relation to a world which, though its constants change, remains one and ever the same.

If we attempt to translate the phenomenology of Husserl, its emphasis upon the way in which the mirror within us distorts (by intention as well as by accident) the phenomena we say we perceive, we are faced with a problem of showing these distortions without suggesting that they are invalid, for who is to say what image is correct? We are faced, perhaps, with presenting a subjective viewpoint whose inconsistencies are clear, but whose coherence is never seriously in question. Higgins does this in his two novels by giving us changing perspectives upon the central characters. He offers us detailed descriptions of persons and scenes, and then further and further descriptions, each one implying a different perception. He moves us back in time, and then forward. He allows third parties to comment for our benefit. We see Helen Langrishe's view of the Otto Beck affair as well as the changing views of Imogen herself, and these last are never quite in the order in which they developed. Longing, nostalgia, and regret may provide a bright and positive vision immediately following a dark and savage one.

This shift in perspective in both novels, and to a lesser degree in the short stories, gives all Higgins's work its ironic cast, and yet irony is not what he is truly after, at least in the narrow point-making sense of the word. Irony can, after all, only be absolutely effective, if there is a standard of truth, and in Higgins there is none. His is a fluid, fluent universe, a movement of tides ebbing and flowing, a series of withdrawals and returns that are only surprising to those who see life, as some of Higgins's characters attempt to see it, as a progress, a Roman road driving straight to a destination foreplanned and foreordained. This ebb and flow movement is not only noticeable in the movements of the plots but also in the way in which the narrator (whoever it may be) shifts perspectives. Thus, in *Balcony of Europe* the Mother's death is contemplated from three different and yet mingling viewpoints. She is seen both in universal and in local terms; naturalistic details follow mythic references, levels of experience mingle and exchange.

> You were dead. You intimated: *Take heed of what you see, my son; for as you see me now, so will you one day be.* You were Sedna the Earth Mother, the old woman who lives under the ice. White birds flew to unknown lands over your head and the aurora borealis danced in the sky, but you heard nothing except the roaring in your head. You were down among the walrus herds and the seal herds and the big fish. You were a deep fish, half that, half human, little soapstone mother.

> They buried her on a grey autumn day, slightly head first (she was always impetuous), put a framework of wreaths on top and left it at that. No thumping of clay on the lid. Not many were there. It was almost nice to be going to earth before the winter.
>
> The grave, *das Grab*; in the old Gaelic poetry it was the "dark school." To prop up the earth with a stone. She belonged to the earth, and it belonged to her. And the past too, and not only her own past. It was there. Hands long still in the grave. Look at the clouds. You had existed as a part of the seminal substance of the universe that is always becoming and never is; and now had disappeared into that which produced you. Many grains of frankincense on the same altar: one falls before, another falls after, but it makes no difference. Some things are hurrying into existence, others are hurrying out of it; and of that which is come into existence a part is already extinguished. (I stood in Doran's snug with my mother, and in my Menswear overcoat thought I would never die.) Everything is only for a day, both that which remembers and that which is remembered. Thou art a little soul bearing a corpse, Epictetus said. St. Paul called the human body a seed. It was sown a natural body; it was raised a spiritual body. Persephone. Xochipilli the Lord of Flowers.
>
> Phrases used by my mother: A drop (or let-down), a land (a harder drop: a disappointment), a windfall. The heel of the hunt; I can't fathom it; a queer fish; it never rains but it pours. It dawned on me. A real Yahoo. A black Protestant. Wall-falling (lassitude, inertia, state of will-lessness).

This final paragraph is one of several in which the narrator withdraws from the detailed scene, from subjective reverie, to gather together key phrases and sum up, with shrewd accuracy, the language of a given person and culture. Thus, at another point in the book, we read: "Sayings of Bob Bayless: Good Faulkner gets better with time, bad Faulkner worse. Stick with me, honey, and in a couple of years you'll be farting through silk. Lace-curtain Irish."

At another point and, significantly, after we have become extremely well acquainted with Charlotte Bayless and have seen her in many intimate postures, we read: "Expressions used by Charlotte: Step-ins (not corset), all washed out (exhausted). Prat, fanny, butt, can, *Dreck*, *guck*, screwball, ass. Happy as clams, ignorant as monkeys in a tree, high-tail it." Here the explanatory parentheses—"(not corset)," "(exhausted)"—established the way in which the narrator's linguistic reactions to phenomena, his verbal picture of the universe differs from Charlotte's. There is much about language itself in all Higgins's work. He is a word-collector, an expert in linguistic patterns. And the language used and the languages brought into the story, all contribute to the shifting patterns of perspective. "'Their language (Andalusian) sounds like heavy raindrops falling down,' said Charlotte." There is no clear division made between what people think and how they move and speak; the movement may tell us more than the words, the manner of speech more than the matter. We record messages on many sensors. Thus Rosa Munsinger is presented to us in terms of thought, movement, and mode of speech.

> Rosa Munsinger had a theory that, given the existing rate of development, carbon monoxide fumes from traffic would make the planet uninhabitable by the first quarter of the next century. No lung-breathing creature would survive into the second half of the twenty-first century, Rosa believed. She had heavy haunches, her thighs quivered, she rolled along monumentally—self-obsessed to an Addisonian degree.
>
> She said: *My* algarroba tree . . .
>
> It was a gnarled old algarroba tree that grew in a siding by the bridge near La Luna. *My* algarroba tree. She had sat under it, surprising a pack-rat in the act of moving a sardine tin into the tree. She threw a stone and it disappeared. I said that I had never heard of a rat living in a tree. Rose assured me that she had seen the pack-rat pushing the tin into the tree.
>
> Was Munsinger a Viennese name? It was her maiden name? No, it was her married name. Her maiden name was awkward to spell, difficult to pronounce, and impossible to remember. She spoke of Klaus Munsinger, who lived in New York and was in the "art racket." He blackened his face at parties, spoke like Henry Fonda.

This style may be called impressionistic, or even possibly cubist. It is certainly rhythmical in its sudden shifts of viewpoint, in its movement forward into a person's mind and its withdrawing back into cool observation. This rhythm of advance and withdrawal is central to both Higgins's novels. It is as central to the affair between Dan Ruttle and Charlotte Bayless, as it is to the affair between Imogen Langrishe and Otto Beck.

Both books are organized cyclically, moreover. In the first we begin with Helen's dying, move on to the Beck affair, and then return to be present at Helen's funeral. In the second we move from Ireland to Spain and then return to Ireland, and the period in Spain is constructed according to the epic formula, beginning early in 1963, moving back to

1962, and then moving forward to the summer and autumn of 1963. In each part of both these novels, there are recurrent images, recurrent themes. The river motif runs through *Langrishe Go Down*, and the sea is ever-present in *Balcony of Europe*. What should be noticed, however, is that some images, and even some sentences and characters, bind together not only the two novels but all three books. In *Killachter Meadow* we have six stories; the first and title story gives us an affair between Imogen Kervick and the German student Otto Klaefisch, and we are also presented with another sister called Helen and with the death by drowning of the third sister, Emily-May. *Langrishe Go Down* reveals to us that some time before the story begins Emily Langrishe had died, (though of phlebitis, not drowning). It is clear that *Killachter Meadow* is the sketch from which *Langrishe Go Down* emerged, but it seems also clear that the link between the two books is not merely the result of creative accident, for the same kind of linking can be detected between the stories and *Balcony of Europe*. In *Tower and Angels* Irwin Pastern's longing for his woman is presented in terms of sea imagery:

> The sky was overreaching the land and cries from the late bathers carried up from below. Above his head, pressed to the darkening window pane, he saw the pale shape of a fish. He thought to himself: *I'll probably run away when she gets out of her clothes.*
>
> As though struggling in the depths of the sea towards a surface ever withdrawing from him, receding because of the very insistence of his longing, his chest rose and sank, rose and sank, rising ever higher to sink ever lower; his lungs contracted, his eyes dilated, fingers shook at his nostrils—his mouth a dark cavern deprived of air.

In *Balcony of Europe* we not only have Dan Ruttle almost taken out by the strong tide; we also have many sexual encounters in the water. At the close of one encounter Dan Ruttle tells us: "I came out of her as the wave went away and we drifted apart. I saw the bell-tower far away. We were certainly far out, perhaps caught in a current that would not let us return. I feel your hands on my breasts. Charlotte said, even when they are not there." In *Langrishe Go Down* we read: "Turning abruptly, he caught her and prssed himself hard against her, kissing her with a very *gros baiser*. She held onto his hand, which had already opened a button lower down, hair about her face, her breathing disturbed.—I feel your hands on my breasts even when they aren't there." The ignorance of Imogen Langrishe and her failure to understand Otto Beck's talk and all his references to the history of her own country is paralleled by Brazill's incomprehending response to Mr. Boucher's farrago of facts and theories in the story *Asylum* as well as by Irwin Pastern's monologue to Annelise in *Towers and Angels*. The catalogue of fish that Otto Beck catches in *Langrishe Go Down* finds a parallel in the many references to fish in *Balcony of Europe*. Within *Langrishe* it exists in series (one might say) with Imogen's description of being eaten alive by the multitude of minnows as she bathes naked in the river. The image of drowning is in all the books. In *Nightfall on Cape Piscator*, we read: "As he laid his hand on her he saw below her woman's dark and anonymous flesh—a brown bay into which he was about to cast himself and be drowned forever. In the end it was to be easy: only thinking about it had made it impossible." This black servant girl reappears in a dream of Dan Ruttle's *Balcony of Europe*, and the theme of thought preventing or obstructing action is present in all the books. At the very end of *Balcony of Europe*, as if to assure us that our suspicion that the book somehow connects with *Langrishe Go Down* is altogether reasonable, we read:

> Martin O'Donnell had told me of the kind Dr. Beck, the German who loved the islands and the islanders and had landed in a helicopter with provisions when Aran was cut off from the mainland in a storm. For twenty years he had been coming on research. Then there was another man, also called Beck but no relation. He had gone back to Germany . . . I had never met either of the Becks, then or later. Mogens Stenicke showed me his paintings and brass rubbings from the old church up to its headstones in sand, but when I was tactless enough to bring up the name of Beck, he cut me short.
>
> I believe you didn't get on too well with the old one, I ventured to say.
>
> The young one was worse, the Dane said, closing the subject.

This took place on Inishere. In *Langrishe Go Down* Otto Beck tells Imogen:

> One day in the middle of that foul winter, I found myself standing in front of the tourist office in Regent Street, before their big plate-glass window. On display there was a photograph enlarged to the size of a door. You could see the black grains. From where I stood in my wretched condition it jumped out at me with the utmost clarity. It was a blown-up photograph of an island, Inishere,

> on the Aran Islands, photographed on a hot summer day. I stood there confronting it, and the reality came floating out at me. I had never been to Ireland, but I was in it that day, in a field of daisies in Inishere. It wasn't a dead and petrified agency still. No, it was the reality that came out at me, breathed on me.

The intension is clearly to tease us with possibilities, as well as to suggest an overlapping of stories, a mingling of lives. I say "clearly" because an examination of the notebooks and work sheets of Aidan Higgins, now lodged in the University of Victoria library, reveals a degree of deliberate planning, a concern with creating mosaiclike patterns of allusion and event, which makes it impossible to believe that the recurrences of names, themes, images, and key locations is accidential.

These notebooks, moreover, reveal another aspect of Higgins's work which is significant. They are crammed with extracts from historians, scholars, linguists, and other writers, and these have not only been used to provide Otto Beck and others with their fund of information on widely diverse subjects but also to set the fiction off by means of allusions to, and near quotations from, other writers. Joyce and Yeats appear often in this form—ghostly presences contributing a sudden sly perspective upon the intelligence and attitude of the narrator. This is particularly the case with Dan Ruttle's narration of *Balcony of Europe*, and it occurs also in the speech of Otto Beck and Mr. Boucher. Thus, we are given a kind of cultural and historical backdrop to the drama, and a hint that this backdrop forms—if I may shift my metaphor—one facet of that distorting mirror which Husserl regards as our consciousness of phenomena we so often regard as being entirely external to us and our characters. The composition of this mirror is complex and is made up of reflecting surfaces stolen from many centuries. In *Balcony of Europe* we find Yeats utilized for his line "Maud Gonne at Howth Station waiting for a train" and Webster pillaged for his description of human flesh as "puff-paste." There are references to and quotations from Pliny, Wagner, Pascal, Husserl (of course), Lewis Carroll, the Nōh drama, Chekhov, Swift, Diego de Rivera, Bonnard, Jan Steen, Rembrandt, Shakespeare, and Defoe—to take a small selection at random. And added to these passing, but precisely attuned, effects, are fragments of historical lore, snippets of philosophy, gobbets of odd information. The pressure of this material is so considerable that one cannot avoid seeing it as a component, almost a scene of the novel. Sir Walter Raleigh's codpiece is repeated in the bulging bikini-briefs of Roger Amory; Dan Ruttle sees himself as "Bonnard in the bathroom at Le Cannet"; Lothar Ebbinghaus repeats, at least in one respect, the role of Alcibiades; the Baylesses recreate, momentarily, King Akhnaton and Queen Nefertiti. Other writers are called into the novel, and with great effect.

Just as Eliot used quotations and near quotations (as did Joyce, as does Beckett) in order to bring into play a whole complex of associations and implications, in order to utilize the viewpoint of, let us say, Shakespeare's Enobarbus or the Buddhist Fire-Sermon, as a part of and counterpoint to his own or his own poems viewpoint, so Higgins uses other books. Thus, as Anthony Kerrigan has pointed out in *Balcony of Europe*, we find fragments of John Montague's poem "Sentence for Konarak." Higgins's two paragraphs run:

> Are not health and corruption said to be incompatible, by the ancient Rhetoricians? She glowed with health and well-being, a ripe-thighed temple dancer. Who then had done this thing to her? What ape's paw had marked her? Her pose was a cajoling one. One of her most endearing and characteristic movements began as a shudder in those ardent hips. A beautiful gentleness glowed from the skin there . . .
>
> . . . Rare, rare, her pierced beauty. The heavy musk of falling hair. In a field of force, the coiling honeycomb of forms, the golden wheel of love.

John Montague's poem must be understood as lying behind this passage, as a comment upon it, as if Montague were writing of Charlotte Bayless, for it is clear that the narrator sees her in terms of Montague's poem. "Sentence for Konarak" runs:

> Extravagantly your stone gestures
> encourage and ease our desires
> till the clamour dies: it is not
> that man is a bare forked animal,
> but that sensuousness is betrayed
> by sensuality (a smell of burning flesh);
>
> though here face turns to face,
> not ashamed (the word barely exists,
> so calm the movement, limpid the smile
> above your monstrous actions)

that we are rebuked to learn
how, in the proper atmosphere,

the stealthy five-fingered hand
is less thief than messenger,
as the god bends towards her
whose head already sways towards him,
pliant as a lily, while round them,
in a teeming richness, move

the ripe-thighed temple dancers
in a field of force, a coiling honeycomb
of forms, the golden wheel of love.

Konarak (or Kanarak) is an Indian village in the state of Orissa, and the setting for the Black Pagoda which is famous for its elaborate erotic sculptures. The allusion to sculpture is taken up two paragraphs after the final quotation from Montague has been given, when Charlie Vine speaks of "Christ's five bleeding wounds sculptured over church portals like bunches of grapes." In this fashion Higgins creates connections and correspondences, a web of echo and allusion which run underneath his novels. They are part of the sensibility of the narrator whose mind, whose mirroring mind, is composed of so many fragments of myth, of poetry, of learning, and of experience; they are also, however, the mind, the consciousness of the novel itself.

Not only is the mirror composed of these deflecting and reflecting fragments of ancient myth and existing literature but also of fragments of the present or near present. There are references to Sybil le Broquy's book on Swift and Stella, to Brendan Behan on Aran, to the features and stance of Harry Kernoff, to Baldwin, Genet, Ginsberg, Mailer—the last-named disguised with careful imperfection. And we (every once in a while, we wonder) to take *Balcony of Europe* as a roman à clef? The answer may be no, but the suspicion makes us restless; fiction and reality move closer together until we are unsure as to whether we are becoming one of those ever-spying ever-rewarded voyeurs about the Spanish beaches, manipulating ourselves into aesthetic ecstasy by creating a self-centered fiction from the realities of others.

The image of the voyeur in *Balcony of Europe* is, of course, more than just another feature of the erotic merry-go-round of the plot; it is an image of that secret—secret because unavailable to all others—pleasure and shame we derive from contemplation of the scene, the passing show. It is an image of the artist, the novelist, Ninbad the Nailer, his hand never still, either at key or crotch. It is an image of that distorting mirror which is our consciousness and beyond whose perspectives we can never see. It is also an image of the repetition within the solitary individual, of acts and events outside him. It is the Fascist Finn recreating and elaborating upon the faith of Nazi Germany; it is Otto Beck writing his philological thesis; it is Bayless studying Byron and Shelley; and it is all our memories, and all our dreams in which we transfigure our appetites and anxieties or are transfigured by them.

It must be obvious by now that while Higgins has been, perhaps inevitably, compared with Joyce, he could equally well be compared with Proust, and it is worth noting in passing that Higgins's third novel in preparation was given the clearly elusive title, *Scenes from a Receding Past*. Certainly he is like Proust in his ability to record with almost hallucinatory precision the sensual details of whatever scene he wishes us to encounter. He has, like Proust, moreover, an exact sense of time. *Langrishe Go Down* is set precisely in the years it states; the clothes, the films, the prices of things, the newspapers are all in period; the same applies to the short stories and *Balcony of Europe*. He has that painstaking thoroughness which set Joyce writing to Dublin for tiny details of this street or that, and which gave *The Remembrance of Things Past* its bewildering impression of total recall. Like Proust and Joyce, Higgins is concerned to recall not only the places and persons but the weight of history, the fragments of the past, under which they struggle. This is particularly the case with Helen's reflection in *Langrishe Go Down*:

> The days draw in. They are soon over. Soon over. The sun rises at eight-thirty; goes up over the trees. Low all day, it sinks out of sight before five. Dusk begins at four in the afternoon. Brief days, brief days. The mornings are dim and overcast, with no sun. Not mornings at all. It might be any hour of the day were it not for the sharpness, the coldness. Through these windows these eyes have watched, have seen. What I see oppresses me. I have looked at it long enough. All old disputed land. My home today. Written of in Exchequer Inquisitions and Chronicles, in the time of Henry VIII and Elizabeth before him. She who, in right of her crown, seized of the Manor of Kildrought, alias Castleton-Kildrought, and one water-mill, all in the County Kildare. Mentioned in Parliamentary Statutes. In the Courts of Exchequer lists dating back six and more centuries. In rolls of forfeited estates. In deeds offices. Ordinance survey records. Statistical surveys, Land Commission files. In private

> documents. In dead men's wills. Forfeited over and over again since the Anglo-Normans. And 74 acres of it mine today—a forgotten battlefield that means nothing to me. Nothing. The grand names and the grand estates. Castletown. Alenscourt. Donycomper where Madame Popoff lives, married to the White Russian. Killadoon where Miss Kitty Clements lives with her mother. The empty Abbey. Oakley Park. Windgates. Rose Lawn. Pickering Forest. Nothing. Napier. Allen. Kane. Conolly. Dease. The Honourable George Cavendish. John Graham Hope de la Poer, the 5th Baron Decies. (Who was it died in the flood?) As it was in the beginning, is now, ever shall be, world without end. Nothing. Invasion after invasion; occupation after occupation. Silent mills, bear testimony. Overgrown ruins, bear silent testimony. Round towers beloved of King John, bear testimony. Disused graveyards, bear testimony. Broken monuments of the Geraldines, bear testimony. Joe Feeney, bear testimony. History ends in me. Now. Today.

Helen may say "History Ends in Me"; the characters in *Balcony of Europe* would perhaps regard history as an ongoing process, even as a perpetual present, a continuing spreading mesh to which there can be no end, an ever-changing surface and depth of tide. Dreams and realities mingle. The dreams recorded in *Balcony of Europe* have the same echoing or mysterious depths as the dreamworld of Joyce's Finnegan or the final soliloquy of Molly Bloom, and the same sensual precision as the elaborate convolutions of Proust's remembrance. Higgins's view of human life is not, however, either Proust's or Joyce's: it lacks the final Assent (however ironically intended and placed) of Molly Bloom and it lacks the mannered distancing of Proust, whose style itself implied a trust, a faith. It is perhaps too early to do more than guess at the final view of Higgins's work; the cunningly placed lacunae in his work suggests that there is more, and it is to be hoped much more, to come. Nevertheless, there are passages which rise out of the novel as the swimmer rises momentarily out of the wave, out of the tugging current, the unceasing flux, the rhythm of withdrawal and return.

> Perhaps nothing ends, he suggested,—only changes. At least this much is certain: for every human being on earth life ends in themselves.
>
> (*Tower and Angels*)

> Oppressed or Oppressor, Otto said, the vain attempts of men to rid

themselves of the inertia of their landscapes, it's that which makes up stories. Anybody's story—or yours or mine. The drama is in man's *angst*, the foreknowledge of one's own death.

(*Langrishe Go Down*)

All prehistory, all the darkly entwined ancient world, world of boulders and animal skins and mankind's first formless and uncoordinated thought, must have been permeated by an immense sexual reverie and longing (heart-beat of lion, brawl of beast, dark and primitive loves, thick hair standing on end on the short bully neck, testicles of goat, tyranny of lust): passion coming from such deep sources.

(*Balcony of Europe*)

And then there are the last two paragraphs of the story

Lebensraum:

The tide rose now until it covered the entire shore. Shallow yet purposeful water embraced the extremity of the seawall. Invisible gulls were complaining, worrying, somewhere over its dark unpeaceful depths. Anxiously the pier lights waged a mile to the south—a remote outfall of light more dingy than the sky, now dropping, now drowned in intervening wave. Michael Alpin walked out of the dark construction of the wall, broken here and there by heavy seas. He stood over her scawlings, her last abuse. Unbuttoning himself he took his stance staring out to sea, his lust or love in the end reduced to this. Retreating to the wall he laid his face against its intolerable surface of freezing stone. As he began to go down the false surf light and the remote light along the pier, diminishing, swung away.

There is no commencement or halfway to that fall: only its continuing.

14

John Montague and the Divided Inheritance

John Montague was born in 1929 in Brooklyn, New York, his parents having left their native Ulster for America a short time before. He returned to Ireland when he was four years old and was brought up by an aunt in the parish of Garvaghey, county Tyrone. Being an Ulster Catholic he soon became aware of the difficulties of belonging to a minority group and of the way in which one particular view of history could be used to oppress and ridicule those who took a different view. He became a student at University College, Dublin, and remained largely in Dublin, with occasional periods in America, until the middle sixties when he moved to Paris with his French wife. He spent some time lecturing in America at Berkeley and at Brown University during this period. In 1973 he returned to Ireland with his second wife and became a lecturer in the English Department of the University of Cork.

With this background, it is hardly surprising that Montague's poems concern themselves with social as well as personal problems and that one motif running through all his books is that of the necessity to identify and explore one's cultural inheritance. In a note on his long poem, "The Rough Field," he wrote: "One explores an inheritance to free oneself and others." Few poets can have had a more divided inheritance.

John Montague's first collection, *Forms of Exile*, was published by the Dolmen Press in 1958, and already one can see the emergence of his main themes. His ambivalent attitude towards religion and the church is revealed in the two poems "Dirge of the Mad Priest" and "A Footnote on Monasticism: Dingle Peninsula." In the former the priest sees "My godhead hung in text of terror on the wall" and believes that the young girls and the blackbirds are mocking him, crying "What is that donkey's cross you carry on your back?" and calling him a "cheerless man in sunshine wearing black." Religion is seen as an infliction, a burden, a terror, and as a denial of simple pleasures and simple beauty. In "A Footnote on Monasticism," however, the hermits, "the lonely dispossessed ones," are viewed sympathetically, and we are told:

> There are times, certainly, looking through the window
> At amiable clustered humanity, or scanning
> The leaves of some old book, that one might wish
> To join their number, start a new and fashionable
> Sect beside the Celtic sea, long favorable
> To dreams and dreamers, people hurt into solitude

The description of the spiritual labors of the hermit may also be regarded as a description of one kind of poetic experience.

> In ceaseless labour of the spirit,
> Isolate, unblessed;
> Until quietude of the senses
> Announces presence of a Guest;
> Desolation final,
> Rock within and rock without
> Til from the stubborn rock of the heart,
> The purifying waters spurt.

This is a presentation of that inwardly searching vision which animates many of Montague's most lyrical and intense poems. It also presents that bare and ascetic landscape which Montague returns to over and over again and which is reflected in the economy of his language and the unadorned directness of the diction in his later poems. This inward probing vision is not infrequently directed towards memory, towards "inheritance," and in Montague's first collection this approach is exemplified most clearly by "The Sean Bhean Vocht." He describes the old woman who is Ireland in harsh and realistic terms.

> As a child I was frightened by her
> Busy with her bowl of tea in farmhouse chimney corner,
> Wrapped in a cocoon of rags and shawls.
> "God be good to all of us:

go ngdeanaidh dia trocaire ar a anam"
She rocked to and fro
A doll's head mouthing under stained rafters.

The vision of the old woman, however, is of a romantic past which contrasts with the ruination of the present.

"The fairies of Ireland and the fairies of Scotland
Fought on that hill all night,
And in the morning the well ran blood.
The dead Queen was buried on that hill.
St. Patrick passed by the cross:
There is the mark of a footprint forever
Where he briefly stood."

Eyes rheumy with racial memory:
Fragments of bread soaked in brown tea
And eased between chambling gums;
Her clothes stank like summer flax,
Watched all day as she swayed
Toward death between memories and prayers
By a farmer's child in a rough play-box.

Here, again, the poem has a double vision. While "Age is neither knowledge or Authority," one must ask "beneath the whorls of the guardian stone What faery queen lay dust?"

This inward probing into both the personal and the collective past is balanced in the collection by tough-minded poems that look outwards at "amiable clustered humanity." We are given deft, precisely adjusted portraits of emigrants, of lovers, of American landscapes, in all of which there is a kind of sweet bitterness, an affectionately clinical precision. There is also a fondness for direct reportage of social phenomena, for documentation. "Downtown America" begins:

The car wipers work against the fretful snow
NEWS OF THE LATEST TRIAL—THE WINNING HORSE—
TROOPS HAVE LANDED—COMMISSION'S REPORT IS
THROUGH
These are normal things and set the heart at rest.

The vast irony that it is difficulty, harassment, crisis which make us feel that life is "normal" is continued through two more verses before we receive the last ferocious verse:

> The car radio suggests our new form of fear,
> TOTAL TERROR AND ECLIPSE ARE HERE—
> ATOMIC MUSHROOMS MAY FLOWER ANYWHERE—
> But these are normal things and set the heart at rest.

This technique of direct newspaper quotation, of documentation, anticipates some of the passages in Montague's long poem, his major work to date, *The Rough Field.* Indeed all the themes and approaches of *Forms of Exile* can be found in that poem, as in his intermediate work. It is rare for a poet's first book to lay out so clearly and fully what lines his later poems are to follow, but *Forms of Exile* does this. There are, of course, new themes in some later poems and many technical developments, but for the most part Montague seems to have known where he was going from the very beginning.

It was two years after the appearance of *Forms of Exile* that *The Rough Field* actually began. It started with a poem called "Like Dolmens Round My Childhood The Old People," which was awarded the May Morton Memorial Prize in Belfast in May 1960 and issued as a pamphlet in a limited edition of one hundred copies by the Dolmen Press in August of that year. The poem clearly developed out of the earlier "Sean Bhean Vocht," the fourth verse of which ran:

> "Mrs MacGurren had the evil eye,
> She prayed prayers on the black cow:
> It dropped there and died
> Dropped dead in its tracks.
> She stood on the mearing and cursed the Clarkes
> They never had a good day since,
> Fluke and bad crops and a child born strange"

"Like Dolmens" consists of five portraits of people, a sixth stanza referring to them collectively, and a final stanza in which the speaker reflects upon his inheritance of "Ancient Ireland."

Like Dolmens Round My Childhood, The Old People

Like dolmens round my childhood, the old people.

I

Jamie MacCrystal sang to himself,
A broken song without tune, without words;
He tipped me a penny every pension day,
Fed kindly crusts to winter birds,
When he died, his cottage was robbed,
Mattress and money box torn and searched
Only the corpse they didn't disturb.

II

Maggie Owens was surrounded by animals,
A mongrel bitch and shivering pups,
Even in her bedroom a she-goat cried.
She was a well of gossip defiled,
Fanged chronicler of a whole countryside;
Reputed witch, all I could find
Was her ravening need to deride.

III

The Nialls lived along a mountain land
Where heather bells bloomed, clumps of foxglove.
All were blind, with Blind Pension and Wireless,
Dead eyes serpent-flicked as one entered
To shelter from a downpour of mountain rain.
Crickets chirped under the rocking hearthstone
Until the muddy sun shone out again.

IV

Mary Moore lived in a crumbling gatehouse,
Famous as Pisa for its leaning gable.
Bag apron and boots, she tramped the fields
Driving lean cattle from a miry stable.
A by-word for fierceness, she fell asleep
Over love stories, Red Star and Red Circle,
Dreamed of gypsy love rites, by firelight sealed.

V

Wild Billy Harbison married a Catholic servant girl
When all his Loyal family passed on:
We danced round him shouting "To Hell with King Billy,"
And dodged from the arc of his flailing blackthorn.
Forsaken by both creeds, he showed little concern
Until the Orange drums banged past in the summer
And bowler and sash aggressively shone.

VI

Curate and doctor trudged to attend them,
Through knee-deep snow, through summer heat,
From main road to lane to broken path,
Gulping the mountain air with painful breath.
Sometimes they were found by neighbours,
Silent keepers of a smokeless hearth,
Suddenly cast in the mould of death.

VII

Ancient Ireland, indeed! I was reared by her bedside,
The rune and the chant, evil eye and averted head,
Fomorian fierceness of family and local feud.
Gaunt figures of fear and of friendliness,
For years they trespassed on my dreams,
Until once, in a standing circle of stones,
I felt their shadows pass

Into that dark permanence of ancient forms.

When this poem was broadcast by the North of Ireland Home Service, the fifth stanza was omitted. It was, in its way, a tribute.

After the awarding of the prize in, ironically, the assembly rooms in a Presbyterian church in Belfast, while the drums rumbled outside in preparation for the festivities of the Twelfth, John Montague had an intuition of a long poem he must write. He later said:

> Bumping down towards Tyrone a few days later by bus, I had a kind of vision, in the medieval sense, of my home area, the unhappiness of its historical destiny. And of all such remote areas where the pres-

ence of the past was compounded with a bleak economic future, whether in Ulster, Brittany, or the Highlands. I managed to draft the opening and the close, but soon realized that I did not have the technique for so varied a task. At intervals during the decade I returned to it, when the signs seemed right. An extreme Protestant organization put me on its mailing list, for instance, and the only antidote I could find against such hatred was to absorb it into *The Bread God*. And ten years later I was given another small prize, again from the North, to complete the manuscript.

Several sections of *The Rough Field* were published as separate pamphlets. *The Hymn to the New Omagh Road* appeared in 1968, *The Bread God* in 1968, *A New Siege* in 1970, and *A Patriotic Suite* in 1966. Other poems included in the whole appeared in the three collections *Poisoned Lands* (1961), *A Chosen Light* (1967), and *Tides* (1970)—the first two being published by MacGibbon & Kee and the last by the Dolmen Press, which also issued the various pamphlets.

From 1960 onwards John Montague's work can, with the percipience of hindsight, be separated into two main streams—one consisting of work which included in, or clearly relates to, *The Rough Field*, and the remainder in which other themes are developed. The distinction is not, however, always easy to make for over and over again the theme of Ireland, of Ireland's past, and the bitterness of Ireland's presence emerges. The very title of Montague's first full-size book, *Poisoned Lands* (1960) points to a central concern with the matter of Ireland. The title poem derives from the practice of laying out poisoned meat on the land to destroy predatory animals. "The practice," Montague says in a prefactory note, "is not highly regarded." The poem itself has no ostensible political message, but the farmer is portrayed as a figure of evil, much whispered about in the countryside, a death-bringer. The last lines read:

> "I dont like country people" he said, with a grin.
> The winter sunlight halved his mottled chin
> And behind, a white notice seemed to swing and say
> "If you too licked grass, you'd be dead today"

The white notice reads, in fact, "These Lands are Poisoned," and the whole poem implies a condemnation of tyranny, a sense of outrage at the slaughter of creatures who are chosen for death because of their race rather than because of their proven acts. In Ulster, one might almost suggest, the attitude of the land-owning Protestant majority to many of the Catholics is that of the farmer.

Another poem reflecting directly upon this theme of man's cruelty to man is "Auschwitz, Mon Amour." The speaker of the poem recalls viewing as a boy the atrocities of Auschwitz in a cinema and reflects:

> To be always at the periphery of incident
> Gave my childhood its Irish dimension; drama of unevent;
> Yet doves of mercy, as doves of air,
> Can tumble here as anywhere.
>
> It takes a decade and a half, it seems,
> Even to comprehend one's dreams:
> Continual operation on the body of the past
> Brings final meaning to its birth at last.
>
> That long dead Sunday in Armagh
> I learned one meaning of total war
> And went home to my Christian school
> And kicked a football through the air.

The tone of this, as of most of the poems in the collection, is cool. The diction is precise yet colloquial, reminding one of the expert balance of the young Auden, and yet the poems lack that touch of conscious superiority, that ironist's élan, which gives Auden's best early poems their harmony of ambiguity. Indeed, when the poems become explicitly critical of the world around them, they do so with a wry grotesquerie, a dark humor, in which there is more of sadness than superiority. Thus even such sardonic poems as "Regionalism" and "Walking the Dog" conclude with lines that dignify the subject rather than the speaker. The poet, while implying ridicule of narrow regionalism, nevertheless contrives to show its necessity to those who can only hope for "anonymity" and, while objecting to the tyranny of the dog that pulls him from "pillar to post," finds himself admiring the dog's independence.

> Pulled from pillar to post
> By this most pampered beast
> I certainly ought to protest—
> Enough's as good as a feast—
> But follow in baffled awe
> Shameless manhood, golden fleece.

It would be a mistake to suggest that the figure of the speaker, of the poet, in Montague's work is invariably that of the victim, the acted-upon rather than the actor, but he accepts this role quite frequently. In part this may be the consequence of Montague's method of constructing poems around images which are made to appear "objective" records by his use of a highly concrete diction expressed without rhetorical flourish. Montague avoids romantic excess with as a great a dedication as Oscar Wilde pursued it. In his second substantial collection, *A Chosen Light*, he identified much of the attitude of his poetry in "The True Song":

> The first temptation is to descend
> Into beauty, those lonely waters
> Where the swan weeps, and the lady
> Waits, a nacreous skeleton.
>
> The second is to watch over
> Oneself, a detached god
> Whose artifice reflects
> The gentle smile in the mirror.
>
> The third, and the hardest,
> Is to see the body brought in
> From the street, and know
> The hand surge towards blessing.
>
> For somewhere in all this
> Stands the true self, seeking
> To speak, who is at once
> Swan
> lady
> stricken one.

Here we have three of the components of Montague's poetry—its love and distrust of the powerful romantic symbol, its relish and suspicion of the artifice of ironic observation, and its cautious yearning for the expression of deep human feeling. It is a portrait of a divided sensibility, perhaps even a sensibility at odds with itself, and yet aware that this unbalance is at the center of the human condition.

Only occasionally does Montague abandon his deft ambiguity, and then, paradoxically, it is usually to present a situation which is itself ambiguous, equivocal. The second verse of "The Siege of Mullingar" makes the point:

In the early morning the lovers
Lay on both sides of the canal
Listening on Sony transistors
To the agony of Pope John.
Yet it did not seem strange, or blasphemous,
This ground bass of death and
Resurrection, as we strolled along:
Puritan Ireland's dead and gone,
A myth of O'Connor and O'Faolain.

Although, to the speaker of the poem, "Everything . . . Seemed to flow in one direction,/ Line simple as a song," the description of the scene is still one of conflict. The poem opens

At the Fleadh Cheoil in Mullingar
There were two sounds, the breaking
Of glass, and the background pulse
Of music

While both sounds may lead in one direction, imply one unifying mood of life acceptance, the images themselves are contraries. Moreover, a second look at the refrain suggests an irony that is not immediately apparent. It was in a strongly romantic poem that Yeats wrote:

Romantic Ireland's dead and gone,
It's with O'Leary in the grave

Might it not be that Montague's parody is intended, slyly, to suggest that, for all the evidence at Mullingar, the puritanism remains, even perhaps reveals itself in the frenzy with which it is denied.

We cannot escape our inheritance. We cannot move freely, even in love, for

There is in love that brief
Jealousy of the other's past
Coming on the charred roots
Of feeling, of ancient grief

("The Water's Edge")

Montague's poems of love almost all present us with contrary impulses, conflicting desires. "Virgo Hibernica" begins with the question "Dare I yet confront/that memory?" and the speaker goes on to say "I feel/the gravitational pull/of love./And fight back." "All Legendary Obstacles" begins with the statement "All legendary obstacles lay between/us." "That Room" opens with the lines

> Side by side on the narrow bed
> We lay, like chained giants

The whole of the poem "The Charm" turns upon the theme of intense yearning, intense fear.

> When you step near
> I feel the dark hood
> Descend, a shadow
> Upon my mind.
>
> One thing to do,
> Describe a circle
> Around, about me,
> Over, against you:
>
> The hood is still there
> But my pupils burn
> Through the harsh folds.
> You may return
>
> Only as I wish.
> But how my talons
> Ache for the knob
> Of your wrist!

In Montague's next collection, *Tides* the same deployment of contraries can be observed. In "A Summer Storm" we read of "pain bleeding/ away in gouts/ of accusation &/ counter accusation." In "Life Class" we are told that the body is "a system/ of checks & balances". "Special Delivery" refers to "the worm of delight/ which turns to/ feed upon itself." The image of the tides, of the ebb and flow of the sea, which is also central to Aidan Higgins's *Balcony of Europe*, pervades the book, and its essential significance is perhaps best summed up in "Boats," which ends with the stanza,

> periodic rhythms of the open sea
> upon which we balance and slide
> hoping for pattern

The sea is for Montague not merely the movement of the individual life, but also that of time. The final poem of the book alludes to Homeric myth by its very title, "Wine Dark Sea," but the text suggests a point of view that qualifies Homer's.

> For there is no sea
> it is all a dream
> there is no sea
> except in the tangle
> of our minds:
> the wine dark
> sea of history
> on which we all turn
> turn and thresh
>   and disappear.

There is a touch of the brooding fatalism of some of the romantics in this short but powerful poem, but the romanticism is qualified by the harsh concreteness of the word "tangle" and the demotic energy of the word "thrash," as by the rejection of the traditional rhetorical sonorities. Nevertheless, one can see behind this poem, as behind all the love poetry of Montague, the victim-lovers of the nineteenth century and even, from time to time, glimpse the hovering shadow of Swinburne's Lady of Pain, Wilde's Sphynx. "The Pale Light" is, from one point of view, a twentieth-century recreation of this figure—twentieth century because of its direct candor, its harshness of imagery, its economy of language.

THE PALE LIGHT

> Again she appears
> The putrid fleshed woman
> Whose breath is ashes,
> Hair a writhing net of snakes!

Her presence strikes gashes
Of light into the skull
Rears the genitals

Tears away all
I had so carefully built—
Position, marriage, fame—
As heavily she glides towards me
Rehearsing the letters of my name
As if tracing them from
A rain streaked stone.

All night we turn
Towards an unsounded rhythm
Deeper, more fluent than breathing.
In the pale light of morning
Her body relaxes: the hiss of seed
Into that mawlike womb
Is the whimper of death being born.

This is, of course, another image of conflict, and of contraries, and a portrait of the Muse in her darkest aspect.

"A Pale Light" may owe something to a symbolism developed by the British romantics of the nineteenth century; it also owes something, however, to Gaelic poetry. The way in which it manipulates internal consonance and assonance, and its harsh clarity of vision, reminds one not only of Gaelic verse forms but of the almost imagist clarities of many Irish lyrics. Montague is a scholar of Gaelic (he could reasonably be regarded as the finest living translator of Gaelic lyrics), and has brought over into English many of the subtleties of the Gaelic tradition. In so doing he has not only exploited a technique but also explored a viewpoint. In his introduction to *The Faber Book of Irish Verse*, he says of "The Hag of Beare" which is included in the anthology in his own translation,

> Behind "The Hag of Beare" lies the struggle between paganism and Christianity, between bodily pleasure and the doctrine of salvation through repentance. It is the ebb and flow of her misery, with sudden crests of remembered pride, which gives this dramatic lyric its structure. . . . it ends as it begins, following the circular aesthetic of Irish art. A thousand years later, the same lonely note is heard, in Maurya's monologue in "Riders to the Sea."
>
> In suggesting that the quarrel between natural and organized religion, between instinct and restraint, is one of the major themes

> of Irish literature, I am not forgetting that the early Church, the civilization of "the little monasteries," as Frank O'Connor called it, had the task of transcribing that oral culture:
>
> > "Not until the coming of Patrick speech was not suffered to be given in Ireland but to three; to a historian for narration and the relating of tales; to a poet for eulogy and satire; to a brehon lawyer for giving judgement according to the old tradition and precedent. But after the coming of Patrick every speech of these men is under the yoke of the white language, that is, the scriptures."
>
> This historical irony is part of the fascination of the period, for while these monks might be ardent Christians, they were also increasingly conscious of being Irishmen.

One cannot apply this view at all points to Montague's work, but it does have a bearing on it. Montague is clearly aware, and intensely aware, of the quarrel he says is a major theme of Irish literature. If one is to judge from the way in which over the years he has translated more and more Gaelic verse and has devoted more and more of his work to the matter of Ulster, one might say too that he has become "increasingly conscious of being an Irishmen," while it is obvious from the way in which he utilizes themes relating to American and European experiences that he is also a cosmopolitan. Indeed, his style owes as much to William Carlos Williams as it does to his Irish predecessors and the British poets of the thirties. Imagism is a part of his inheritance, as well as the prose-poetry of surrealism and post-surrealism. He has learned from Patrick Kavanagh and from Robert Graves, from Robert Lowell and from Austin Clarke. His style is, one might say, syncretic, which is, of course, not to deny its individuality.

The syncretic nature of Montague's style, as well as its intense Irishness, is most apparent in "The Rough Field," his long poem about Ulster, and about more than Ulster. In 1969, having been building the poem ever since "Like Dolmens" came to him in 1960, he saw violence break out in the north. In a comment on the "Rough Field," he said

> Although as the Ulster crisis broke, I felt as if I had been stirring a witch's cauldron, I never thought of the poem as tethered to any particular set of events. One explores an inheritance to free oneself and others, and if I sometimes saw the poem as taking over where the last bard of the O'Neills left off, the New Road I describe runs

> through Normandy as well as Tyrone. And experience of agitations in Paris and Berkeley taught me that the violence of disputing factions is more than a local phenomenon. But one must start from home—so the poem begins where I began myself, with a Catholic family in the townland of Garvaghey, in the county of Tyrone, in the province of Ulster.

The point is hammered home by two preliminary quotations on the title page of the book.

> I had never known sorrow.
> Now it is a field I have inherited, and I till it.
>
> from the Afghan

> The Greeks say it was the Turks who burned down
> Smyrna. The Turks say it was the Greeks.
> Who will discover the truth?
> The wrong has been committed. The important thing
> is who will redeem it.
>
> George Seferis

"The Rough Field" (Garvaghey: Garbh acaidh, a rough field) is made up of ten sections and an epilogue. It is both a deeply personal and an astringently political poem. It shifts easily from the poignant to the sardonic, from the telegraphic to the melifluous, from the romantic to the Augustan. Collage is used in many places; fragments of history, quotations from letters, shreds of ancient rhyme, gobbets from political pamphlets are used as prefatory material to the individual sections, placed in the margin as counterpointing statements, and fitted into the body of the poem itself. The viewpoint also shifts. It is sometimes, and most frequently, that of the returned exile recalling the rough field in which he was raised. It is sometimes that of the historian recalling the past of Ulster and of county Tyrone in particular. It is sometimes that of the cultured European, seeing Ulster's predicament in the context of European culture. It is, indeed, a poem of many voices, many devices, but all is brought together into unity by the central all-informing passionate intelligence.

Certainly this is Montague's chef d'oeuvre. It is a masterwork in the way in which Skelton's *Garlande of Laurell* is a masterwork, for it displays mastery of many modes. Consider the variety of tone and technique in the following fragments:

Vast changes have taken place, and rulers have passed away, dynasties fallen, since that glorious autumn day when Lord Mountjoy, accompanied by his land steward, arrived by coach in Omagh . . .

Catching a bus at Victoria Station,
Symbol of Belfast in its iron bleakness,
We ride through narrow huckster streets
(Small lamps bright before the Sacred Heart
Bunting tagged for some religious feast)
To where Cavenhill and Divis, stern presences,
Brood over a wilderness of cinemas and shops,
Victorian red-brick villas, framed with aerials,
Bushmill hoardings, Orange and Legion Halls,
A fringe of trees affords some ease at last
From all this dour despoiled inheritance,
The shabby through-otherness of outskirts:
"God is Love," chalked on a grimy wall
Mocks a culture where constraint is all.

In this passage the heroic couplet, implied subtly at the commencement of the paragraph by the assonantal and consonantal chimings of the end words, is allowed to come openly into view with the last two lines that could have been written in the age of Swift, or that of Cromwell.

Ulster's Pride

"O'Neill: A name more in price than to be called Caesar."
Sir George Carew

Con Bacach O'Neill, 1542

1
Heralded by trumpeters,
Prefaced by a bishop,
Sided by earls, Con
The lame limps down
The palace at Greenwich.
Twenty angels for
A fur lined gown,
Ten white pounds
To the College of Arms
For a new escutcheon
That he may kneel on
The deep strewn rushes
To hear Henry's command;
When the bugles sound—
Forty shillings, by custom,
Must go to the captain—
His knee lifts rustily
From English ground:
Arise, Earl of Tyrone.

The marginal note identified Con as Con Bacach O'Neill, and the time as 1542. There are no interpretive epithets, no elaborations, as in the passage above. All is objective, cleanly and economically stated; it is the impartial voice of history which speaks. Again, however, the structure is interesting. The lines are once again linked tightly by means of consonance and assonance. The last words of the first two lines have a *p* and sibilance in common; the third and fourth lines almost rhyme; the fifth line is in consonance with the seventh, and the "for" at the end of line six is echoes of the "fur" in line seven, while the eighth and ninth lines again are almost rhymed. One could reasonably suggest that Gaelic devices have been used to present this piece of Irish history, just as English cadences have been used to present Victorian Belfast in the earlier passage.

A Grafted Tongue

An Irish
child weeps at school
repeating its English.
After each mistake

The master
gouges another mark
on the tally stick
hung about its neck

Like a bell
on a cow, a hobble
on a straying goat.
To slur and stumble

In shame
the altered syllables
of your own name;
to stray sadly home

and find
the turf cured width
of your parent's hearth
growing slowly alien:

In cabin
and field, they still

speak the old tongue.
You may greet no one.

To grow
a second tongue, as
harsh a humiliation
as twice to be born.

Decades later
that child's grandchild's
speech stumbles over lost
syllables of an old order.

Here while consonance and assonance still play a part, the verse structure is balanced beautifully upon a tight organization of the step by step process of thought. Each of the three longer lines in each stanza adds one single perception or concept, makes one further small and deliberate step towards an inevitable conclusion. It is true wit. The same dexterous and witty use of form appears in the section, *Hymn* "To the New Omagh Road" which opens with a "Balance Sheet," itemizing first the losses, then the gains, and then concluding with a passage which is presented typographically as if it were the inscription upon a tombstone. One of the verse paragraphs on the debit side of the ledger reads:

Item: The shearing away of an old barn
criss-cross of beams where pigeons moan
high small window where the swallow built
white-washed dry-stone walls

The last paragraph on the credit side and the final paragraph of the whole read:

Item: The dead of Garvaghey Graveyard (including my grandfather have an unobstructed view—the trees
having been sheared away for a carpark—of the living
passing at great speed, sometimes quick enough to come
straight in:

Let it be clear
That I do not grudge my grandfather

This long delayed pleasure!
I like the idea of him
Rising from the rotting boards of the coffin
With his J.P.'s white beard
And penalising drivers
For travelling faster
Than jaunting cars

This counterpointing technique is also used in the second part of this section where the main verse is interrupted by the stanzas of an old song, thus producing a savage and bitter portrait of the destruction of natural beauty by the new road, as well as a contrast between the nineteenth and the twentieth centuries' approach to the landscape.

GLENCULL WATERSIDE

Glen chuil: the Glen of the Hazels

From the quarry behind the school
the crustacean claws of the excavator
rummage to withdraw a payload,
a giant's bite

Tis pleasant for to take a stroll by Glencull Waterside
On a lovely evening in spring (in nature's early pride);
You pass by many a flowery bank and many a shady dell,
Like walking through enchanted land where fairies used to dwell

Tuberous tentacles
the topsoil of a living shape
of earth lifts like a scalp
to lay open

The trout are rising to the fly; the lambkins sport and play;
The pretty feathered warblers are signing by the way;
The blackbirds' and the thrushes' notes, by the echoes multiplied,
Do fill the vale with melody by Glencull waterside.

slipping sand
shale, compressed veins of rock,
old foundations, a soft chaos
to be swallowed wholesale,
masticated, regurgitated
by the mixer.

Yet another structure is used in the section, "A New Siege." Here the lines themselves have a rocking motion, a rhetorical energy, that reminds one of the system of balances in the early bardic poetry.

Lines of history
        lines of power
the long sweep
        of the Bogside
under the walls
        up to Creggan
the black muzzle
        of Roaring Meg
staring dead on
        cramped houses
the jackal shapes
        of James's army
watching the city
        stiffen in siege

SMALL SHOT HATH
        POURED LIKE HAIL
THE GREAT GUNS
        SHAKEN OUR WALLS
a spectral garrison
        no children left
sick from eating
        horseflesh, vermin
curs fattened on
        the slain Irish
still flaunting
        the bloody flag
of "No Surrender"
        GOD HAS MADE US
AN IRON PILLAR
        AND BRAZEN WALLS
AGAINST THIS LAND.

Lines of defiance
        lines of discord
under Walker's arm
        brisk with guns
British soldiers
        patrol the walls
the gates between
        Ulster Catholic
Ulster Protestant
        a Saracen slides
past the Guildhall
        a black Cuchulain
bellowing against
        the Scarlet Whore
twin races petrified
        the volcanic ash
of religious hatred

symbol of Ulster
        these sloping streets
blackened walls
        sick at heart and
seeking a sign
        the flaghung gloom
of St. Columb's
        the brass eagle of
the lectern bearing
        the Sermon on the Mount
in its shoulders
        "A city that is
set on a hill
        cannot be hid."

This brief glance at the rich variety of style in *The Rough Field* has certainly not brought more than a small part of its extraordinary technical successes into view. It has, however, shown how Montague has not only made full use of a variety of methods which derive from the ancient Irish, the traditional British, and the twentieth-century collage and cut-up techniques. It has also, perhaps, revealed how the shifting viewpoint intensifies the thrust of the poem, preventing it from ever becoming on the one hand overpersonal, overautobiographical, or on the other hand too intellectually bitter, too distanced from ordinary human experience. It also shows how the lyrical, epic, and satirical are brought together with the meditative and philosophical modes in the whole.

The heart of the poem itself, however, remains the personal testimony, the record of an individual experience of pain, bewilderment, and lost loveliness, which has led to a final reconciliation.

> I go to say goodbye to the Cailleach
> that terrible figure who haunted my childhood
> but no longer harsh, a human being
> merely, hurt by event

While the speaker feels again that “ancient awe” at confronting the Sean Bhean Vocht, he finds also that

> Memories have wrought reconciliation
> between us, we talk in ease at last,
> like old friends, lovers almost,
> sharing secrets

The last movement of the poem, the epilogue, relates the whole to the lost dream of a rural Ireland, to the lost country childhood, and recalls how this vision (essentially one of innocence) has been presented by Palmer, Chagall, and Goldsmith.

> Palmer’s softly lit Vale of Shoreham
> commemorates it, or Chagall’s lovers
> floating above a childhood village
> remote but friendly as Goldsmith’s Auburn—
>
> Our finally lost dream of man at home
> in a rural setting! A giant hand

as we pass by, reaches down
to grasp the fields we gazed upon

Harsh landscape that haunts me,
well and stone, in the bleak moors of drean
with all my circling a failure to return
to what is already going,

going

GONE

Though Montague does not sentimentalize over the discomforts and brutalities of the Hiring Fairs, the peasant servitude, here he is lamenting the destruction of that ancient tradition and wisdom which is lamented by so many Irish writers over the centuries. He has shown himself typical of Irish Letters in his nostalgia, in his character as Revenant. He is at one with Synge in the landlord's garden in county Wicklow, with Yeats in his recallings of his dead friends, with Kinsella in his Parnassian yearnings, and even with Wilde, whose nostalgia was for the glories of Greece rather than those of ancient Ireland. One might even remember that one of Yeats's earliest poems, his sixth to appear in print in 1885, began

The woods of Arcady are dead,
And over is their antique joy;
Of old the world on dreaming fed;
Grey Truth is now her painted toy;
Yet still she turns her restless head.

Here is another version of that quarrel which Montague sees in "The Hag of Beare" and in all Irish literature, the quarrel between dream and reality, between romantic fantasy and clear-eyed realism, between (one might say) the heart and the head. Montague reveals himself, indeed, to be at the very center of the Irish tradition in terms of theme, to have brought Irish and English and American and European verse techniques together in his work, and to have built from the contraries of his own and his country's divided inheritance a poetry that is both national and international, both personal and universal. It is an astonishing achievement.

Epilogue

It was Oscar Wilde's misfortune, perhaps, to be born into a time when an Anglo-Irish writer could not easily perceive the value of exploring native Irish tradition. Influenced by Mahaffy's classicism, he therefore found himself playing the Irish role of revenant in Greek costume. Yeats, who inherited the same English romantic tradition, became quickly aware that he had also inherited an Irish tradition, and in his themes and craftsmanship both, he contrived to progress by way of these "contraries." Both men differed with and profitted from the approaches of AE and J. M. Synge. Synge himself in his Petrarch translation attempted to unify both European and Irish romanticism and, in his other works, made some attempts at suggesting a political and social philosophy which might heal his country's wounds. Susan L. Mitchell wittily commented upon the contrary personalities of her day and saw the humor in the situation of Ireland. Sean O'Casey perceived the conflicts also, and he tackled them with vigor, setting romantic feeling against the realities of Irish life. Jack B. Yeats contrived to express the complexity of his own inheritance by means of an all-embracing creativity that fused romantic symbolism with a shrewd observation of life in Ireland. Robert Graves attempting to bring two traditions into unity, brought Celtic prosody into a poetry with classical and Jonsonian antecedents. MacNeice contrived to create a verse in which classical and Gaelic methods of construction were brought together and, in this, anticipated a similar fusion of traditions in both Thomas Kinsella and John Montague. Aidan Higgins brought his concerns for Ireland and his observations of continental Europe together.

All these writers have clearly been aware of a divided inheritance, and all have, in one way or another, utilized the "contraries" they have experienced. They are not the only Irish writers to have done this during the period of time which the work discussed in this book covers. Nor has their awareness of a divided inheritance been, in all cases, the central compulsion behind their work. Nevertheless, it seems to me that in the poetry, fiction, and drama of these writers we can detect something which is central to Irish writing from the 1870s, when Wilde visited Rome, to the 1970s, when Higgins published *Balcony of Europe*, Kinsella his *Selected Poems*, and Montague *The Rough Field*. John Montague has identified this central element as a "quarrel between natural and organized religion, between instinct and restraint." I have suggested that the "contraries" can also be seen in other terms and that they involve tensions between native Irish and British literary traditions, between the impulse towards regionism (or nationalism) and that towards internationalism, and between nostalgic romanticism and clear-eyed realism, even between antiquarianism and modernism.

All literature may spring, in part, from an awareness of the divided nature of man. We can see the theme clearly in Shakespeare's *Anthony and Cleopatra* and *Measure for Measure*; we can see it, obviously, in *Faust*; we can see it in Milton, Blake, Wordsworth, and Browning. We can see it particularly clearly, however, in the Irish writers of the last hundred years. It may be that the silver lining in the black cloud of Ireland's centuries of suffering and confusion is an inherited awareness of a central fact in human nature and is a compulsion, somehow or other, to harness those contraries and to employ them for the advancement of human understanding and the further development of art.

Index

CELTIC CONTRARIES

was composed in 10 on 12 Galliard on a Merganthaler Linotron 202
by Eastern Graphics;
printed by sheet-fed offset on 50-pound, acid-free Glatfelter Natural Hi-Bulk,
Smyth-sewn and bound over binder's boards in Holliston Roxite B,
with dust jackets printed in 2 colors
by Braun-Brumfield, Inc.;
designed by Victoria Lane;
and published by

SYRACUSE UNIVERSITY PRESS

SYRACUSE, NEW YORK 13244-5160